THE LAW OF AGENCY

Second Edition

Leonard Lakin
Professor Emeritus of Law
Bernard M. Baruch College
City University of New York

Martin Schiff
Adjunct Associate Professor of Law
John Jay College of Criminal Justice
City University of New York
and
Adjunct Associate Professor of Social Sciences
New York University

KENDALL/HUNT PUBLISHING COMPANY
4050 Westmark Drive   Dubuque, Iowa 52002

ISBN 0-7872-2318-2

Printed in the United States of America

10 9 8 7 6 5 4 3 2

TO RITA, JILL, NIDIA, AMBER-DAWN, AND TIFFANY HEATHER

CONTENTS

CASES

82 Multiple Choice.

PREFACE

This is the second edition of a book that we published in 1984. As with the earlier edition, this book is intended for practicing attorneys and for law students who are studying the subject of business organizations. Such a course is typically divided into the three subject areas of agency, partnerships, and corporations. Our experience is that the available materials dealing with the law of agency are either too superficial or overly-detailed in certain areas of agency to the exclusion of others. Therefore, the student or lawyer is ill-served by either in the pursuit of his education in this important area which forms the bedrock of a proper understanding of the law of partnerships and corporations. A student cannot understand the rights, duties, and liabilities of partnerships and corporations without a thorough grasp of agency law.

We believe that the understanding of the rules of agency law can be enhanced by treating it as a separate discipline of study rather than as part of another course of study and by examining the rationale of the rules of agency law and its major applications.

This second edition contains ten significant recent court cases in agency law including the growing field of municipal tort liability. The newer cases together with those in the earlier edition illustrate the application of major rules of agency law to common business situations which the student will encounter in his or her professional career. We have also included all of the multiple choice questions dealing with the subject of Agency which have appeared on the CPA law exam since the 1984 edition to supplement the questions at the end of each chapter. All questions have been placed in a new interactive format to allow students to remove them for self-testing and study purposes. The new format should promote classroom discussion and test preparation and assist those students who will eventually take the bar exam, or the CPA Law Exam, which is a Uniform Examination prepared by the American Institute of Certified Public Accountants and given in all fifty states to over 100,000 CPA candidates each year. The CPA Examination is recognized as the most difficult professional licensing examination in the United States because of its low passing percentage rate of approximately 30%-35%.

We have also included a bibliography of the most significant legal research on the law of agency since the first edition of the book was published in 1984. We have retained the extensive documentation of the earlier edition with numerous citations to more than 350 cases and over 100 law review articles as well as other legal literature including the Restatement of Agency prepared under the sponsorship of the American Law Institute for students and professors who wish to pursue the subject matter in greater depth. We have also liberally cited the classic early writings on the subject by such eminent authorities as Professors Floyd R. Mechem and Warren Seavey.

The First Restatement of Agency was completed in 1933 by Professor Seavey from the work initiated by Professor Mechem after Professor Mechem died. The Second Restatement of Agency was completed in 1957. Both Restatements were sponsored by the American Law Institute. The Restatement of Agency has been recognized as the authoritative compilation of the common law of agency in the United States, and the three volume Second Restatement, constantly referred to in judicial decisions, represents important material to be studied by the student as part of the course on the law of agency.

We have endeavored to present the subject matter in a concise, readable and interesting manner. We have tried to anticipate most of the questions that students have raised in our classes when studying the subject and to provide the answers together with the rationale for the particular major rules of agency law.

It is our earnest hope that this book will contribute to the reader's education and assist him or her in the journey through the law of business organizations, a field which pervasively dominates so much of our economic lives.

Leonard Lakin
Martin Schiff

CHAPTER 1

THE NATURE AND CHARACTER OF THE AGENCY RELATIONSHIP

1. Definitions and background of the agency relationship.

The law of agency in the United States has evolved over the last two hundred years, taking on added impetus during and after the explosive nineteenth century industrial revolution when businesses expanded rapidly and found it necessary or desirable to multiply their presence in the ever-growing marketplace by employing others as their agents to transact business on their behalf. The operative effect of the agency relationship is that today, in the United States, more than three million corporations, one million two hundred thousand general and limited partnerships, and fifteen million sole proprietorships, acting as principals, employ millions of others as their agents to transact business on their behalf in over 180 countries. The employment of millions of agents in the United States to negotiate contracts and to buy and sell more than two trillion dollars of real property, goods and services annually enables business organizations to function effectively and operate at optimum profitability levels. Thus, the legally permitted use of agents effectively allows the principal to be legally present in many different places at the same time and to contract with many more third parties than he could personally contract with. Indeed, without the juridical recognition that principals can transact business through their agents, our American economy and society would be vastly different today, analogous to the anachronistic pre-industrial revolution society.

The law of agency defines the rights, duties, and liabilities of the principal, the party who employs the agent to contract for him, the agent, and the third party with whom the agent deals.[1] The essential nature and character of the agency relationship is that the principal authorizes his agent to contract on his behalf with one or more third parties.[2] The agent may be either an employee of the principal or an independent contractor who is not the principal's employee, such as an attorney, accountant, or auctioneer. Although an employee may be an agent for his employer-principal, some employees may never become agents because they are not employed to contract with third parties on their employer's behalf (e.g., janitor, mechanic, or typist). The legal relationship between such an employer and employee continues to be traditionally designated as the "master-servant relationship" (a term coined some seven centuries ago), which is not an agency relationship.[3] Thus, every agent is not an employee and every employee is not an agent. While the master-servant relationship does not contemplate the servant entering into contracts on behalf of his master with third parties, the law of agency nonetheless applies for the limited purpose of defining the rights, duties, and liabilities of the master, servant, and injured third parties when the servant commits a tort (civil wrong) against a third party during the scope of the servant's employment.[4]

2. Examples of agents and non-agents.

The American workforce of over 125,000,000 includes millions of agents who contract daily with third parties on behalf of their principal. Salespeople are the largest single group but virtually every industry and business employs many kinds of agents who contract on behalf of their principal to purchase or sell every conceivable type of personal property, real property, or service. For example, personnel officers who hire employees for their principals, bank employees, airline ticket agents, stockbrokers, and building agents who rent apartments and commercial offices are only a few of the significant business activities where agents routinely transact billions of dollars business annually on behalf of their principals. Furthermore, certain business entities such as corporations and partnerships may contract with third parties only through the agents, who are either their employees or independent contractors engaged by them to do so. In a partnership, each partner is by statute an agent for the partnership,[5] and the legal relationship of partners to each other is said to be one of mutual agency.[6]

The term "agent" does not apply to the servant in the master-servant relationship. Nor does the term "agent" apply to independent dealers who are associated with others, such as the more than 25,000 automobile dealers in the United States who purchase more than ten million automobiles annually from the domestic and foreign manufacturers and then resell them to the public. Although, for example, called a General Motors dealer, he is not an agent, servant, or employee of General Motors. He does not contract or act for General Motors or bind General Motors when he contracts to sell its automobiles. He is in business for himself.[7] By contrast, one who received goods "on consignment" from his supplier for the purpose of resale and sells such goods and remits the proceeds, less his commission, to his supplier, occupies the legal position of agent, though he is not generally referred to as an agent in the marketplace.

A real estate broker is not an agent for the seller or buyer in the absence of an express agreement because he is not authorized by the seller to contract on the seller's behalf with a prospective buyer. Rather, he serves as an intermediary who introduces the seller and buyer to each other so that they can consummate the sale and purchase of the real property. Accordingly, a real estate broker may properly be paid by both seller and buyer for introducing each to the other.[8]

The existence of the family relationship does not of itself automatically constitute one spouse the agent of the other. Thus, one spouse may not lawfully act as agent for the other without the latter's consent.[9] Although a husband has been held liable for necessities purchased by his wife where he has failed to provide them or the means of purchasing them, the legal result is not reached on the basis of an agency relationship. Rather, the husband is liable on the theory of restitution, which requires that he pay the fair and reasonable value of the goods or services furnished to his wife instead of the contract price.[10]

In summary, the inclusion or omission of the term "agent" by the parties in their contract will not of itself determine whether an agency relationship legally exists between the parties. Rather, substance prevails over form and courts will consider the manifested intention of the parties, prior dealings, if any, course of dealing and course of performance to answer the sometimes elusive question: did the parties enter into an agency relationship?[11]

References

"The airport operator: air carrier's agent or independent contractor?" by Giuseppe Guerreri, 17 *Air and Space Law* 231-234, Sept. 1992.

Notes

1. The Restatement, Second, Agency, Sect. 1 (1), (1958), defines agency as "the fiduciary relation which results from the manifestation of consent by one person to another that the other shall act in his behalf and subject to his control, and consent by the other so to act"; see, also, Tonka Corp. v. Commissioner of Taxation, 169 N.W. 2d 589, 593 (Minn. 1969); Brilliant v. Raidy, 189 Misc. 561, 70 N.Y.S. 2d 126 (1947); In Re Fitzpatrick's Estate, 17 N.Y.S. 2d 280 (1940); Cadman Memorial Congregational Soc. of Brooklyn v. Kenyon, 197 Misc. 124, 95 N.Y.S. 2d 133 (1950); United Packinghouse Workers v. Maurer-Neuer, Inc., 272 F. 2d 647 (10th Cir. 1959).

   Some of the earliest works on agency are William Paley, *A Treatise On The Law Of Principal And Agent, Chiefly With References To Mercantile Transactions* (2d Am. ed. 1822); Joseph Story, *Commentaries On The Law Of Agency As A Branch Of Commercial And Maritime Jurisprudence* (1839); Oliver Wendell Holmes, Jr., "History of Agency", in 3 *Select Essays On Anglo-American Legal History* 368 (1909), reprinted from 4 *Harvard Law Review* 345, 5 id. 1 (1891); other early works on agency are cited in 1 Floyd R. Mechem, *Cases on Agency* 10 (2d. ed. 1914).

   For an excellent analysis of the First Restatement of Agency, see Warren A. Seavey, "Agency Since The Restatement", *American Bar Association Journal,* 23:503-510, July 1937. See, also, Basil H. Pollitt, "Some Comments On The Restatement Of Agency", *Georgetown Law Journal,* 17:177-195, April 1929 and 17: 283-306, June 1929.

   For a very brief early overview of the law of agency, see "Principal and Agent", *The Solicitor's Journal,* 72:32-33, January 14, 1928.

   For a recent concise analysis of the law of agency, see, Ronald C. Wyse, "A Framework Of Analysis For The Law Of Agency", *Montana Law Review,* 40:31-59, Winter 1979.

2. The authority of an agent to make representations for his principal and the legal effect of his utterances are analyzed in Merton Ferson, "Agency To Make Representations", *Vanderbilt Law Review,* 2: 1-26, December 1948.

For a capsule synopsis of the consensual basis of agency, see, "Agency-Consent: The Basis of the Agency Relationship," *Washburn Law Journal,* 5:281-285, Spring 1966.

The concept of agency as we know it today was in fact unknown in Roman contract law. If one party authorized a second party to contract on his behalf with a third party, the contract was held to be strictly between second and third parties unless and until the second party assigned the contract to the first party. See W. Buckland and A. McNair, *Roman Law and Common Law* 218 (2d rev. ed. 1965); see 3 E. Rabel, *The Conflict of Laws, A Comparative Study,* note 14, at 128 (1962); F. Lawson, *The Roman Law Reader,* note 16 at 103.

3. See, for example, McKenna v. Stayman Mfg. Co., 112 N.Y.S. 1099 (1908); Massey v. Tube Art Display, Inc., 551 P.2d 1387 (Ct. App. Wash. 1976); Cimorelli v. N.Y. Central Railroad Co., 148 F.2d 575 (1945). The essence of agency, in contrast to the master-servant relationship, is the power of the agent to act for another so as to affect directly the other's legal relations, and agency has been analyzed in these terms in the common law world for over a century.

4. See, "Principal and Agent: Torts: Liability of principal for torts of his agent," *Cornell Law Quarterly,* 11:403-408, April 1926; "Agency-Implied Authority-Liability of Master. Peterson v. Crossley," 185 Atl. 926 (N.J.), *Boston University Law Review,* 17:96-102, January 1937.

A master is liable to a third person for the intentional torts of his servant against third parties even though the servant exceeds his authority or the torts are willfully or maliciously committed, if such acts are incidental to and in furtherance of the business of the master. See, "Agency: Liability of the Master to Third Persons for Intentional Torts of the Servant," *Oklahoma Law Review,* 29:946-57, Fall 1976.

Under the doctrine of respondeat superior, the master is liable for the servant's torts committed within the scope of employment even though the servant was acting in an unauthorized manner. See, "Agency-Master Is Liable for Servant's Negligence in Colliding with Stranger While Servant Was Running Along Sidewalk. . . . ," *Georgetown Law Journal,* 32:308-309, March 1944.

The question of determining which employer is liable for a tort in the case of a borrowed servant is examined in "Agency-Liability For Torts Of Borrowed Servant," *Ohio State Law Journal,* 28:550-558, Summer 1967.

The master is normally not criminally liable for the crimes of his servant committed within the scope of his employment unless the master's criminal intent can be established. See, "Agency: Criminal Law: Criminal Liability of Master for Acts of Servant," *Oklahoma Law Review,* 1:52-54, May 1948.

5. Holloway v. Smith, 88 S.E.2d 909 (Sup. Ct. Va. 1955). Partnerships are governed by the Uniform Partnership Act (U.P.A.), which has been adopted in all states but Georgia, Louisiana, and Mississippi, and by any agreements among the partners. The U.P.A. section 9(1) and the New York Partnership Law, Sec. 20 state that "Every partner is an agent of the partnership for the purpose of its business. . . ."

6. Id; see, also, U.P.A. secs. 11-17.

7. A general employer is not ordinarily responsible for the negligence of an independent contractor or the independent contractor's servants. Scammon v. Chicago, 25 Ill. 425, 437 (1861); 2 Mechem, *Agency* (2d ed. 1914), sect. 1917; "Responsibility For The Torts of An Independent Contractor," *Yale Law Journal,* 39:816-873, April 1930.

The independent contractor is analyzed in King v. Young, Brown, and Beverly, Inc., 107 S.2d 751 (Fla. App. 1958); Uppington v. City of New York, 165 N.Y. 222, 59 N.E. 91 (1901); Klein v. Mr. Transmission, Inc., 318 So.2d 676 (Ala. 1975).

The question of whether a person hired is an employee or independent contractor is often difficult to answer when there is ambiguity concerning the right to control the work to be done and the means used to accomplish it. See, P. Streer, J. Boyd. "Employee or independent contractor? Proposed guidelines may lessen the controversy," *Taxes,* 56:489-495, August 1978; see, also, L. G. Harter, Jr. "Are they employees or independent contractors?", *Labor Law Journal,* 29:779-785, December 1978. Professors Dave N. Stewart and John L. Kramer of Brigham Young University in a statistical analysis of 139 federal court cases found that there are eleven factors used to determine whether a worker is an employee or an independent contractor. These are: (1) supervision; (2) degree of integration of the worker's services into the employer's business activities; (3) right of worker to delegate; (4) continuing relationship; (5) set hours of work; (6) having control over the place of work; (7) independent trade; (8) method of payment; (9) payment of business and/or traveling expenses; (10) furnishing of tools and materials; (11) realization of profit or loss. See, "An Empirical Answer to the Problem of Determining 'Employee' or 'Independent Contractor' Status," *Taxes,* 58:747-757, November 1980; see, also, "Agency-Independent Contractor And Agent," *Notre Dame Lawyer,* 15:250-252, March 1940. The Restatement, Second, Agency, Sect. 220(2) (1958) sets forth criteria to distinguish a servant from an independent contractor.

8. Knudson v. Weeks, 394 F. Supp. 963 (Okla. 1975). Where a real estate broker is given an exclusive right of sale for a stated time for the purpose of finding a buyer for a property, the seller may not terminate such agency during the stated time, sell his property on his own or through another, or unreasonably withhold approval of a prospective buyer presented by such an agent without breaching the exclusive right of sale agreement; see, McDonald v. Davis, 389 S.W. 2d 494 (Texas 1965). See, also, Lickus v. O'Donnell, 321 Ill. App. 144, 52 N.E. 2d 271 (1943); Rindeikis v. Coffman, 231 Ark. 422, 329 S.W. 2d 550 (1959); Elliott v. Brooks, 184 S.W. 2d 929 (Tex. Civ. App. 1944). However, where a real estate broker is given an exclusive agency, the seller can sell the realty by himself without being liable for a commission as long as he does not use another broker. See, Restatement, Second, Agency, Sect. 449 c (1958); and Bagley v. Butler, 59 Misc. 2d 1029, 301 N.Y.S. 2d 148 (1969).

9. However, if the husband customarily permits his wife to purchase household supplies while withholding his formal

consent, the wife's authority may nevertheless be implied, or apparent authority may be created to make such purchases, making the husband liable as principal. See, for example, The Restatement, Second, Agency, Sect. 22, Comment b (1958); and Melton v. Mire, 268 So. 2d 123 (La. 1972).

10. The Restatement, Restitution, Sect. 113 (1936). Gorco Const. Co. v. Stein, 256 Minn. 476, 99 N.W. 2d 69 (1959). Similarly, there is no implication of agency merely from the fact of a parent-child relationship; see, Wilks v. Stone, 339 S.W. 2d 590 (Mo. App. 1960).

11. NAACP v. Overstreet, 221 Ga. 16, 142 S.E.2d 816 (1965); Groh v. Shelton, 428 S.W.2d 911 (Mo. 1968); King v. Earley, 274 Ala. 116, 145 So.2d 831 (1962); Lee v. People's Cooperative Sales Agency, Inc., 201 Minn. 266, 276 N.W. 214 (1937); Appleby v. Kewanee Oil Co., 279 F. 2d 334 (10th Cir. 1960); United States v. German-American Vocational League, Inc., 153 F.2d 860 (3d Cir. 1946); Riss & Co. v. Association of Western Rys., 159 F. Supp. 288 (D.D.C. 1958).

CHAPTER 2

CREATION OF THE AGENCY RELATIONSHIP

3. Creation of the agency relationship: by contract.

An agency relationship may be created either by agreement between the parties or by operation of law. The usual agency relationship between principal and agent is created as a result of contract between the parties. Thus, the agency relationship is consensual, and the rights, duties and liabilities of principal and agent to each other are governed by both the common law rules of contract law and agency law as well as any applicable statutes.[1]

The contract between principal and agent creating the agency relationship may be express or implied. It will be an express agency contract if the parties use words, oral or written, to create their agency relationship. The express agency contract between principal and agent may be oral or written unless an applicable statute requires a written contract. It will be an implied agency contract if the parties create an agency relationship by their conduct (not words) which manifests a mutual intention that one should represent the other for the purpose of contracting on his behalf with a third party. Whether there is an express or implied agency contract between principal and agent, the question arises whether the agent is bound by his agency contract where he has agreed to act without compensation. If the common law rules of contract were applied, the principal could not enforce the contract against the agent because he did not give the agent any consideration for the agent's promise to act for the principal. However, under the law of agency applicable to such a case, the principal can enforce the contract against his agent.[2] Some states reach this result, such as New York, by holding that consideration is not legally required for the creation of an agency relationship. Other states do not go so far and hold that the party's gratuitous promise to act as a noncompensated agent is enforceable against him by the principal only if the agent caused the principal to refrain from having the act done by other available means, or if he subsequently fails to notify his principal that he will not perform the requested act while other means are still available to his principal. In such cases, courts apply the doctrine of promissory estoppel and hold that the principal's reasonable reliance on the agent's gratuitous promise will render it enforceable against the agent in order to avoid resulting injustice to the principal. Similarly, the principal will also be bound by the contracts made on his behalf by his non-compensated agent.

4. Formalities of the principal-agent contract required by statute.

In most states, by statute, commonly called the Statute of Frauds, a contract which cannot be performed within one year from the date the contract was made is unenforceable unless it is in writing and signed by the party against whom enforcement is sought. Therefore, where a principal orally employs another to be his purchasing agent for five years, the contract is unenforceable because it violates the Statute of Frauds, and the party who is sued on the employment contract may raise the defense of the Statute of Frauds and thereby void liability under the contract to the other party. Thus, to satisfy the Statute of Frauds the principal and agent will usually execute a written contract where the contract cannot

Pursuant to statute
Agency by estoppel

be performed within one year from the date their contract is made.[3] However, if the duration of the oral contract between principal and agent is unstated or indefinite, as is the case in many employment contracts between principal and agent where the principal prefers to employ the agent without a fixed term, the Statute of Frauds does not apply. This is so because the contract may possibly be performed within one year from the date made regardless of how long the duration of the contract actually becomes. Thus, the oral contract for an unstated or indefinite time is enforceable by either party against the other.[4] Such an agency of unstated or indefinite duration is called an agency at will and may be lawfully terminated by either party at any time upon reasonable notice if their contract is silent as to how much advance notice of termination must be given.

Moreover, if the principal-agent contract can be performed within one year from the date made, the Statute of Frauds will not require such a contract to be written and signed by the party against whom enforcement is sought even though the contract made by the agent on his principal's behalf with the third party is required by the Statute of Frauds to be in a signed writing. Thus, a principal may hire an agent for nine months or for an indefinite term pursuant to an oral contract without violating the Statute of Frauds even though the agent will contract on his principal's behalf to sell goods to third parties at a price of $500 or more. In such a case, only the agent's contract on behalf of his principal with the third party must be in writing and signed by the party against whom enforcement is sought to satisfy the Statute of Frauds requirements of the Uniform Commercial Code governing the sale of goods (Section 2-201) even though the principal-agent contract may be oral.

Many states have also enacted statutes which require a written contract between principal and agent, which must be signed by the principal when the principal authorizes an agent to contract on his behalf concerning real estate, such as entering into contracts to buy, sell, or mortgage real property.[5] And in some twenty six states, including New York, an agent's authority to offer his principal's real property for sale must be created by written instrument signed by the principal. However, such statutes applicable to real estate contracts generally do not require an agent's authority to lease real property for his principal for less than one year, whether as landlord or tenant, to be evidenced by a writing signed by the principal.

5. Creation of the agency relationship: by operation of law.

An agency relationship may be created by operation of law. In such a case an agency relationship is imposed upon the principal and the agent without the voluntary consent of the principal and without the formality of any contract between the parties. When an agency relationship is created by operation of law it is done either pursuant to a statute or pursuant to the legal principle adopted by the courts called agency by estoppel.

Two examples of statutes creating an agency relationship by operation of law are those statutes enacted in every state which provides that every corporation, foreign and domestic, doing business in the state and every nonresident owner of a motor vehicle where the statute applies designates the Secretary of State as the agent for the corporation or the owner of a motor vehicle to receive service of legal process (summons and complaint) on behalf of the corporation (principal) or motor vehicle owner (principal). The significant effect of these two statutes is that a plaintiff may obtain legal jurisdiction over a defendant corporation (principal) or motor vehicle owner (principal) by serving legal process upon the statutory agent. Such statutes require that the Secretary of State mail a copy of the summons and complaint to the party designated in the certificate of incorporation of the corporation or to the owner of the motor vehicle.[6] Thus 10,000,000 motor vehicle owners and more than 3,000,000 corporations are governed by such statutes.

Another way an agency may be created by operation of law in certain circumstances is by the court-adopted principle of law called agency by estoppel. Under the principle of agency by estoppel, a court under certain circumstances will estop or preclude a principal from denying the existence of an agency relationship between himself and another party. The significant effect of the application of agency by estoppel is to hold a principal liable on contracts made by a person on the principal's behalf even though the person has no actual authority to act for the principal. Agency by estoppel is discussed in chapter 5.

Notes

1. Richardson v. Sibley, 101 N.H. 377, 143 A.2d 414 (1958); Arkansas Valley Feed Mills, Inc. v. Fox De Luxe Foods, Inc., 171 F. Supp. 145 (W.D. Ark. 1959). The character of the principal-agent relationship as distinguished from that of a master-servant relationship is examined in "Distinction Between Servants And Agents," *University of Pennsylvania Law Review,* 67: 136-150, April 1919; see, also, chapter one, note 4. The question of determining whether an agency exists is examined in "Establishing Agency," *Law Quarterly Review,* 84: 224-244, April 1968.
2. The mere fact that the agent is not to receive compensation for performance does not relieve him of liability. See, Isham v. Post, 141 N.Y. 100, 35 N.E. 1084 (1894); 1 Mechem, *Agency* (2d ed. 1914), sect. 1258, 1283; Comment, "Insurance-Liability of Gratuitous Agent for Negligence," *Illinois Law Rev.,* 26:916-918, April 1932.
3. See, for example, New York General Obligations Law 5-703.
4. id.
5. The Restatement, Second, Agency, Sect. 193 (1958) states that while an agent's signature is sufficient in a real estate transaction, some states also require that the agent's authority be in writing. New York General Obligations Law 5-1111 requires an agent's authority to be in writing from his principal to execute real property contracts. When the appointment of an agent is in writing, it is usually called a power of attorney. See, Gittings Neiman-Marcus, Inc. v. Estes, 440 S.W. 2d 90 (Tex. Civ. App 1969); Park v. Appeal Bd. of Mich. Employment Sec. Commission, 355 Mich. 103, 94 N.W. 2d 407 (1959); Restatement, Second, Agency, Sect. 46 (1958).
6. The relationship between service under the Nonresident Motorist Statute New York Vehicle and Traffic Law, Sect. 253 and service under the Civil Practice Laws and Rules (CPLR), Sects. 302 and 313, under each of which the Secretary of State is a statutory agent, is somewhat obscure, but apparently the CPLR is meant to supplement but not supersede the Nonresident Motorist statute. Therefore if a plaintiff has a cause of action against a nonresident motorist, he has a choice between the two statutes.

Power of Attorney

Case 1
Siegel v. Spear & Co.
234 N.Y.479 (1923)

Introduction

Sometimes a party agrees to enter into an agency agreement and to perform as an agent for his principal even though no consideration is given to the agent for doing so. The question arises whether in such a case the agent is bound by his gratuitous promise if the principal sues him for not properly performing his agency. The following leading case illustrates how courts rationalize the judicial result reached.

Crane, J.

The plaintiff commenced this action in the City Court of the City of New York, to recover his loss sustained by failure of the defendant to insure his household furniture stored in its storehouse. The action is based upon an alleged agreement to insure made with the defendant's creditman. So far the plaintiff has been successful, the Appellate Division, however, certifying that in its opinion there is a question of law involved which should be reviewed by this court.

In August of 1917 and January of 1918 the plaintiff purchased of the defendant certain household furniture for the sum of $909.25 and took it to his apartment in New York City. He gave back to the defendant two chattel mortgages, which provided for monthly payments of the purchase price, and also that the furniture should not be removed from the plaintiff's residence without the written consent of the mortgagee.

By May of 1918 the plaintiff had paid in all $295. In that month, desiring to move from the city for the summer months and give up his apartment, the plaintiff went to the defendant's place of business in New York City to see about storing his furniture until his return. It was arranged with the defendant's creditman, McGrath, that the plaintiff should send his furniture by his own truck to the defendant's storehouse and that the defendant would keep it for him free of charge. It is claimed that McGrath at the time of making these arrangements also promised and agreed to insure the furniture for the plaintiff's benefit. The furniture had not been insured by the plaintiff at any time. The conversation is given by Mr. Siegel as follows: "At that time he said, 'You had better transfer your insurance policy over to our warehouse.' I said 'I haven't any insurance. I never thought of taking it out, as I never had time to take it out.' But I said: 'Before the furniture comes down I will have my insurance man, who insures my life, have the furniture insured and transferred over to your place.' He said, 'That won't be necessary to get that from him; I will do it for you; it will be a good deal cheaper; I handle lots of insurance; when you get the next bill—you can send a check for that with the next installment.'"

The furniture was sent to the defendant's storehouse about the 15th of May and about the 15th of the following June was destroyed by fire. No insurance had been placed upon it.

Upon these facts the plaintiff has recovered the amount of his loss. The defendant raises at least two objections to this result. It claims first, that there was no consideration for the alleged agreement made with McGrath to insure the furniture and, second, that McGrath had no authority to make any such contract even if he did.

We are inclined to think that if the contract were made—and we must assume that it was as there is evidence to sustain the finding of the jury to this effect—there was in the nature of the case a consideration sufficient to sustain the promise. It is, of course, a fact that the defendant undertook to store the plaintiff's property without any compensation. The fact that it had a chattel mortgage upon the property did not affect its relationship as a bailee without pay. Under these circumstances it was liable for the destruction of the goods by fire unless due to its gross neglect. . . . There is no such element in this case.

But if in connection with taking the goods McGrath also voluntarily undertook to procure insurance for the plaintiff's benefit, the promise was part of the whole transaction and was linked up with the gratuitous bailment. The bailee, if such a contract were within McGrath's agency, was then under as much of an obligation to procure insurance as he was to take care of the goods.

When McGrath stated that he would insure the furniture it was still in the plaintiff's possession. It was after his statements and promises that the plaintiff sent the furniture to the storehouse. The defendant or McGrath entered upon the execution of the trust. It is in this particular that this case differs from Thorne v. Deas (4 Johs.84,99) so much relied upon by the defendant. In that case A and B were joint owners of a vessel. A voluntarily undertook to get the vessel insured but neglected to do so. The vessel having been lost at sea it was held that no action would lie against A for the non-performance of his promise, although B had relied upon that promise to his loss. It was said that there was no consideration for the promise. In that case there was the mere naked promise of A that he would insure the vessel. B parted with nothing to A. He gave up possession of none of his property to A, nor of any interest in his vessel. The case would have been decided differently, no doubt, if he had. As Chancellor Kent said in referring to the earlier cases: "There was no dispute or doubt, but that an action upon the case lay for a misfeasance, in the breach of a trust undertaken voluntarily."

The same may be said regarding the case of Brawn v. Lyford. (103 ME. 302)

In the case of Rogers v. Lucet . . . the law on this point was stated to be as follows:

A mere agreement to undertake a trust, in futuro, without compensation, it is true, is not obligatory; but when once undertaken, and the trust actually entered upon, the bailee is bound to perform it, according to the terms of his agreement. The confidence placed in him, and his undertaking to execute the trust, raise a sufficient consideration; a contrary doctrine would tend to injure and deceive his employer, who might be unwilling to consent to the bailment on any other terms.

In Hammond v. Hussey . . . the court, quoting Professor Parsons, says: "If a person makes a gratuitous promise, and then enters upon the performance of it, he is held to a full execution of all he has undertaken."

Where one had gratuitously undertaken to carry the money of a bailor to a certain place and deliver it to another and after receiving the money the bailee gave it to a neighbor who undertook to make delivery and lost it, it was held that the bailee had violated his trust in handling the money, that he was guilty of gross negligence in not fulfilling the terms of the bailment. . . .

From this aspect of the case we think there was a consideration for the agreement to insure. This renders it unnecessary to determine whether the plaintiff in refraining from insuring through his own agent at the suggestion of McGrath surrendered any right which would furnish a consideration for McGrath's promise.

I find that Thorne v. Deas (supra) has been seldom cited upon this question of consideration and whether or not we would feel bound to follow it today must be left open until the question comes properly before us.

As to McGrath's authority to act in this manner, we do not find the point raised by any sufficient exception.

For the reasons here stated, the judgment must be affirmed, with costs.

Discussion questions

1. How could McGrath's employer effectively given notice to Siegel that McGrath had no authority to insure Siegel's furniture?
2. If a person agrees to act as agent without consideration, could he ever change his mind thereafter without liability to his principal?

Name: ____________________

PROBLEMS

Date: ____________________

Section Number: ____________________

1. P has decided to expand the scope of its business. In this connection, it contemplates engaging several agents. Which of the following agency relationships is within the Statute of Frauds and thus should be contained in a signed writing?

_____ a. An irrevocable agency.

_____ b. A sales agency where the agent normally will sell goods which have a value in excess of $500.

_____ c. An agency for the forthcoming calendar year which is entered into in mid-December of the prior year.

_____ d. An agency which is of indefinite duration but is terminable upon one month's notice.

2. P appointed A as its agent. It was essential that P's identity be kept secret. Therefore, A was to act in the capacity of an agent for an undisclosed principal. The duration of the agency was for exactly one year commencing Wednesday of the following week. As a result of this agreement between P and A, P

_____ a. Is not liable on the agency contract unless it is in writing

_____ b. Cannot ratify the unauthorized acts of Doe.

_____ c. Can rely upon the parol evidence rule to avoid liability to third parties if the contract is in writing.

_____ d. Cannot be held liable for torts committed by A while acting as an agent.

3. A power of attorney is a useful method of creation of an agency relationship. The power of attorney

_____ a. Must be signed by both the principal and the agent.

_____ b. Exclusively determines the purpose and powers of the agent.

_____ c. Is the written authorization of the agent to act on the principal's behalf.

_____ d. Is used primarily in the creation of the attorney-client relationship.

4. Elliot mentioned to Martin, his friend, that he was going to attend an auction sale the next day at 10 A.M. at the premises of Norton Manufacturing Company which had gone bankrupt. Elliot said he was interested in buying a particular pressing machine for his business. Martin stated that he was also interested in attending the auction and bidding up to $5,000 for a particular lathe for his business. Elliot volunteered to bid on the lathe for Martin so that Martin would not have to attend the auction. Martin agreed and authorized Elliot to bid up to $5,000 for the lathe. That night at 7:45 P.M. Elliot learned that the pressing machine was not in good repair and decided not to go to the auction, but he did not notify Martin of his decision. The lathe was sold for $4,000 at the auction.

a. Is Elliot liable to Martin? Why?

____

____

____

b. Would your answer to (a) be different if Elliot telephoned Martin at his home the night before the auction three times between 8:00 P.M. and midnight to tell Martin that he was not going to the auction and there was no answer? Why?

____

____

____

c. Would your answer to (a) be different if Elliot telephoned Martin at his home at 8:00 P.M. on the night before the auction and left a message on Martin's telephone answering machine that he was not going to the auction and that Martin should make other arrangements to have someone else attend the auction on behalf of Martin? Why?

____

____

____

____

d. Would your answer to (a) be different if Elliot telephoned Martin not at 7:45 P.M. but at 11:30 P.M. on the night before the auction and left a message on Martin's telephone answering machine as stated in (c), which Martin did not play and hear until after the auction was held? Why?

____

____

____

____

5. Work Corp. has decided to expand the scope of its business. In this connection, it contemplates engaging several agents. Which of the following agency relationships is within the statute of frauds and thus should be contained in a signed writing?

_____ a. A sales agency where the agent normally will sell goods which have a value in excess of $500.

_____ b. An irrevocable agency.

_____ c. An agency which is of indefinite duration but which is terminable upon one month's notice.

_____ d. An agency for the forthcoming calendar year which is entered into in mid-December of the prior year.

6. Which of the following actions requires an agent for a corporation to have a written agency agreement?

_____ a. Purchasing office supplies for the principal's business.

_____ b. Purchasing an interest in undeveloped land for the principal.

_____ c. Hiring an independent general contractor to renovate the principal's office building.

_____ d. Retaining an attorney to collect a business debt owed the principal.

7. Forming an agency relationship requires that

_____ a. The agreement between the principal and agent be supported by consideration.

_____ b. The principal and agent **not** be minors.

_____ c. Both the principal and agent consent to the agency.

_____ d. The agent's authority be limited to the express grant of authority in the agency agreement.

8. A principal and agent relationship requires a

_____ a. Written agreement.

_____ b. Power of attorney.

_____ c. Meeting of the minds and consent to act.

_____ d. Specified consideration.

CHAPTER 3

TYPES OF AGENTS AND SPECIAL AGENTS

6. Introduction.

In the business world, principals employ many different kinds of agents, some of whom specialize in performing certain services for their principals. Principals and agents sometimes also create special agencies to accomplish a specific business purpose. As expected, the courts have judicially established special rules applicable to the rights, duties, and liabilities of each type of agent. The most common types of agents and agencies in the business world are those which will be discussed in the sections that follow: general agent, special agent, subagent, factor, del credere agent, universal agent, real estate broker, insurance broker, insurance agent, auctioneer, and two special agencies, agency for security and agency coupled with an interest.

7. General agent and special agent.

In the judicial development of the rules of agency, courts divided agents into two classes, general agents and special agents, for the purpose of determining the rights, duties and liabilities of the principal, the particular kind of agent, and third parties who dealt with such an agent.[1] Similarly, the Restatement on Agency distinguishes between a general agent and a special agent.[2]

An agent is a general agent when his principal gives him authority to transact all of the principal's business of a particular kind over a period of time with continuity of service.[3] Accordingly, the agent is a general agent even though his authority is limited to a particular business, as where the agent is employed as sales manager of the principal's stationery store.

By contrast, an agent is a special agent when his principal gives him authority to conduct only one transaction or a series of transactions for the principal where there is no continuity of service or where the agent's authority is extremely limited and circumscribed, in terms of time or purpose of the agency.[4] Consequently, an agent is a special agent where his principal employs him to buy or sell a particularly valuable diamond, painting collection, or several tracts of land suitable for shopping centers.

The major significance between a general agent and special agent is that the general agent usually has more actual authority, express and implied, and more apparent authority to bind his principal to a third party than does a special agent. Accordingly, a third party who deals with a special agent is charged by law with notice that the authority of a special agent is generally limited to the express authority given to him by his principal and that the special agent's implied authority is limited to such authority as is reasonably necessary to carry out his express authority. The special agent has very little apparent authority. The cumulative effect of these rules is that a principal is not bound by the contracts made in his name by his special agent if the special agent exceeds his express authority. Thus, third parties who deal with a special agent act at their peril if they do not ascertain his actual express authority before contracting with him. Unless the special agent acts within the scope of his actual express authority, the principal will not be bound by the contracts made by special agent in his name. In such a case, the third party will be able to hold the special agent personally liable on the contract based upon his breach of warranty because every agent impliedly warrants to the party he contracts with that he has actual authority to make the contract for his principal. This subject is fully discussed in Chapter 5.

In determining judicially whether an agent is a general agent or special agent, courts consider substance more than form. Thus, the use of the term "general agent" or "special agent" by the parties is not controlling. Rather, the courts examine the functions to be performed by the agent, the nature of the services to be rendered, the purpose of the agency and the period of time during which the agency is to be performed and whether or not there is a continuity of service required.[5]

The implied authority of a general agent is much greater than a special agent. Thus a general agent employed to manage the principal's drug store has implied authority to make contracts usually made in that business or incidental to it, or reasonably necessary to carry on the business.[6] Such implied authority includes authority to (1) hire, promote, and discharge employees, (2) purchase merchandise, (3) purchase necessary equipment and fixtures, (4) establish prices of goods to be resold to the public, (5) make necessary repairs, (6) collect money due his principal, (7) pay bills, and (8) do all other acts reasonably necessary or appropriate to manage the principal's business. By contrast, a special agent who is employed by his principal to make a single purchase of drugs has no implied authority or apparent authority to make a purchase of other items.

8. Subagent.

A subagent is a person appointed by an agent to perform some or all of his duties. The legal effect of such an appointment is that the agent has delegated performance of some or all of his duties. An agent may properly appoint a subagent without his principal's permission only if the agent's duties do not involve any discretion or judgment.[7] Accordingly, an agent has no authority to appoint a subagent if the agent's duties include the use of discretion or judgment unless his principal consents to such an appointment.[8] The principal's consent may be expressed or implied and such implied consent will be found by courts based upon the nature of the agency and the circumstances involved, as where the principal knows that the agent cannot personally perform, or where a sudden emergency arises, or where the custom and usage of trade allow an agent to employ one or more subagents.[9]

Assuming the agent has express or implied consent to appoint a subagent, and thereby delegate some or all of his duties, the agent must exercise reasonable care in selecting the subagent. If the agent acts negligently in appointing a subagent, as where he does not investigate his background before hiring him, he will be liable for any loss proximately caused by his negligence in appointing the subagent. However, if the agent acts with reasonable care in making the appointment of the subagent, he will not be liable for any subsequent loss caused by the wrongful acts, omissions or negligence of the subagent.[10]

In the event the agent's appointment of the subagent is properly made there will be privity of contract between the principal and the subagent and the principal and subagent will have the same rights, duties, and liabilities towards each other as does the principal and his agent.[11] Moreover, the principal will have the same liability to third parties on contracts made by his subagent as by his agent.[12] By contrast, if the agent's appointment of a subagent is not properly made because the principal did not consent expressly or impliedly, then there is no agency relationship between the principal and the subagent and the principal will not be bound by the subagent's torts or by any contract made in the principal's name with a third party.[13] This subject is discussed more fully in section 69.

9. Factor.

A factor is an agent to whom the principal has delivered his goods with authority to sell them for the principal in return for what is called a factoring commission. He is often called a "commission merchant" or "commission agent". The factor is given authority to sell the goods in his own name and at the time and for the price he thinks best, to sell on reasonable credit terms, to receive payment and to give warranties concerning said goods if it is usual to do so.[14] A factor has a lien on the principal's goods in his possession for expenses incurred in his capacity as a factor and for any unpaid amount due him from his principal, such as advances made by the factor to his principal.

10. Del credere agent.

A del credere agent is a factor who sells his principal's goods on credit and for a fee guarantees that the buyers will pay the purchase price. Thus, the del credere agent is a surety and is liable to his principal on his guaranty. Since his guaranty is considered as having been given for his own benefit, it is not required to be in writing to satisfy the Statute of Frauds.

11. Universal agent.

An agent is a universal agent when he is authorized to do anything his principal may properly and legally authorize an agent to do. In the business world it is extremely rare for a principal to appoint a universal agent.

12. Attorney-at-law.

An attorney-at-law is a lawyer duly licensed by law to engage in all legal acts both in and out of court which are necessary or incidental to the authority conferred upon him. The word "attorney" means "agent" or "representative".

13. Attorney-in-fact.

An attorney-in-fact is not a lawyer but an agent authorized to perform one or more acts for his principal under a written power of attorney. The term is usually applied to all agents having written authority from their principal. Where the power to act or contract is restricted to a certain period of time and to specific transactions, it is a limited power of attorney. However, where the authorization is to do any and all things necessary to carry out the principal's affairs, it is a general power of attorney.

14. Real estate broker.

A real estate broker is a person employed to negotiate the sale of real property. He is usually authorized to find either a purchaser or seller for his principal upon the terms and conditions set by the principal. The duly licensed broker earns his commission when he produces a purchaser or seller who agrees to the principal's terms and conditions even though the principal and his purchaser or seller never conclude the sale or purchase. To avoid this result, the principal and broker will usually expressly agree that the broker's commission will be earned and payable only when the sale or purchase has actually been concluded and the deed conveyed.

The principal may give the broker an exclusive agency pursuant to which the principal agrees not to employ any other broker but reserves the right to sell on his own without the aid of the broker and without paying any broker's commission if he succeeds in doing so.[15] Alternatively, the principal may give the broker the exclusive right of sale, in which case the principal cannot sell the property himself without paying the broker his commission.

A real estate broker who is authorized to "sell" his principal's property has authority only to find a purchaser and to bring him to his principal. He has no authority to execute a contract for his principal. In an agreement between the seller, as principal, and the real estate broker, the words "sell" or "to sell" have a well-understood legal meaning, and, in the absence of any contrary language in the agreement, do not confer authority in the broker to execute any contract in his principal's name.

15. Insurance broker.

An insurance broker is not an agent of the insurance company. Rather, he is the agent for the insured party who makes the application to the insurance company and negotiates with it and receives the insurance policy. Since the broker usually guarantees the payment of the premium by the insured party, the insured pays the premium directly to the broker.

16. Insurance agent.

An insurance agent is the agent for the insurance company. In the case of life insurance, he forwards the application to the company for its acceptance. In the case of other types of insurance, it is not unusual that the insurance agent is authorized by the company to accept applications, fix the rate, prepare, sign, and deliver policies, and collect the premiums.

17. Auctioneer.

An auctioneer is a person duly licensed by law to sell property to another at a public sale. When a principal employs an auctioneer as his agent to sell his property at a public sale the auctioneer's implied and apparent authority is limited in the absence of any agreement to the contrary. Thus, he may receive bids and sell to highest bidder for cash only. He may not make a private sale, may not accept anything but money as the price, may not give any warranties concerning the property he sells, may not deliver except upon payment of the price in money, may not sell on credit, may not modify or cancel the sales contract, and may not delegate his authority to conduct the public sale to another. If the auctioneer does any of the enumerated acts, his principal will not be liable to the third party on the contract made by the auctioneer in his name.

When the auctioneer accepts a bid he acts simultaneously as agent of the buyer and seller for purposes of preparing and signing a memorandum of sale as required by the Statute of Frauds. Today, sales by auction are also governed by Article 2-328 of the Uniform Commercial Code.

18. Agency for security.

In many commercial transactions a creditor who lends money to a debtor wants to assure repayment by becoming the agent of the debtor for the purpose of collecting money, in the name of the debtor, from third parties who owe money to the debtor, and applying the collections to repay the debt owed to the creditor. Thus, a bank that lends money to the owner of a commercial building will usually take a real estate mortgage on the building as collateral for the loan. However, the bank knows that the cash flow generated monthly by the tenants' payment of rent is what the landlord will use to pay off the loan. In such a case it is a common bank requirement to have the borrower, as principal, appoint and authorize the bank, as agent, to collect rents for the principal. Such authorization may begin immediately or become effective only in the event the principal defaults under the terms of the mortgage and will authorize the bank to apply the collections to the debt and account to the principal for the balance, if any. The agency described is called an agency for security because the agency has been created to give the agent security by giving him authority to collect money due his principal for the purpose of applying it to reduce a claim the agent has against his principal.

An agency for security cannot be terminated by the act of the principal, and his attempt to terminate the agency for security has no legal effect while the principal is indebted to his agent. However, an agency for security will be terminated by operation of law, by the death of the principal or agent,[16] the destruction of the subject matter of the agency, or the repayment of the debt. Applying these rules, tenants who have been paying rent directly to the bank-agent pursuant to the agency for security may properly continue to do so without liability to the landlord where the landlord is indebted to his bank-agent even though the landlord-principal has notified the bank-agent and the tenants that the bank-agent's authority to collect rents has been terminated and that he demands that the tenants pay rent directly to him.

However, in an agency for security, the agent-creditor does not have a lien or security interest in the future rent payments, which is the major difference between an agency for security and an agency coupled with an interest, which is discussed in the next section.[17]

19. Agency coupled with an interest.

In many commercial transactions a creditor who lends money to a debtor is not satisfied to have an agency for a security, which gives him only the right to collect money on behalf of his principal-debtor from third parties as it becomes due. Instead, the creditor wishes to have actual collateral in his possession, such as stocks or bonds, inventory or other valuable property owned by the debtor or a non-possessory security interest in specified property owned by the principal. In such a case, the creditor also wants authority to act with respect to said collateral in the event the debtor defaults. To accomplish this objective, the principal-debtor and agent-creditor may properly create what is called an agency coupled with an interest. When properly created, the principal-debtor gives his agent-creditor either possession of the collateral or a legal interest therein, called a security interest under Article 9 of the Uniform Commercial Code, and authority to dispose of the collateral and to apply the net proceeds realized to repay the debt. However, the mere recital in the agency agreement that it is the intention of the parties to create an agency coupled with an interest is insufficient without the agent receiving a present legal interest in the principal's property which is substantial and not nominal.[18]

In view of the foregoing, an agency coupled with an interest provides greater protection to the creditor than an agency for security. Accordingly, an agency coupled with an interest cannot be terminated by the act of the principal-debtor and his attempt to terminate the agency coupled with an interest has no operative legal effect while the principal is indebted to his agent. Moreover, contrary to the rule applicable to an agency for security, the death of the principal also will not terminate the agency coupled with an interest if the principal dies while still indebted to his agent. Thus, the only two events which will terminate an agency coupled with an interest is the destruction of the subject matter of the agency and the repayment of the entire debt.[19]

In examining the legal nature and concept of an agency for security and an agency coupled with an interest, the principal in both cases relinquishes legal control over the subject matter of the agency to the agent who exercises control for his own benefit rather than for the benefit of his principal. In this context, the agent is not a true agent according to the classic definition of the principal-agent relationship.[20]

Current References

"Agency property as collateral: legal issues for the secured lender," by Craig M. Tighe, 28 *Uniform Commercial Code Law Journal,* 115-151, Fall 1995.

Notes

1. Butler v. Maples, 76 U.S. (9 Wall.) 766 (1869). For an analysis of the factors used by courts to distinguish general agents from special agents, the writings of Basil H. Pollitt are especially relevant. See his "Special Agency," *Minnesota Law Review,* 17:17-46, December 1932; "Agency, General and Special," *Kentucky Law Journal,* 21:407-431, May 1933; and "Agency, General and Special—A Further Study," *Kentucky Law Journal,* 22:11-62, November 1933.
2. Restatement, Second, Agency, Sect. 3 (1958) distinguishes between a general agent and a special agent.
3. Corklite v. Rell Realty Corp., 249 N.Y. 1, 162 N.E. 565 (1928).
4. O.A. Skutt, Inc. v. J. and H. Goodwin, 251 App. Div. 84, 295 N.Y.S. 772 (1937).
5. Clearly, the liability of the principal cannot be settled by the parties calling the agent either general or special. If the act done by the agent, general or special, was within the actual or apparent scope of his authority, the principal will be found liable See "Agency—Distinction Between General and Special Agents," *Texas Law Review,* 11:540-541, June 1933.
6. The fact that the authority of an agent is limited to a particular business does not make the agency a special one. It may be general, in regard to that particular business, as if its range was unlimited. See Magnus v. Platt, 62 Misc. 499, 115 N.Y.S. 824 (1909).
7. Grinnel v. Buchanan, 1 Daly 538 (1866). See Floyd R. Mechem, "Delegation of Authority By An Agent," *Michigan Law Review* 5: 94 (1906).
8. People ex rel Cohoes Ry. Co. v. Public Service Commission, Second Dist., 143 App. Div. 769, 128 N.Y.S. 384 (1911).
9. Skutt, Inc. v. Goodwin, 251 App. Div 84 (1937).
10. White v. Bronson, 120 Misc. 73, 197 N.Y.S. 583 (1922); Cardot v. Barney, 63 N.Y. 281 (1875).
11. Friedman v. Irving Trust Co., 164 Misc. 811, 300 N.Y.S. 51 (1937); Buck v. State, 198 Misc. 575, 96 N.Y.S.2d 667 (1950); Gold v. Serrell, 6 Misc. 124, 26 N.Y.S. 5 (1893). For an analysis of the problems in establishing existence of a fiduciary relation between principal and subagent, see "Contracts - Agency - Fiduciary Relation Between Principal And Sub-Agent," *Illinois Law Review,* 26: 700-702, February 1932.
12. However, such liability exists only if the delegation of authority to the subagent does not exceed the authority granted to the original agent. See, Allegheny Corp. v. James Foundation of N.Y.S. Inc., D.C.N.Y., 115 F. Supp. 282 (1953).
13. Skutt, Inc. v. Goodwin, 251 App. Div. 84, 295 N.Y.S. 772 (1937); Palmer v. Holland, 51 N.Y. 416 (1873). The agent who appointed the subagent without consent of the principal will be bound, however, by the subagent's contracts with a third party and will be liable to the subagent for his compensation. See, Taylor v. Nostrand, 134 N.Y. 108, 31 N.E. 246 (1892). See, also, Warren Seavey, "Subagents and Subservants," *Harvard Law Review,* 65:658-671, February 1955.
14. For a concise analysis of the functions performed by a factor, see J.L.A. Ormiston, "Factoring and the smaller company," *New Law Journal,* 130:6-9, March 13, 1980 (supplement). For an excellent historical account of the factor in the English legal system and how it came to be applied in United States commerce, see Roderick Munday, "A Legal History of the Factory," *Anglo-American Law Review,* 6:221-260, October-December 1977.
15. Bagley v. Butler, 301 N.Y.S.2d 148 (1969). The Restatement, Second, Agency, Sect. 449(c) (1958) distinguishes between a real estate broker's exclusive agency and his exclusive right of sale.
16. Terwilliger v. Ontario Carbondale and Scranton R.R. Co., 149 N.Y. 86 (1896); Hunt v. Rousmanier, 8 Wheaton 173 (1823).
17. In Re Tabbagh's Estate, 167 Misc. 156, 3 N.Y.S.2d 542 (1938); Piper v. Wells, 175 Md. 326, 2 A.2d 28 (1938).
18. In Re Jarmakowski's Estate, 169 Misc. 463, 8 N.Y.S.2d 35 (1938); In Re Lohnert's Estate, 137 Misc. 442, 243 N.Y.S. 757 (1930).
19. The irrevocability of an agency coupled with an interest is discussed in, "Agency: Power coupled with an interest: Agency in terms irrevocable for purpose of agent's compensation," *Cornell Law Quarterly,* 19:267-271, 1934. See, also, Floyd R. Mechem, "An Agent's Right To Sue Upon Contracts I," *University of Pennsylvania Law Review,* 59:517-531, May 1911; Floyd R. Mechem, "An Agent's Right to Sue Upon Contracts II," *University of Pennsylvania Law Review,* 59:587-596, June 1911; "Agency - Irrevocable Powers - Power Coupled With An Interest," *Illinois Law Review,* 19:596, March 1925; "Agency - Irrevocable Powers - Power Coupled With An Interest," *Georgetown Law Journal,* 17:156-158, February 1929; "Agency - Power Coupled With An Interest - Contract Not To Reduce Agent's Share Below That of An Heir," *Columbia Law Review,* 34:549-561, February 1934; "Agency: Power coupled With An Interest: Agency in terms irrevocable for purpose of agent's compensation," *Cornell Law Quarterly,* 19:267-271, February 1934.
20. See the Restatement, Second, Agency, Sects. 14H, 138, and 464 (1958) which distinguish between these two types of agencies but observe that neither one involves strict fiduciary duties to the principal. See In Re Jarmakowski's Estate, 8 N.Y.S.2d 35 (1938).

Name: ____________________

PROBLEMS

Date: ____________________

Section Number: ____________________

1. A is a sales agent for P. A has assumed an obligation to indemnify P if any of A's customers fail to pay. Under these circumstances, which of the following is correct?

_____ a. A's engagement must be in writing regardless of duration.

_____ b. Upon default, P must first proceed against the delinquent purchaser-debtor.

_____ c. The above facts describe a del credere agency relationship and A will be liable in the event his customers fail to pay P.

_____ d. There is no fiduciary relationship on either A's or P's part.

2. Foremost Realty, Inc., is a real estate broker that also buys and sells real property for its own account. Hobson purchased a ranch from Foremost. The terms were 10% down with the balance payable over a 25 year period. After several years of profitable operation of the ranch, Hobson had two successive bad years. As a result, he defaulted on the mortgage. Foremost did not want to foreclose, but instead offered to allow Hobson to remain on the ranch and suspend the payment schedule until Foremost could sell the property at a reasonable price. However, Foremost insisted that it be appointed as the irrevocable and exclusive agent for the sale of the property. Although Hobson agreed, he subsequently became dissatisfied with Foremost's efforts to sell the ranch and gave Foremost notice in writing terminating the agency. Foremost has indicated to Hobson that he does not have the legal power to do so.

   Can Hobson terminate the agency? Explain.

3. On January 2, Lawrence loaned Barton $50,000. Barton owned a valuable painting for which the Modern Museum had offered him $75,000 one month earlier. On January 19, Barton gave Lawrence a written instrument authorizing Lawrence to sell the painting to the Modern Museum for $75,000 at any time after April 15 if Barton did not repay the loan by that date and to retain out of the proceeds the amount of the loan, and to return the surplus to Barton. On April 15 Barton informed Lawrence that he could not repay the loan and that Lawrence's authority to sell the painting was revoked. On the same day Barton informed the curator of the Modern Museum by letter that his painting was not for sale under any circumstances. Five days after the curator received Barton's letter, Lawrence showed the January 21 written authorization to the curator and they executed a contract for the sale of the painting for $75,000. Lawrence signed the contract as agent for Barton.

   a. Does Barton have any remedy against Lawrence for contracting in his name to sell the painting to the Modern Museum? Explain.

b. Does Barton have any liability to the Modern Museum if he refuses to deliver his painting pursuant to the terms of the contract? Explain.

4. Maxwell, a manufacturer, turned over certain merchandise to Abbot, a factor or commission merchant. Pursuant to the terms of their written agreement, Abbot undertook to sell the merchandise at stated prices on a factoring basis under which Abbot was to retain as his compensation any overage that he would receive above a $25,000 advance that he had made to Maxwell upon receipt of the goods. Abbot thereby acquired an irrevocable property interest in the subject matter of the agency. Before Abbot sold any of the merchandise, two events occurred. First, Maxwell died. Second, two weeks after Maxwell's death, all the merchandise turned over to Abbot was completely destroyed by fire without negligence on Abbot's part.

   Was the irrevocable agency terminated by the occurrence of either event? Explain fully.

5. Stanton, a manufacturer, delivered certain merchandise to Zayre, a factor or commission merchant. Pursuant to their written agreement, Zayre agreed to sell the merchandise at stated prices on a factoring basis. Zayre was to receive as his compensation any money he received above a $25,000 advance he made to Stanton upon receipt of the goods, and to apply the money received to the advance. Before Zayre sold any merchandise, two events occurred. First, Stanton died. Second, one week after Stanton's death all the merchandise delivered to Zayre was completely destroyed by fire without negligence on Zayre's part.

   a. Was the agency terminated by Stanton's death? Why?

   b. Was the agency terminated by the destruction of the merchandise? Why?

6. Basso borrowed $20,000 from Lee and delivered to Lee several valuable autographs by United States Presidents with authority to sell all of them for $20,000, to collect the price, and apply it to the amount of the loan. Before Lee was able to offer the autographs to any prospective collector, Basso revoked Lee's authority. Nevertheless, Lee sold the autographs to Thompson who had no knowledge of the facts.

   a. Is the sale binding on Basso? Why?

   b. Suppose Basso died immediately before the sale to Thompson. Is the sale binding on the estate of Basso? Why?

7. Philips, the owner of an apartment house, borrowed $150,000 from Apple Realty Corp. and executed and delivered to Apple a mortgage on the apartment house as security for the repayment of the loan, and authorized Apple to collect rents due from tenants at a commission of ten percent. Shortly thereafter Philips died.

   a. Does Philips' death terminate Apple's authority to collect rent? Why?

   b. Suppose that Philips had assigned to Apple the rents due from tenants and had authorized Apple to apply the rents collected to the loan after deduction of the commissions. Would Philips' death terminate Apple's authority to collect the rents? Why?

8. Baxter borrowed $50,000 from Lomax for the purchase of a computer. Baxter then leased the computer to Terrence for two years at a monthly rental of $4,000 and authorized Lomax to collect the rent from Terrence and apply it to the amount of the loan. After Lomax collected $24,000 in rent Baxter notified Lomax that this authority to collect rent from Terrence was revoked.

   a. Is the revocation effective or may Lomax nevertheless collect the rent until the loan is repaid? Why?

b. Suppose Baxter died after Lomax collected $24,000 in rent from Terrence. May Lomax lawfully continue to collect rent from Terrence until the loan is repaid? Why?

____

____

____

____

9. An agency coupled with an interest will be created by a written agreement which provides that a (an)

_____ a. Borrower shall pledge securities to a lender which authorizes the lender to sell the securities and apply the proceeds to the loan in the event of default.

_____ b. Employee is hired for a period of two years at $40,000 per annum plus 2% of net sales.

_____ c. Broker is to receive a 5% sales commission out of the proceeds of the sale of a parcel of land.

_____ d. Attorney is to receive 25% of a plaintiff's recovery for personal injuries.

10. Pell is the principal and Astor is the agent in an agency coupled with an interest. In the absence of a contractual provision relating to the duration of the agency, who has the right to terminate the agency before the interest has expired?

	Pell	*Astor*
a.	Yes	Yes
b.	No	Yes
c.	No	No
d.	Yes	No

11. Orr gives North power of attorney. In general, the power of attorney

_____ a. Will be valid only if North is a licensed attorney at law.

_____ b. May continue in existence after Orr's death.

_____ c. May limit North's authority to specific transactions.

_____ d. Must be signed by both Orr and North.

12. Anker wishes to give Mix power of attorney. In general, the power of attorney

_____ a. May limit Mix's authority to specific transactions.

_____ b. Must be signed by both Anker and Mix.

_____ c. Will be valid only if Mix is a licensed attorney at law.

_____ d. May continue in existence after Anker's death.

13. Noll gives Carr a written power of attorney. Which of the following statements is correct regarding this power of attorney?

_____ a. It must be signed by both Noll and Carr.

_____ b. It must be for a definite period of time.

_____ c. It may continue in existence after Noll's death.

_____ d. It may limit Carr's authority to specific transactions.

CHAPTER 4

LEGAL CAPACITY OF PRINCIPAL AND AGENT

20. Legal capacity of principal: introduction.

In accordance with common law rules of contract law, anyone who has legal capacity to contract in his own behalf with a third party may do so through his agent. Conversely, if the principal does not have any legal capacity to contract, he may not do so through an agent even if the agent himself has legal capacity to contract.[1] The question then arises under what lawful circumstances, if any, may each of the following lawfully act as a principal: infant, incompetent person, married woman, alien, partnership, joint parties, corporation, and unincorporated association, society or club. Each will be discussed in the sections that follow.

21. Infant as principal.

In the case of an infant principal (under 18 in almost all states), it has long been the rule that an infant principal has legal capacity to enter into an agency relationship and to appoint an agent, subject, however, to his right to disaffirm his contracts in accordance with common law rules of contract law. Thus, the infant principal may subsequently disaffirm the contract with his agent as well as any contract made on his behalf by his agent with a third party. In such a case both the contract creating the agency relationship and the resulting contract made by the agent on behalf of his principal with the third party are voidable at the infant principal's election provided he disaffirms such a contract in a timely manner.[2] If the subject matter of the contract involves personal property or services, he may disaffirm the contract during his infancy or within a reasonable time after he reaches his majority. However, if the subject matter of the contract involves real property, he may not disaffirm the contract until he reaches his majority or within a reasonable time thereafter. If he does not disaffirm the contract in a timely manner or he affirms the contract after reaching his majority by his words or conduct, he will be bound on the contract made by his agent while he, the principal, was an infant.[3]

While the infant principal has the right to disaffirm the agency contract and the resulting contract made by his agent with a third party, it is well settled that neither the agent nor the third party may disaffirm the contract with the infant principal. The rationale of this rule of law is that infancy is a personal defense available only to the infant principal and not to those who contract with the infant principal. Thus, agents and third parties who contract with infant principals do so at their peril. However, in such a case, the third party may hold the agent personally liable even though the agent contracted in the name of his infant principal where the agent knows his principal is an infant and he knows that the third party is ignorant of the principal's infancy. This result flows from the rule that every agent who contracts on behalf of his principal impliedly warrants to the third party that his principal has legal capacity to contract if he knows or has reason to know of such lack of capacity and of the third party's lack of knowledge of such incapacity and yet fails to inform the third party of such fact. Since an infant principal does not have capacity, the agent has breached his implied warranty to the third party in such circumstances and is liable for any loss incurred by the third party when the infant principal disaffirms the contract. Thus, an agent who contracts with a third party on behalf of an infant principal with such knowledge does so at his peril. Of course, if such an agent is without sufficient assets, the maxim may be observed: third parties who contract with financially poor agents do so at their peril.

22. Incompetent person as principal.

A principal who is insane or otherwise mentally incompetent but who has not been so adjudicated by a court of law has legal capacity to enter into an agency relationship and to appoint an agent, subject, however, to his right to disaffirm his contract in accordance with common law rules of contract law. Thus, such a principal may disaffirm the contract with his agent and any resulting contract made on his behalf by his agent with a third party. The contracts made by such a principal are voidable. However, if such a principal has been judicially declared incompetent, his contracts are no longer voidable but absolutely void and he has no legal capacity to contract thereafter.[4] If a nonadjudicated incompetent disaffirms his contract, he must restore the other contracting party to the condition which prevailed prior to the execution of the contract.[5] By contrast, if the other contracting party knew that the principal was mentally incompetent or if the principal was an adjudicated incompetent, then the principal has no such duty.[6] Before adjudication of incompetency, the principal's mental incompetency is a defense available only to such a principal and not to the agent or third party who contracts with a mentally incompetent person. Thus, the third party is bound on the contract if the principal does not elect to disaffirm. By contrast, after adjudication of incompetency, the agent and third party may also disaffirm any contract thereafter made with him.[7]

23. Married woman as principal.

For several hundred years it was the common law rule in England and the United States that a married woman had no legal capacity to contract in her own name (presumably for her own benefit). This rule disqualified her from lawfully acting as a principal or from employing others to act as her agent. This rule was abolished by statutes enacted in every state during the nineteenth century that expressly granted her legal capacity to contract in her own name during marriage. Thus, since then a married woman has legal capacity to contract in her own name for any purpose and in any capacity, including as a principal with full legal capacity to appoint others as her agents.[8]

24. Alien as principal.

An alien residing in a country at war with the United States is an enemy alien and may not lawfully appoint an agent to act in the United States. The prohibition is directed against the enemy alien's attempt to do business in this country through an agent. By contrast, if the enemy alien resides in the United States, he may act here through an agent as long as he is not prohibited by local or federal statute. Of course, an alien friend, wherever he resides, may appoint an agent to act for him in this country.

25. Partnership as principal.

A general or limited partnership may act as a principal. Moreover, under the Uniform Partnership Act, each general partner is also a principal and an agent of all the partners and the partnership for the conduct of transactions within the scope of the partnership business.[9] Thus, there is a statutory foundation for the application of agency law to partnership transactions.

26. Joint parties as principals.

Joint parties may become joint principals only by the consent of all. Accordingly, the fact that they have joint interests does not of itself authorize only one or several of the joint parties to appoint another an agent for all, or for one or several joint parties to act as agent for all. In the absence of a contrary intent, any authority given to an agent by joint principals refers only to matters in which they could act as joint principals. If the authority is to sell, it extends only to property which they jointly own.

27. Corporation as principal.

A corporation has the powers that are conferred upon it by the certificate of incorporation and by statute. Generally, they include the express power to appoint agents to transact business in behalf of the corporation. However, even in the absence of such express power the corporate power to appoint agents is implied.

28. Unincorporated association, society, and club as principal.

It is well-settled that an unincorporated association, society or club can act lawfully as a principal only if such an organization has a constitution or by-laws which confers authority upon any member, officers or board of directors to act as its agent. If so, each member is bound as a principal on any authorized contract or transaction made by the agent which is within the scope of the purposes for which the organization was formed, unless he terminates his membership before the contract or transaction occurs.[10]

29. Liability of agent where principal lacks legal capacity to contract.

In the event the principal lacks legal capacity to contract, he is not liable to his agent or to the third party with whom his agent contracted. However, in such a case, the third party may recover against the agent who contracted on behalf of the principal based upon breach of implied warranty of capacity. This rule applies because a person who contracts on behalf of a principal impliedly warrants to the third party with whom he contracts that his principal has legal capacity to contract with the third party. If the principal does not, because of any reason other than his infancy, such as where the principal is insane, the agent will be personally liable on the contract to the third party for breach of the implied warranty of legal capacity.[11] Thus, an agent who acts as an agent for a principal who lacks legal capacity to contract, does so at his peril. However, where the principal is an infant, the liability of the agent for breach of implied warranty of capacity is as set forth in section 21.

30. Legal capacity of agents: introduction.

In accordance with common law rules of contract law, anyone who has legal capacity to contract in his own behalf may act as agent for another unless a statute applies to prohibit a party from acting as an agent in connection with particular contracts. However, under agency law, a person who has no legal capacity to contract on his own behalf may act as agent for another unless a statute applies to prohibit a party from acting as an agent in connection with particular contracts. Thus, under agency law, a person who has no legal capacity to contract on his own behalf may lawfully act as an agent for another under certain circumstances.[12] In such a case, the resulting contract made by the agent on the principal's behalf will bind the principal to the third party if made within the scope of the agent's actual or apparent authority. The question then arises under what circumstances a party may lawfully be an agent when the party proposing to act as an agent is: an infant, unlicensed, incompetent, a married woman, a partnership, a corporation or joint parties. Each will be discussed in the sections that follow.

31. Infant as agent.

In the United States there are approximately 20,000,000 persons between the ages of 13 and 18. Many of these teenagers work part-time or full-time as agents, primarily as salespersons. Under the common law rules of contract law, an infant (under 18 in almost all states) has no legal capacity to contract in his own name. Therefore, an infant may disaffirm his contracts. However, under the general rules of agency law, an infant may lawfully act as an agent for a principal if he possesses sufficient mental capacity, business judgement and acumen.[13] The significant effect of this rule of law is that any contract made by an infant agent on behalf of his principal with a third party, which is within the actual or apparent authority of the agent, is binding on the principal and the third party. By contrast, an infant agent may disaffirm his own contract with his principal and may also avoid any contract liability with the third party with whom the infant agent contracts on behalf of his principal. However, the defense of infancy is personal and available only to the infant agent and not to the principal or third party, both of whom are liable to each other on the contract made by the infant agent even though the infant agent disaffirms his agency contract with his principal. This legal result is based upon the rationale that the contract made (albeit through the instrumentality of an infant agent) is in fact and law between the principal and the third party. Indeed, the infant agent is not a legal party to the contract between the principal and third party where the agent contracted in the name of his principal. Thus, a principal may not disaffirm the contract made on his behalf by his infant agent on the ground that his agent was an infant even if the principal lacked knowledge of the agent's infancy when he appointed the agent.

32. Unlicensed person as agent.

If the law requires a person to have a license to act as an agent for another, he cannot lawfully act as agent without such a license (e.g., attorney, real estate agent, insurance agent). The significant legal effect of this rule is that the unlicensed agent may not enforce the contract he has with his principal even though he has fully performed his contract with his principal. Applying this rule, an agent who is not a licensed real estate broker as required by statute, who finds a buyer for his neighbor's house for an agreed 6% commission, will not be able to enforce his contract against his principal and will recover nothing. By statute in many states, an attorney-at-law is authorized to act individually as a real estate broker without a separate real estate broker's license.[14] However, he may not employ others to engage in the real estate brokerage business without first obtaining a real estate broker's license.

33. Incompetent as agent.

A person who is insane or mentally incompetent has no legal capacity to be an agent. Consequently, a principal who appoints such a person as his agent without knowledge of such incompetency, as where he communicates with him by mail, may disaffirm the contract with his agent and any resulting contract made on his behalf by such an incompetent agent. However, it has been held that such a person has legal capacity to act as an agent for a principal who appoints him with knowledge of such incompetency.[15] In that event, the principal will be bound by his contract with his agent and by the resulting contract made by his agent on his behalf if the agent acted within the scope of his actual or apparent authority.

34. Married woman as agent.

As noted earlier in the section on a married woman as principal, a married woman today may lawfully act as agent for another.[16] Thus the sixty million women in the American workforce have the same legal capacity as men to act as agents.

35. Partnership as agent.

A partnership may act as an agent for a principal. To accomplish this result, a partner may act as an agent for the partnership for the conduct of transactions within the scope of the partnership to enable the partnership to become an agent for a principal.

36. Corporation as agent.

A corporation which has express or implied power to do so may act as an agent for a principal.[17] To accomplish this result, any agent who acts within the scope of his actual or apparent authority will enable the corporation to become an agent for a principal.

37. Joint parties as agent.

Joint parties may act as agents, but they must act together. Thus, a principal who appoints two parties as his joint agents to contract with third parties on his behalf will be bound by contracts only if made by both of the joint agents. If the principal appoints two or more persons as his agents, without stating whether they shall act jointly or severally (separately) in contracting on his behalf with third parties, courts will determine whether such agents must act jointly or may act separately based upon the intention of the principal according to the terms of the power conferred, the surrounding circumstances and course of dealing. If no intent can be found to indicate that the authority to act as agent may be exercised by each without the other, then it is legally presumed that the agents must act jointly in order to bind the principal.

Notes

1. Corcoran v. Scolaro, 46 N.Y.S. 2d 278 (1943); In Re Peters Estate, 71 Misc. 2d 662, 336 N.Y.S. 2d 712 (N.Y. Sur. 1972); In Re Farley, 213 N.Y. 15, 106 N.E. 756 (1914). Some courts, however, have granted exceptions to this rule by permitting a minor to appoint an agent for the limited purpose of contracting for the minor's necessities of life. See, Casey v. Kastel, 237 N.Y. 305, 142 N.E. 671 (1924).
2. Goldfinger v. Doherty, 153 Misc. 826, 276 N.Y.S. 289 (1934); see, "The Capacity Of An Infant To Appoint An Agent," *Modern Law Review,* 18:461, September 1955.
3. Anderson v. Middle States Util. Co., 231 Mo. App. 129, 98 S.W. 2d 163 (1936). The only contracts to which an infant may be held even if he chooses to disaffirm are those contracts related to necessaries or, in New York, to reasonable business contracts made between April 13, 1941 and September 1, 1974 if he is an infant businessman; see, for example, New York General Obligations Law 3-101.
4. Figueroa v. City of New York, 279 App.Div. 771, 109 N.Y.S. 2d 126 (1951); Wittkugel v. State, 5 Misc. 2d 886, 160 N.Y.S. 2d 242 (1955), affirmed 5 A.D. 2d 958, 172 N.Y.S. 2d 576 (1958).
5. Smith v. Ryan, 191 N.Y. 452, 84 N.E. 402 (1908).
6. Merritt v. Merritt, 43 App. Div. 68, 59 N.Y.S. 357 (1899).
7. Frankel v. Heinrichs, 187 Misc. 532, 67 N.Y.S. 2d 333 (1946).

8. See, for example, New York General Obligations Law 3-301; Gott v. Scott, 199 So. 460 (La. App. 1940).
9. Uniform Partnership Act, Section 9; see, also, chapter one, notes 5 and 6.
10. Winona Lumber Co. v. Church, 6 S.D. 498, 62 N.W. 107 (1895).
11. See, Restatement, Second, Agency, Sect. 322 (1958). See, also, Goldfinger v. Doherty, 153 Misc. 826, 276 N.Y.S. 289 (1934), where a New York court held that an agent is not liable to the third party unless the agent knew or had reason to know of his principal's lack of full capacity and had reason to believe that the third party was in ignorance of this fact.

The Restatement, Second, Agency, Sects 329-331 (1958) describe generally an agent's implied warranty of authority on matters other than the capacity of his principal even if he makes no express representations as to his authority. To prevent liability, the agent should expressly state that he does not warrant his authority to bind his principal (Sect. 331). This rule applies even though the agent reasonably believes that he was authorized to act.

12. Chastain v. Bowman, 9 S.C. (1 Hill) 270 (1833).
13. Butler v. Moore, 125 Ga. App. 435, 188 S.E. 2d 142 (1972); Smith v. Smith, 41 Ala. App. 403, 139 So. 2d 345 (1961).
14. Under Sect. 442-f of the New York Real Property Law, an attorney is not required to be licensed as a real estate broker as long as he is licensed as an attorney in New York. See, Weinblatt v. Parkway, St. Johns Place Corp., 136 Misc. 743, 241 N.Y.S. 721, aff'd 229 A.D. 865, 243 N.Y.S. 810 (1930).
15. Sims v. Slovin, 42 Del. Ch. 216, 207 A. 2d 597 (1965).
16. Cobuzzi v. Parks, 315 Mass. 199, 51 N.E. 2d 965 (1943); Spartan Petroleum Corp. v. Curt Brown Drilling Co., 446 P. 2d 808 (Okla. 1968).
17. United Bonding Insurance Co. v. Banco Suizo-Panameno, S.A., 422 F. 2d 1142 (5th Cir. 1970).

Case 2

Goldfinger v. Doherty et al.

276 N.Y.S.289 (1934)

Introduction

Infants frequently enter into contracts through adult agents. In such a case, the question arises what is the liability of the infant principal and his agent when the principal elects to disaffirm the contract made in his name by his agent. The following case illustrates the different implied warranties that an agent makes to a third party when he contracts with the third party in the name of his infant principal.

Shientag, Justice

The plaintiff sued the defendant Doherty, disaffirming certain purchases of stock, made in her behalf by her duly authorized agent, alleging that she was an infant at the time of the transactions, and that she now elected to rescind and offered to return the stock, together with the stock and cash dividends received thereon. The defendant Doherty thereupon obtained an order permitting him to serve a supplemental summons and complaint on the agent Samuel Goldfinger, pursuant to section 193, subdivision 2, of the Civil Practice Act. No question is raised on this appeal with reference to the propriety of this order. . . . The supplemental pleading alleged, in substance, that the agent purchased the stock from Doherty on behalf of the alleged infant "without disclosing the infancy of his principal." It further alleged that, if plaintiff should recover against Doherty, then the defendant Goldfinger, plaintiff's agent, will be liable to defendant Doherty for damages sustained through the rescission of the contracts by plaintiff, "on the ground that defendant Samuel Goldfinger has breached his implied warranty that he was authorized to enter into binding contracts for the plaintiff."

The supplemental pleading was dismissed below for insufficiency, no opinion being rendered. From that determination, the defendant Doherty has appealed to this court.

The fair inference to be drawn from the pleading is that at the time of the transactions in suit the infant was at least 16 years old; that she has disaffirmed, not the authority of the agent to act in her behalf, but the transactions entered into by her duly authorized agent. The relationship between the infant and the agent is not disclosed by the pleading, nor is there any allegation that, at the time of the transaction, the agent knew, or had reasonable cause to know, of his principal's infancy, or that the other contracting party, Doherty, was in ignorance thereof.

A contract made by an infant is not void. He has the capacity to enter into an agreement which will bind the other contracting party. An infant's contract is said to be voidable. Another way of putting it is that the law, for the protection of the infant, gives him the privilege, under certain conditions, of disaffirming his contract. This privilege is not without its limitations. . . .

An infant's appointment of an agent is not void; it is merely voidable, like any other contract he makes. "Notwithstanding numerous general statements in the books, sound principles compel the conclusion that no satisfactory distinction can be drawn between a sale and delivery by the infant and a sale and delivery by an agent for him. . . . Dicta and general statements to the contrary are no longer respectable authority." . . .

There is, therefore, no basis for the contention of the appellant that disaffirmance by the infant of a contract entered into on his behalf by his agent renders the transaction void ab initio, so that the agent is deemed to have acted without any authority. The infant, without questioning the authority of his agent, may disaffirm the contract entered into on his behalf, in the same manner as if he had made the contract directly. The infant may disaffirm the contract of agency; he may disaffirm the contract entered into by his agent. Either contract is voidable; neither is void.

The general rule is that, if, in making a contract in the name of the principal, the agent acts without authority or beyond it, be becomes liable. As the agent assumes to represent the principal he cannot be heard to say that he had no authority, or that there was, in fact, no principal to be bound; he impliedly warrants that there is a principal, and that he is authorized to act for him.

"The agent does not warrant the capacity of the principal." . . . An agent does not warrant that his principal has full contractual capacity, any more than he warrants that his principal is solvent. Thus an agent for one not of legal age is not necessarily liable if the infant avoids the obligation of the contract made on his account." Comment (a) on section 332, Restatement of the Law of Agency. An agent who misrepresents the capacity of his principal to contract is liable as for any other misrepresentation, and this whether he misrepresents tortiously or innocently.

In the absence of misrepresentation, under what circumstances, if any, is an agent acting for an infant, who subsequently disaffirms, not the agency, but the transaction of the agent, liable to the other contracting party? It must appear that the agent knew or had reason to know of his principal's lack of full capacity, and it must further appear that the other contracting party was in ignorance thereof. The theory of breach of warranty of authority is that one dealing with an agent has been misled by him. This could hardly be deemed to have occurred, if all the facts are known. "It is material, in these cases, that the party claiming a want of authority in the agent should be ignorant of the truth touching the agency.". . . If the agent "acts within his instructions, and in good faith, especially when the facts are equally known to both parties, he is not personally responsible, although it may happen that the authority itself is void." . . .

Assuming that the agent knows or has reason to know of his principal's lack of full capacity, and of the other party's ignorance thereof, what, if any, is the agent's liability?

Clear authority on this point is lacking. Ordinarily, the duty to speak has been limited to a situation where there is either a pre-existing fiduciary relationship, or one expressly created by a repose of confidence, or where the contract itself calls for disclosure.

In a case as here presented, however, the duty imposed, if any, must rest on a broader basis. Concealment involves a suppression of truth, and, when accompanied by a statement in itself true, they together may create such a misleading impression as to cause the statement made to be in effect false and actionable. "Half the truth may be a lie in effect. . . .

The basis of the liability of an agent, in a situation such as we are here considering, is that he has produced "a false impression upon the mind of the other party; and, if this result is accomplished, it is unimportant whether the means of accomplishing it are words or acts of the defendant, or his concealment or suppression of material facts not equally within the knowledge or reach of the plaintiff." . . . We believe that the correct rule is that set forth in the Restatement of the Law of Agency as follows: "332. Agent of partially incompetent principal. An agent making a contract for a disclosed principal whose contracts are voidable because of lack of full capacity to contract, or for a principal who, although having capacity to contract generally, is incompetent to enter into the particular transaction, is not thereby liable to the other party. He does not become liable by reason of the failure of the principal to perform, unless he contracts or represents that the principal has capacity or unless he has reason to know of the principal's lack of capacity and of the other party's ignorance thereof."

We believe that this rule is based, not only upon the requirements of fair business practice, but that it embodies sound legal principles. . . .

If, therefore, the liability of the agent is to be based on his failure to disclose facts in connection with his principal's lack of full capacity to the other contracting party, it must appear (1) that the agent knew or had reason to know the facts indicating his principal's lack of full capacity; (2) that the other contracting party was in ignorance thereof and the agent had reason so to believe; and (3) that the transaction is one in which lack of full capacity was a material fact.

Drawing the most favorable inferences from the pleading under consideration, we find that it fails to set forth enough facts to constitute a cause of action.

We feel, however, that the defendant Doherty should have an opportunity to amend, if he be so advised, so as to conform his pleading to the requirements herein set forth.

The order dismissing the supplemental complaint is affirmed, with $10 costs and disbursements, with leave to the defendant to serve an amended supplemental complaint within six days after service of order entered hereon upon payment of said costs.

Discussion questions

1. Does an agent impliedly warrant that his principal (a) has capacity to contract? (b) is solvent? (c) has authorized him to contract on his behalf?
2. When is an agent liable to the third party he contracted with where his infant principal subsequently and properly disaffirms the contract made by the agent in the infant principal's name?
3. Is an agent liable to a third party he contracts with where the infant principal properly disaffirmed the contract creating the agency and the particular contract made by the agent in the infant principal's name?
4. What provision should the third party include in his contract with an agent that will entitle the third party to recover from the agent in the event the principal subsequently disaffirms the contract made by the agent in his principal's name with the third party?

PROBLEMS

Name: __________

Date: __________

Section Number: __________

1. Peter, 17, engaged his 22 year old brother-in-law Adam, as his agent for the purchase of a used sports car from Tom. Adam knew that Peter was a minor, and that Tom did not know this, but made the purchase to accommodate Peter. He acted without compensation and with a written authorization to make the purchase. At the time of the sale Adam exhibited the authorization to Tom and signed the contract in such a way as to clearly indicate he was acting in an agency capacity. Peter, after driving the car for several days, decided he would obtain a better deal elsewhere. He informed Tom that he disaffirmed the contract, stopped all payments and returned the car to Tom. Tom seeks to enforce the contract against either Peter or Adam.

   a. In an action by Tom against Peter, judgment for whom? Explain.

   b. In an action by Tom against Adam, judgment for whom? Explain.

2. The Fidelity Surety Company executed a power of attorney naming Adams, Baker and Cole agents with authority to issue fidelity bonds on behalf of the company. Adams issued a fidelity bond on behalf of the company to the Excelsior Bank pursuant to which the company insured the faithful performance of duties by certain bank employees.

   a. Is the Fidelity Surety Bank liable on the bond if it promptly notifies the Excelsior Bank that Adams had no authority on his own to issue the fidelity bond? Why?

b. Is the Fidelity Surety Company liable on the bond if it accepts the premium paid by the Excelsior Bank without knowledge that Adams alone issued the fidelity bond? Why?

3. Nikal hired Youngblood, 17 years old, to sell automobiles. Youngblood made a very good sale, and Nikal wishes to hold the buyer liable on the contract. The customer claims that a minor cannot lawfully act as an agent and, consequently, there is no enforceable contract.

   In an action by Nikal against the customer, judgment for whom? Explain.

CHAPTER 5

AUTHORITY OF AN AGENT

38. Actual authority: distinction between express and implied.

When the agent acts within the scope of the actual authority conferred upon him by his principal, the resulting contract made by the agent on his principal's behalf with a third party will bind both the principal and third party. The actual authority given by the principal to his agent may be either express or implied. The agent's authority is express authority when the principal by his words, oral or written, specifically authorizes his agent to make one or more contracts on his behalf with one or more third parties in accordance with the principal's specific terms, such as the specific personal property or real property to be bought or sold, price to be sold or purchased for, and the terms of payment. By contrast, an agent's actual authority may be implied only where there is no express authority conferred upon the agent to make a particular contract on behalf of the principal.[1]

39. Implied authority: introduction.

When a principal enters into an agency relationship with his agent, he will usually tell him the nature and extent of his general authority (e.g., salesman) and any specific limitations on his general authority. However, he rarely tells his agent every specific detail as to what constitutes his actual authority because it is virtually impossible for the principal to state the exact actual authority the agent will have in connection with every possible transaction or action that the agent may become involved in on behalf of the principal. To the extent the principal confers specific authority on his agent, the agent has express authority. However, if an agent's actual authority were limited by law to the express authority given to him, he would not be able to perform his duties in a satisfactory and efficient manner because he would have to first obtain express authority each time he wanted to act for his principal if his proposed action was not expressly authorized. Moreover, the agent would be liable to his principal where he acted without express authority even if he acted in furtherance of his principal's business interests.

Accordingly, the common law rules of agency expanded the agent's actual authority to include not only the express authority given but also implied authority. The judicial recognition that an agent has actual authority that is implied enables the agent to function more effectively and legally protects the agent in his dealing with his principal when the agent acts within the scope of his implied authority. Further, third parties who contract with agents are legally protected because they may enforce contracts against the agent's principal based upon the implied authority the agent has, without having to inquire or prove that express authority existed.

It is a well-settled rule of agency law that an agent has implied authority to do whatever is reasonably necessary to perform the express authority given to him by his principal.[2] If the agent acts within the scope of his implied authority, his principal will be liable on contracts made on his behalf by his agent and the agent will have no liability to his principal for so acting.[3]

To determine whether or not an agent had implied authority to act on behalf of his principal, when there is a conflict between the principal and third party, courts will examine a number of factors to resolve the issue of whether the principal is liable to the third party on the contract made by his agent on his behalf. The factors examined by the courts to determine the nature and extent of the agent's implied authority as it relates to a specific dispute between principal and third party include: (1) prior course of dealing between principal and agent,[4] (2) custom and usage of trade or business in the geographical area where the agent acts,[5] (3) the relation between the authority exercised by the agent and the actual express authority conferred,[6] (4) the circumstances under which express authority was conferred upon the agent,[7] (5) the principal's limitations or prohibitions placed upon the agent's actual express authority, and (6) what a "reasonable man", acting in the agent's position, would understand his implied authority to be under the same circumstances.[8]

When a court evaluates the enumerated factors to determine whether or not the agent had implied authority to bind the principal to the third party, it will ignore the principal's secret intentions or limitations which he has not communicated to his agent. Moreover, where the principal uses ambiguous language in telling his agent what his express authority is, the agent will not be liable to his principal if he reasonably interprets the ambiguous language even if the resulting action taken by the agent binds his principal and is not what the principal intended.[9] By contrast, if the principal tells his agent of the limitations on his actual express authority, the agent has no express or implied authority to act on his behalf with respect to those transactions or actions expressly limited or prohibited. In such a case, the agent has no implied authority no matter what the custom or usage of trade or business may be to the contrary. Therefore, the third party who seeks to enforce the contract against the principal will have to prove that the contract was made by the agent while acting within the scope of his apparent authority because the agent had neither express nor implied authority to bind the principal on the contract to the third party. Apparent authority is discussed later in this chapter.

It will be useful to examine the nature and extent of an agent's implied authority in different circumstances or situations.

40. Implied authority: emergencies.

It is a well-settled rule of agency law that an agent's implied authority expands during an emergency that affects his principal. Thus, during an emergency the agent has implied authority to do whatever is reasonably necessary to protect his principal's interests unless the principal has expressly precluded such action under all circumstances.[10] However, before the agent acts he must make every reasonable effort to reach his principal in order to obtain express authority unless the nature of the emergency requires immediate action and there is no opportunity to communicate with the principal. The agent's implied authority during the emergency includes the unlimited right to use the broadest discretion as well as lawful force to protect his principal's interest. The actions taken and the contracts made by the agent on the principal's behalf during the emergency will bind the principal to the third party even where the principal seeks to repudiate the contract because he would have acted differently. Furthermore, the agent will have no liability to his principal for what he did during the emergency provided what he did was reasonably necessary to protect his principal's interest under the circumstances. Indeed, even if the agent departs from his general authority in order to take emergency action he will not be liable to his principal provided he acts within the general scope of his employment and reasonably believed that his departure from instructions was justifiable under the circumstances because the emergency was not contemplated by his principal.[11]

To determine if an agent had implied authority to do what he did during an emergency, a court will examine the nature and degree of the emergency, the feasibility and availability of communication with the principal, and the relation between the cost of the action taken and the value of the principal's interest to be protected. If the agent's action was reasonable under the circumstances, the court will find that the agent had implied authority to act and to bind his principal to a third party and that the agent has no liability to his principal for what he did during the emergency.

41. Implied authority: authority to sell.

The question frequently arises whether an agent has implied authority to sell his principal's goods when he has been given possession of them by his principal for a limited purpose, other than resale, such as storage or only to procure an offer where the agent is not a merchant who deals in goods of that kind. The rule is well-settled that such an agent has no implied authority to sell, and, as we shall see later in this chapter, no apparent authority to sell such goods either. Applying this rule, a principal can recover his goods which he gave to his agent only for storage which his agent wrongfully sold to an innocent buyer who had no knowledge that someone else was the owner of the goods.

By contrast, where a principal gives possession of his goods to his agent and gives him actual express authority to sell them, but nothing is said as to payment terms, he has implied authority to sell for cash only. This rule changes, however, where there is an established usage or custom known to the principal for such a sale to be made on credit terms. In such a case the agent has implied authority to sell on credit terms if the actual express authority is silent on the matter.

When an agent is authorized to sell his principal's real estate the question arises as to what implied authority the agent has. The rule is well-settled that the agent has implied authority to receive a down payment but no implied authority to receive the balance of the purchase price, or to make any representations as to the real property, or to rent, mortgage, or exchange it for other property,[12] or to execute any contract on behalf of the seller-principal.

42. Implied authority: authority to buy.

An agent has implied authority to buy whatever is reasonably necessary to enable him to perform his duties, if he is unable to obtain it otherwise. This rule applies even though the actual express authority conferred upon the agent is silent on the matter. Whether the agent buys pursuant to express authority or implied authority, it is well-settled that he has implied authority to buy for cash only and to make payment only upon or after delivery of the goods. Applying this rule, he has no implied authority to execute a negotiable instrument in his principal's name, such as a promissory note, on behalf of his principal in payment of the purchase price. However, if the principal has not given his agent the necessary funds to buy, the agent has the implied authority to buy on the principal's credit. And if the agent advances his own funds for the purchase, he is entitled to reimbursement from his principal for any reasonable purchase he made.

43. Implied authority: authority to receive payment.

An agent has implied authority to receive the purchase price where he has been given possession of his principal's goods and express authority to sell them.[13] Similarly, where an agent is given express authority to collect a debt, he has implied authority to execute and deliver a receipt in his principal's name to the debtor.[14] If the debt to be collected is evidenced by a negotiable instrument, such as a promissory note, the agent has the implied authority to surrender the instrument to the debtor upon full payment or to note thereon a partial payment. However, an agent has no implied authority to receive payment before maturity or to sell or transfer the instrument or to extend the time of payment or to compromise or settle the claim.

44. Implied authority: authority to issue commercial paper.

As a general rule, an agent does not have implied authority to issue or endorse commercial paper, such as checks and promissory note, in his principal's name.[15] An exception has been recognized in the limited case where an agent endorses commercial paper in the principal's name for the sole purpose of depositing it in the principal's checking account. Although an agent's authority to issue commercial paper is not required to be express or in writing,[16] implied authority to do so will be narrowly construed.[17] Thus, implied authority to issue commercial paper will be found only in an emergency situation or where necessary to complete a loan transaction.[18]

45. Implied authority: authority to modify contracts.

If an agent has express authority to enter into a contract on behalf of his principal, the question arises as to whether the agent has any implied authority to modify or rescind it at a later time. The rule is well-settled that in the absence of express authority to do so, he has no implied authority to do so. However, he does have implied authority to correct any mistakes or errors contained in the contract.[19]

46. Apparent authority: nature and extent.

In the business world agents frequently exceed the authority given them (accidentally or intentionally) or sometimes enter into contracts which they have expressly been denied authority to do. Thus, the conflict arises as to whether the principal should be legally immunized from liability to the third party on an unauthorized contract made by his agent on his behalf or whether the innocent third party should be able to enforce the unauthorized contract against the principal. The law of agency has resolved this conflict in favor of the innocent third party based upon the legal concept called "apparent authority," sometimes called "ostensible authority", provided certain conditions are met.

The effect of the rule of law that a principal will be liable on his agent's unauthorized contract where the agent acts within the scope of his apparent authority is rationalized upon the ground that it is the principal's words or conduct which have cloaked his appointed agent with the appearance of actual authority and that a third party who acts reasonably and in good faith in believing and relying upon the appearance of actual authority ought to be able to enforce the unauthorized contract against the principal in order to fulfill his reasonable expectations.[20] Thus, in such a case, the loss on an unauthorized contract is imposed by law upon the principal who, by his words or conduct, placed his agent in the stream of commerce with the appearance of actual authority. Consequently, where an agent acts within the scope of his apparent authority, his principal will be liable to the third party on the unauthorized contract.[21]

The nature and extent of an agent's apparent authority and whether the agent has sufficient apparent authority to bind his principal on an unauthorized contract the agent makes on his behalf with a third party always depends on all the facts and circumstances of each case. Courts will carefully examine the following six factors to determine whether an agent has apparent authority to bind his principal: (1) the agent's title, (2) the agent's job function, (3) prior dealings between the agent and third party, if any, (4) similarity of contract in question with prior contracts made between agent and third party, (5) third party's knowledge of any revocation or limitation on agent's actual authority, and (6) custom and usage of the trade or industry as to what an agent's authority includes.

A third party who seeks to enforce a contract against the agent's principal has the burden of proving that the agent acted either within the scope of his actual authority or apparent authority when he contracted on behalf of his principal with the third party. If the third party can prove the agent had actual authority, express or implied, to enter into the contract he does not have to prove that the agent also acted within the scope of his apparent authority. However, where in fact the agent had no actual authority (express or implied) to contract on his principal's behalf, the only way the third party can enforce the unauthorized contract against the principal is to prove by a preponderance of the evidence that the agent acted within the scope of his apparent authority.[22] If the third party can do so, the principal is liable even though the principal expressly prohibited the agent from acting on behalf of the principal or the agent now wants to unilaterally rescind the unauthorized contract he made on behalf of his principal with the third party.[23]

Courts will find apparent authority when three conditions are met: (1) the principal by his words or conduct manifested to either his agent or to a third party that he appointed him as an agent, (2) the principal held out the agent to the third party as possessing greater authority than actually existed, and (3) the third party acted reasonably in relying on such authority.

The principal's act of holding out his agent may be based on either (1) the agent's continuing authority or (2) the title the principal confers upon his agent. These will be examined in the next two sections.

47. Apparent authority: based upon continuing authority.

The question of whether or not a principal has sufficiently "held out" his agent to create apparent authority (and thus bind the principal on unauthorized contracts), where the agent in fact has no actual authority, will be decided in part on whether the principal previously gave the agent actual authority to act on a continuing or only occasional basis. Where the principal previously gave his agent actual authority to act for him on a continuing basis, such as to make purchases or collect rents, and thereafter revokes or limits his agent's authority, the rule of law is that the agent thereafter has sufficient apparent authority to bind the principal to third parties who previously dealt with the agent before his authority was revoked or limited and who have no actual knowledge that the agent's authority to act has been revoked or limited.[24] As we shall see in Chapter 9, the principal can avoid the undesirable result of having liability imposed upon him after he revokes or limits his agent's authority based upon apparent authority by simply giving both actual notice of the revocation or limitation of the agent's authority to all third parties who previously contracted with the agent and constructive notice, by publication, to the rest of the world.[25]

By contrast, where the agent has previously acted on behalf of the principal only on an occasional basis the rule of law is that the agent has no apparent authority to do so after the principal revokes or limits his authority. In such a case, the principal will not be bound thereafter on any unauthorized contract made by the agent with anyone, including a third party who previously dealt with the agent at the time when the agent had actual authority, even where the third party had no actual knowledge that the agent's authority had been revoked.

48. Apparent authority: based upon agent's title.

When a principal confers a title upon his agent and holds out his agent with such a title, the principal by his action makes a representation to those with whom the agent deals that the agent has the authority indicated by his title. Thus, a corporation that confers titles upon its officers, such as president and vice-president, cloaks them with authority to conduct the ordinary business of the corporation. And a partnership cloaks its partners with authority to engage in transactions within the scope of the partnership business. Therefore, third parties who contract with such agents may enforce such contracts against the corporation or partnership which are within the scope of the business because third parties may reasonably believe and rely upon the fact that an officer in a corporation and a partner in a partnership have the authority that persons with such a title usually have. Moreover, third parties who reasonably rely in good faith upon the title of the agent will not be bound by the principal's secret limitations upon the agent's authority of which the third party had no knowledge. This result is achieved by finding that the agent, by reason of his title, has apparent authority, if not actual authority, to enter into the particular contract. Here again, the principal can avoid the undesirable result of having liability imposed upon him by communicating to third parties what limitations exist with respect to the agent's authority. Thus, the principal's printed sales contract with a third party can include a provision that the principal's agent has no authority to make any representations or warranties beyond those stated in the contract or that the contract does not become binding upon the principal until approved by the home office or that another person's approval is required where the sale amount or the quantity involved exceeds a certain figure.

49. Agency by estoppel: distinguished from apparent authority.

Although many courts and legal commentators have often used the terms apparent authority and agency by estoppel interchangeably,[26] there is a significant legal distinction between the two terms. Moreover, the legal principles of apparent authority and agency by estoppel require a different set of conditions before each principle of law can be applied to hold a principal liable on an unauthorized contract. We have discussed the three conditions which must be met to find apparent authority in the preceding section. Let us now examine what conditions must be met to find that an agency by estoppel exists.

Courts will apply the equitable principle of agency by estoppel only where the principal has not actually appointed another party as his agent and when four conditions are met: (1) the person holds himself out as the agent for a principal, (2) the principal by his silence, inaction, or other conduct does not object to the other person holding himself out as his agent, (3) the third party reasonably relies on the person holding himself out as an agent of the principal, and (4) the third party materially changes his position in reliance thereon.[27] The rationale of the agency by estoppel rule is that when all four conditions are met, it would be inequitable to permit a party to deny that another person is his agent, where his own conduct, whether benign or intentional, causes the third party to contract with another in the name of the principal. Thus, the application of this equitable principle places the loss on the party whose conduct caused it. Of course, the principal could avoid the imposition of liability under the agency by estoppel principle by taking prompt, effective and appropriate action against the person holding himself out as the other person's agent as well as notifying interested third parties. Such appropriate action, depending upon the circumstances, would include obtaining an injunction against the purported agent to restrain him from holding himself out as his agent or notifying the third party that the person purporting to be his agent is not his agent where he knows the identity of the third party or publishing a newspaper notice to the effect that the person who is holding himself out to the public at large as his agent is not his agent. In such a case, the party holding himself out as agent would be liable for general damages and punitive damages and reasonable legal fees incurred by the purported principal.

Thus, apparent authority is different than agency by estoppel. A third party who seeks to enforce an unauthorized contract against the principal based upon the agent's apparent authority must first prove that the principal appointed the other party as his agent and that the agent then acted within the scope of his apparent authority even though he exceeded his actual authority, and that the third party acted reasonably in relying on such apparent authority.[28] By contrast, a third party will seek to apply the principle of agency by estoppel when the principal did not appoint another as his agent but the person holds himself out as an agent for another, the purported principal does not object thereto, and the third party reasonably relies thereon and materially changes his position in reliance thereon. The legal difference between apparent authority and agency by estoppel may be illustrated by the following two examples:

Example of apparent authority

P authorized A as his agent to sell his property for not less than $100,000. A contracted in P's name to sell it for $95,000 to T, who had no knowledge of P's limitation on A's authority. When P discovered what A did he immediately notified T that A had no actual authority to sell P's property at that price and repudiated the contract. T sues P for breach of contract.

Held

T wins. A had apparent authority to sell for $95,000 because P manifested to his agent that he had authority to sell P's property. T's reliance on A's apparent authority was reasonable, based upon all the circumstances. T is not bound by P's secret limitations on A's actual authority and P is bound by the contract. P's sole recourse is against A who is liable to P for his loss because A breached his contract by violating P's instructions.

Example of agency by estoppel

P knows that A is stating to T that A is P's agent with authority to sell P's goods. P has never appointed A as his agent and has never given A any such authority. However, P does nothing and T buys the goods and pays A the purchase price. P refuses to deliver the goods to T asserting that A is not his agent. T sues P for breach of contract.

Held

T wins. A does not have actual or apparent authority to sell P's goods because P has not manifested to A or to T that A has any authority. However, the equitable principle of agency by estoppel applies because the third party changed his position materially in reasonable reliance on the holding out (by paying A) while P, by his conduct or silence did nothing to object thereto, so that it would be inequitable to permit P to avoid liability on the resulting contract. In such a case, the operative effect of applying the equitable principle of agency by estoppel is to preclude, bar or estop the principal from denying the actual lack of authority by the person who purports to be his agent. P's sole recourse is against A for any loss suffered by P because of A's wrongful conduct.

In summary, a third party who wishes to enforce an unauthorized contract made in the principal's name will have to prove either that the agent acted within the scope of his apparent authority or, failing such proof, that an agency by estoppel exists. If the third party cannot prove either, he cannot enforce the unauthorized contract against the named principal. In such an event, the only recourse the third party has is to recover from the person who made the contract in the principal's name because of the person's breach of the implied warranty of authority. This is so because every party who contracts in the name of another impliedly warrants to the third party with whom he contracts that he has authority to contract for his principal. Where he does not, he is personally liable to the third party for breach of his implied warranty of authority. Thus, an agent who contracts in his principal's name without authority does so at his peril.

50. Apparent authority: based upon possession of another's goods; common law rule and Uniform Commercial Code rule.

The early common law rule recognized that an agent did not have apparent authority to sell the principal's goods based upon the agent's possession of them even where the agent was in the business of selling similar goods if the buyer knew the goods he bought from the agent were owned by the principal.

The application of this rule did not prejudice such a buyer because he knew he could not rely on the agent's apparent authority to sell based upon naked possession. In such a case, the buyer would insist that the agent furnish him with evidence of actual authority to sell the principal's goods. Otherwise, the buyer acted at his peril and the owner-principal could recover his goods from the buyer in a conflict between the two parties.

The more difficult issue to resolve between the conflicting claims of owner and buyer arose when an owner gave possession (but not title) of his goods to a person who dealt in goods of that kind for the limited purpose of procuring offers, for storage or safekeeping, or for repairs and that person wrongfully sold them to a buyer who did not know the goods were owned by another and were sold without the owner's authority. In such a case the issue arises whether the owner is entitled to recover his goods from the innocent buyer. A strong argument may be made in favor of the innocent buyer that the seller had apparent authority to sell the owner's goods or that there is an agency by estoppel. The rationale of such an argument is that the owner has cloaked the seller with the *appearance* of ownership when he entrusted possession of his goods to another who deals in goods of that kind and that the buyer acted reasonably in regarding the seller as owner of the goods he bought.

Despite this strong argument in favor of the innocent buyer, many courts, including those in New York, held that the owner was entitled to recover his goods from the innocent buyer. These courts ruled that the owner's delivery or entrusting of his goods to another party for the limited purposes mentioned was a reasonable act of ownership even if that party was a merchant dealing in such goods and the buyer had no knowledge of the facts. This common law rule was widely criticized and was changed by statute in 49 states when the Uniform Commercial Code was enacted.[29]

51. Power to sell: Uniform Commercial Code.

The Uniform Commercial Code has changed the common law rule by providing that "any entrusting of possession of goods to a merchant who deals in goods of that kind gives him power to transfer all rights of the entruster to a buyer in ordinary course of business." The Code further provides that "entrusting" includes "any delivery and any acquiescence in retention of possession regardless of any condition expressed between the parties to the delivery or acquiescence and regardless of whether the procurement of the entrusting or the possessor's disposition of the goods have been such as to be larcenous under the criminal law."

The operative effect of this important rule of law is that the party who entrusts his goods to a merchant who deals in goods of that kind, no matter for what limited purpose, gives the merchant power to transfer whatever rights the entruster has to a buyer in the ordinary course of business. A buyer in the ordinary course of business is defined by the Code to mean "a person who in good faith and without knowledge that the sale to him is in violation of the ownership rights or security interest of a third party in the goods buys in ordinary course from a person in the business of selling goods of that kind but does not include a transfer in bulk or as security for or in total or partial satisfaction of a money debt."

This rule is illustrated by the following examples:

Example

P entrusts goods he owns to A for repair, storage, safekeeping, or to procure offers. A is a merchant who deals in goods of that kind. A wrongfully sells P's goods to T, a buyer in the ordinary course of business, who buys in good faith and without knowledge that the sale to him is in violation of P's rights and interest in the goods. P seeks to recover his goods from T.

Held

T acquires P's rights and P cannot recover his goods from T. P's sole recourse is against A.

Example

X, a thief, steals P's goods and entrusts them to A, a merchant who deals in goods of that kind, for the purpose of resale. A does not know the goods are stolen and sells them to T, a buyer in the ordinary course of business who buys in good faith and without knowledge that the sale is in violation of P's rights and interest in the goods. P seeks to recover his goods from T.

Held

T does not acquire P's rights to the goods and P can recover his goods from T because T acquires only the rights of the entruster. X, the thief, as entruster, had no rights to the stolen goods and therefore A had no title to convey to T.

Example

P entrusts goods he owns to A for repair, storage, safekeeping, or to procure offers. A is a merchant who deals in goods of that kind. A wrongfully sells P's goods to T in connection with A's sale of his entire business to T or A wrongfully delivers P's goods to T as collateral for a debt A owes T. P seeks to recover his goods from T.

Held

T does not acquire P's rights and P can recover his goods from T because the Code expressly provides that under such circumstances T is *not* a buyer in the ordinary course of business.

52. Agency by ratification: introduction.

As stated previously, it is a fundamental rule of agency law that a principal will be liable on contracts made by his agent on his behalf only where his agent had actual or apparent authority to contract or where an agency by estoppel is created. Therefore, when an agent enters into a contract on his principal's behalf where the agent had no actual or apparent authority, neither the principal nor third party can enforce the unauthorized contract against the other. These two salutary rules protect the principal and the third party and place the loss arising from the unauthorized contract on the agent who acted without actual or apparent authority. However, in the business world, an agent often contracts on his principal's behalf without actual or apparent authority, as where he contracts to buy property which he has no authority to buy because he thought his principal wanted it. In some cases, the principal, when so informed, might decide he wants the benefit of the unauthorized contract, is willing to perform its terms and wants to enforce it against the third party. The question then arises, in terms of agency law, whether there is any legal prejudice against the third party if a principal is allowed to ratify an unauthorized contract and to enforce it against the third party. Upon careful legal analysis there is no legal prejudice because the third party intended to enter into the contract with the principal which would bind both him and the principal according to its terms. Thus, the third party obtains exactly what he bargained for.

The legal theory of ratification is that the principal's words or conduct manifest his intention to be bound by the originally unauthorized contract. Thus, his ratification, when legally effective, operates to supply the agent retroactively with original authority to do the act as if it had been originally authorized.[30] Accordingly, the principal may ratify his own agent's unauthorized contracts or even the contracts of a party with whom the principal had no agency relationship at the time the party contracted on behalf of the principal.[31] Consequently, the principal's liability to a third party on an unauthorized contract that he ratifies is not based on apparent authority or agency by estoppel.[32]

53. Agency by ratification: requirements.

In order for a principal to ratify an unauthorized contract made on his behalf, all of the following six requirements must be met:

1. Agent or purported agent must contract on behalf of the principal.

The unauthorized contract must have been made in the name of the principal by the agent or purported agent.[33] This requirement is met when the unauthorized contract discloses the name of the principal as where the contract is signed "Peter Principal by Arthur Adams, agent". By contrast, if the agent or purported agent enters into an unauthorized contract in his own name, even where he intends the unauthorized contract to be for the benefit of his undisclosed principal, the principal cannot ratify.[34] Moreover, in such a case the third party cannot enforce the unauthorized contract against the principal even if the principal announced his ratification, because his attempted ratification has absolutely no legal effect. In such a case only the agent or purported agent will be able to enforce the contract or be liable thereon to the third party since the contract was made only in the name of the agent or purported agent.

2. Principal must ratify the entire unauthorized contract.

The principal who wishes to ratify must ratify the entire unauthorized contract. If he attempts to ratify only part, his ratification is ineffective. Thus, he cannot ratify the beneficial part of an unauthorized contract and reject the remainder.[35] Furthermore, where a principal properly ratifies an unauthorized contract, he becomes liable not only on the ratified contract to the third party but also for any torts committed by his agent against the third party or anyone else during the course of the agent's employment in connection with the unauthorized contract being ratified.

3. Principal must ratify the unauthorized contract with full knowledge of the material facts.

A principal cannot ratify an unauthorized contract unless he has full knowledge of all the material facts except where he intends to ratify without full knowledge of all the material facts.[36] Thus courts hold that ratification will not be presumed as to unauthorized contracts or acts where the principal was ignorant of the material facts at the time he attempts to ratify.[37] Furthermore, if the principal's knowledge of the material facts is partial or imperfect, the principal's ratification will have no legal effect and he will not be liable on the contract despite his intended ratification. The party who alleges that the principal has ratified the unauthorized contract has the burden of proving that the principal had adequate and actual knowledge of the material facts at the time he ratified.[38]

4. Principal must ratify the unauthorized contract within a reasonable time and before the third party rescinds the contract.

The principal may ratify the unauthorized contract by words, oral or written, or by his conduct, including silence.[39] However, if a statute requires the principal's authorization to be in a signed writing, as where the sale or purchase of the principal's real property is involved, then the ratification must be in a signed writing because ratification must comply with the same formalities as authorization. When words are used, no special language is required. The principal may communicate his ratification either to the agent or third party with whom the agent contracted on the principal's behalf. However, a third party may rescind the unauthorized contract at any time prior to the principal's effective ratification.[40]

Ratification may be by active conduct, as where the principal uses the property purchased from the third party by his agent without authority, or passive conduct, as where the principal receives, accepts and retains the benefit of an unauthorized contract.[41] Regardless of how the principal ratifies an unauthorized contract, the rule is well-settled that he must ratify within a reasonable time after he is informed of the unauthorized contract and before any event occurs which makes ratification inequitable or unfair to the third party. What constitutes a reasonable time within which a principal must ratify an unauthorized contract depends upon all the facts and circumstances of each case, including whether the subject matter is perishable or the price of the subject matter fluctuates in the marketplace between the time the unauthorized contract was made and the date it was ratified. However, even where the principal ratifies the unauthorized contract within a reasonable time, he still must do so before the third party exercises his right to rescind the unauthorized contract or his ratification will not be effective to bind the principal or third party to each other. Moreover, the agent or purported agent and third party may each rescind or modify the unauthorized contract at any time before the principal ratifies it even though the third party knew that the agent had no actual authority.[42] However, in the event the agent unilaterally rescinds the unauthorized contract, he will be personally liable to the third party for breach of the implied warranty of authority, as discussed in section 55 hereafter.

5. Principal must have had legal capacity to contract both at the time the unauthorized contract was made and at the time of ratification.

It is well-settled that in order to ratify an unauthorized contract, the principal must have had legal capacity to contract at the time the unauthorized contract was made.[43] This is required because ratification operates retroactively to the date the unauthorized contract was made. Therefore, if the principal was not in legal existence or did not have legal capacity to contract on the date the unauthorized contract was made, the principal could not enter into the contract if he wished to do so in the first instance.[44] Accordingly, he cannot ratify an unauthorized contract that he did not have legal capacity to enter into. Applying this rule, a corporation may not legally ratify contracts made by promoters on its behalf before the corporation came into legal existence because the corporation had no legal capacity to contract when the pre-incorporation contracts were made. However, in such a case, the corporation may *adopt* pre-incorporation contracts because adoption does not operate retroactively and therefore does not require legal capacity to contract at the time the pre-incorporation contract was made.

6. Unauthorized contract must be lawful contract when made and ratified.

It is well-settled that an unauthorized contract can be ratified only if it was a lawful contract both at the time made and later ratified.[45] Thus, a principal cannot ratify an unauthorized contract which was void, illegal, or violated public policy either at the time it was made or ratified.[46] An exception to this rule of law has been provided by the Uniform Commercial Code (Section 3-404 (2)) which declares that a person may ratify a forgery of his signature on a check, note or draft unless he promises to withhold information of the crime from the police. Moreover, a person cannot ratify an act done by another which public policy requires he do himself, such as marry or vote.

54. Effect of ratification.

If the principal ratifies an unauthorized contract, the agent has no personal liability to his principal or the third party on the ratified contract arising out of his original lack of authority. Thus, following ratification, the third party is not entitled to recover damages from the agent or purported agent based on breach of implied warranty of authority, and the principal is not entitled to recover damages from his agent or purported agent for exceeding the authority originally given.[47] Moreover, since ratification is equivalent to prior actual authority, the agent is entitled to recover compensation in connection with the originally unauthorized contract he made on the principal's behalf. However, where the principal ratifies an agent's or purported agent's tort (wrongful act), the agent continues to be personally liable for his own tort to an injured third party,[48] and he must indemnify or reimburse his principal for any loss the principal incurs to the insured third party as a result of the agent's tort. Similarly, under the Uniform Commercial Code, the person ratifying the forgery of his signature is entitled to pursue his rights against the forger. (Section 3-404(2))

55. Liability of agent to third party when unauthorized contract is not ratified.

In the event the principal does not ratify the unauthorized contract or his attempted ratification is ineffective, he cannot enforce the contract against the third party. Moreover, if the third party cannot prove that the unauthorized contract was made within the scope of the agent's apparent authority or that an agency by estoppel exists or that it was ratified, the third party cannot enforce the contract against the principal. However, the third party is not without any remedy. In such a case, the third party may enforce the unauthorized contract against the person who contracted on behalf of the purported principal based upon his breach of his implied warranty of authority. This rule applies because a person who contracts on behalf of a principal impliedly warrants to the third party with whom he contracts that he has actual authority to enter into the contract on behalf of the principal named in the contract. If he does not have such actual authority and the principal does not ratify the unauthorized contract, he will be personally liable to the third party for breach of his implied warranty of authority.[49] Thus, a person who acts as an agent for a principal without actual authority, express or implied, does so at his peril. Moreover, where the agent or person purporting to act as an agent for a principal knows he has no authority to enter into the particular contract and he expressly warrants to the third party that he has authority to contract with him, he has committed fraud and is liable therefore to the third party.

Current References

"The agent's apparent authority: paradigm or paradox" (United Kingdom) by Ian Brown, *Journal of Business Law*, 360-372, July 1995.

"Embezzling agent's consent to extend time is valid," by A. Breault, K.M. Kess and D.H. Ager, 23 *Taxation for Lawyers* 183 (1), Nov.-Dec. 1994.

"Ratification, retroactivity and reasonableness" (United Kingdom) by Ian Brown, 110 *Law Quarterly Review*, 531-536, October 1994.

Notes

1. See, Floyd R. Mechem, "The Nature And Extent Of An Agent's Authority," *Michigan Law Review*, 4:433 (1906). Mechem gives twenty illustrations of when implied authority of an agent does and does not exist in "Implied Authority Of Agent To Purchase Personal Property", *Yale Law Journal*, 17: 257 (1908). See, also, Quist v. Zerr, 12 Wash. 2d 21, 120 P.2d 539 (1941).
2. Burke v. Bonat, 255 N.Y. 226, 174 N.E. 635 (1931).
3. For an analysis indicating that an agent for a disclosed principal cannot be liable on the contract barring unusual circumstances, see, "Personal Liability of an Agent", *Law Quarterly Review*, 85:92-103, January 1969.
4. Presley v. Commercial Credit Corp., 177 A. 2d 916 (D.C. Mun. App. 1962); Harvey v. J.P. Morgan and Co., 166 Misc. 455, 2 N.Y.S. 2d 520 (1937).
5. Peter Pan Mfg. Corp. v. Lady Royal Mfg. Co., 272 A.D. 418, 71 N.Y.S. 2d 97 (1947); Winslow v. Kaiser, 313 Pa. 577, 170 A. 135 (1934).
6. O. A. Skutt, Inc. v. J. and H. Goodwin, 251 App. Div. 84, 295 N.Y.S. 772 (1937); Siedhoff v. Campbell, 141 Kan. 255, 40 P. 2d 404 (1935), which held that a special agent authorized to buy shares from a shareholder at a specified price

did not have further authority to agree that his principal would also pay certain debts of the corporation.

7. Atwater v. Lober, 133 Misc. 652, 233 N.Y.S. 309 (1929); Alterman v. Lydick, 241 F. 2d 50 (7th Cir. 1957); Lynch v. Maw, 3 Utah 2d 271, 282 P. 2d 841 (1955).
8. Vaughn v. Great Am. Ins. Co., 390 S.W. 2d 622 (Mo. App. 1965); Lucey v. Hero International Corp., 281 N.E. 2d 266 (Mass. 1972), which held that the agent has no implied authority to do those acts which are not incidental, not usually done or not reasonably necessary.
9. Makousky, Inc. v. Stern, 285 Minn. 202, 172 N.W. 2d 317 (1969); Welsh v. Feyka, 119 Pa. Super. 44, 179 A. 810 (1935).
10. Huebner v. Farmers Co-operative Assn., 283 Minn. 258, 167 N.W. 2d 369 (1969). The implied power of an agent to act in an emergency beyond the scope of his actual authority is examined in "Agency-Emergency Power Of Agent To Summon Medical Aid For Injured Employees Of Principal", *University of Pennsylvania Law Review,* 78: 101-102, November 1929. Similarly, a stranger without any authority may act for the benefit of another in an emergency; see Walter B. Williston, "Agency of Neces-sity", *Canadian Bar Review,* 22: 492-508, June-July 1944, and "Agency By Necessity", *Columbia Law Review,* 25:464-470, April 1925. See, also, Restatement, Second, Agency, Sect. 47 (1958).
11. Sauter v. New York Tribune, 305 N.Y. 442, 113 N.E. 2d 790 (1953).
12. Chelsea Exchange Bank v. Weinstein, 226 App. Div. 601, 236 N.Y.S. 185 (1929). In the absence of any trade usage, the power to sell does not carry with it or imply the power to barter or exchange. See "Agency—Ostensible Authority—Custom", *Wisconsin Law Review,* 3: 190-191, April 1925.
13. Hedman v. Security Title and Guaranty Co., 245 App. Div. 224, 281 N.Y.S. 565 (1935).
14. An agent in possession of goods for sale customarily has authority to receive payments. Ronald A. Coco, Inc. v. St. Paul's Methodist Church, Inc. 78 N.M. 97, 428 P. 2d 636 (1967); Degen v. Acme Brick Co., 228 Ark. 1054, 312 S.W. 2d 194 (1958).
15. Massey-Ferguson, Inc. v. Fargo Nat'l Bank, 270 F. Supp. 227 (D.N.D. 1967); Bogue Elec. Mfg. Co. v. Coconut Grove Bank, 269 F. 2d 1 (5th Cir. 1959); Provident Trust Co. v. Interboro Bank & Trust Co., 389 Pa. 548, 133 A. 2d 515 (1957). Peoples Cotton Oil Co. v. Hunt Foods & Indus., Inc., 147 So. 2d 687 (La. App. 1962).
16. Atlantic National Bank v. C.A. Edmund, 108 Ga. App. 63, 132 S.E. 2d 103 (1963); Rakestraw v. Rodrigues, 8 Cal. 3d 67, 500 P. 2d 1401, 104 Cal. Rptr. 57 (1972).
17. Hensinger Hardware Co. v. First Nat'l Bank, 364 S.W. 2d 851 (Tex. Civ. App. 1963); Nielson v. Suburban Trust & Sav. Bank, 37 Ill. App. 2d 224, 185 N.E. 2d 404 (1962); Wagner v. Nichols, 5 A.D. 2d 191, 170 N.Y.S. 2d 542 (App. Div. 1958).
18. There is no implied authority, however, to issue commercial paper from an agent's actual authority merely to borrow, Kenneally v. First National Bank, 400 F. 2d 838 (8th Cir. 1968), cert. denied 393 U.S. 1063 (1969).
19. Ingle v. Market Tree Equip. Co., 244 Ark. 1166, 428 S.W. 2d 286 (1968).
20. System Inv. Corp. v. Montview Acceptance Corp., 355 F. 2d 463 (10th Cir. 1966); Grummitt v. Sturgeon Bay Winter Sports Club, 197 F. Supp. 455 (E.D. Wisc. 1961). Professor Seavey argues that the doctrine whereby a principal is responsible for the unauthorized acts of his agents within the scope of the agent's usual authority does not fall within the usual bases of liability: actual authority, ratification or apparent authority. See his "Agency Powers", *Oklahoma Law Review,* 1:3-20, May 1948. However, Professor Seavey notwithstanding, the weight of authority holds that the principal will not be liable unless he created some appearance of authority for the agent's unauthorized act. See note 21.
21. Kugler v. Romain, 110 N.J. Super, 470, 266 A. 2d 144 (1970); Clements v. Jungert, 90 Idaho 143, 408 P. 2d 810 (1965); Tel-Ads, Inc. v. Trans-Lux Playhouse, Inc. 232 F. Supp. 198 (D.D.C. 1964); S. S. Silberblatt, Inc. v. Seaboard Sur. Co., 417 F. 2d 1043 (8th Cir. 1969); Roth v. Ducks Hockey Club, 52 Misc. 2d 533, 276 N.Y.S. 2d 246 (1966); Wen Koy Realty Co. v. Public Nat. Bank & Trust Co. of New York, 260 N.Y. 84, 183 N.E. 73 (1932); Farr v. Newman, 14 N.Y. 2d 183, 250 N.Y.S. 2d 272, 199 N.E. 369 (1964). The contemporary application of the doctrine of apparent authority to create liability in cases of franchising and product liability is analyzed in "Apparent Agency—An Extension Of The Deep Pocket Theory", *South Carolina Law Review,* 23: 826-838, 1971. In his classic work "Rationale of Agency", *Yale Law Journal,* 29:859, at 861, 872-874 (1920), Professor Seavey points out that the liability of a principal for unauthorized acts must be based on public policy. Although both principal and third person are innocent, "one of two persons both innocent" must suffer. "It is good business sense to hold that when one employs another in the performance of acts for the benefit of a business, that business ought to pay for the mistakes, negligence and errors of judgment of one employed", including knowingly entering into unauthorized contracts.
22. The third party must actually know of and rely in good faith upon such apparent agency authority and must lack knowledge of any secret limitation upon the agent's authority if he is to hold the principal liable. See, Karetzkis v. Cosmopolitan Nat'l Bank, 37 Ill. App. 2d 484, 186 N.E. 2d 72 (1962); Duluth Herald & News Tribune v. Plymouth Optical Co., 286 Minn. 495, 176 N.W. 2d 552 (1970); Shipley v. Ohio National Life Ins. Co., 199 F. Supp. 782 (W.D. Pa. 1961); Healy v. Larsson, 323 N.Y.S. 2d 625 (1971); Falta v. Edgerton, 137 N.Y.S. 226 (1912); Perry v. New York Life Ins. Co., 22 N.Y.S. 2d 696 (1940); Ernst Iron Works v. Duralith Corp., 270 N.Y. 165, 200 N.E. 683 (1936).
23. There is liability for a principal when he has created the appearance of authority in an agent. See, Enright v. Asplundh Tree Expert Co., 271 App. Div. 847, 65 N.Y.S. 2d 871 (1946); Skutt, Inc. v. Goodwin, 251 App. Div. 84, 295 N.Y.S. 772 (1937). The principal is not responsible for acts done under an appearance of authority caused by someone who purports to be an agent. See, Paul Armstrong Co. v. Majestic Motion Picture Co., 87 Misc. 141, 149 N.Y.S. 1039 (1914). Nor is the principal liable for the acts of someone else who purports to be a principal. See, Stanton v. Hawley, 193 App. Div. 559, 184 N.Y.S. 415 (1920). For an excellent analysis of just what is the scope of employment

authority when an agent deviates from his instructions, see "Agency-Scope of Employment", *Texas Law Review,* 10: 69-71, December 1931. See, also, "Principal And Agent-Apparent Authority of Agent", *Illinois Bar Journal,* 28:90-91, November 1939.

24. H. Michaelyan, Inc. v. New Jersey Fidelity and P.G. Ins. Co., 229 App. Div. 123, 241 N.Y.S. 142 (1930).
25. The rule that revocation of an agent's authority must be conveyed to a third party in order to be effective is analyzed in "Agency—Revocation—Notice", *University of Cincinnati Law Review,* 4: 225-227, March 1930. See, Bussing v. Lowell Film Productions, Inc., 233 App. Div. 493, 253 N.Y.S. 719 (1931).
26. See, "Agency-Secret Limitations Upon Agent-Apparent Authority-Estoppel. Simons v. Northeastern Finance Corp. (Mass. 1930), 171 N.E. 643", *Boston University Law Review,* 11: 242-245, April 1931. For the view that apparent authority is based on contract rather mere estoppel so that not only is the principal liable for the third party's change of position in reliance on the agent's appearance of authority but the third party is also liable to the principal, see Cook, "Agency by Estoppel", *Columbia Law Review* 5:36 (1905); Ewart, "Agency by Estoppel", *Columbia Law Review,* 5:354 (1905); Cook, "Agency by Estoppel: A Reply", *Columbia Law Review,* 6:34 (1906).
27. See, Restatement, Second, Agency, Sect. 8 (1958) on apparent authority and Sect. 8B on estoppel, change of position. The First Restatement of Agency drew a distinction between apparent authority and authority by estoppel which created much confusion and was strongly criticized. See, "Analysis of 'Apparent Authority' In Principal And Agent", *The University of Chicago Law Review,* 1:337-340, November 1933. Professor Bernard J. Rubinstein, calling the doctrine of apparent authority the second most difficult problem in the study of law (the Rule Against Perpetuities being the most difficult), analyzed incisively the distinction, now often overlooked, between apparent authority and agency by estoppel in "Apparent Authority: An Examination of a Legal Problem," *American Bar Association Journal,* 44:849-852, Spring 1958. See, also, Michael Conant, "The Objective Theory Of Agency: Apparent Authority And The Estoppel Of Apparent Ownership," *Nebraska Law Review,* 47:678, July 1968, for an analysis of the theoretical foundations of the liability of a principal to third parties in contract including the distinction between apparent authority and agency by estoppel.
28. English law is virtually identical with American law in its treatment of apparent authority. See, "The Apparent Authority Of An Agent Of A Company," *Law Quarterly Review,* 50:224-242 (1934). See, also, "Apparent Authority," *Canadian Bar Review,* 16:757 (1938); F. Tiffany, *Agency,* sect. 16 (2d ed. 1924); R. Powell, *Law of Agency,* 68-72 (2d ed. 1961).
29. Even before passage of the Uniform Commercial Code, mere possession was sufficient in all states to give the possessor actual or apparent authority to dispose of the property of the owner as his agent if the possessor to whom the goods were entrusted was a factor. The factor is given the authority to sell the goods in his own name, and the buyer of such goods, therefore, is protected as a third party bonafide purchaser. See, New York Personal Property Law (McKinney's Comp. 1917), sect. 43, repealed effective September 27, 1964 and now covered by the Uniform Commercial Code, Sect. 9-101 et seq.; 1 Mechem, *Agency* (2d ed. 1914), sect. 720; "Sales—Apparent Authority—Bonafide Purchase Of Property Entrusted To A Factor," *Tulane Law Review,* 5:670-672, June 1931.
30. Rakestraw v. Rodrigues, 8 Cal.3d 67, 500 P.2d 1401, 104 Cal. Rptr. 57 (1972); Prudential Ins. Co. of America v. Clark, 456 F.2d 932 (5th Cir. 1971); In re. Eastern Supply Co., 267 F.2d 776 (3d Cir. 1959); State ex rel. Riley Const. Co. v. East Liverpool City School Dist. Board of Education, 10 Ohio St.2d 25, 225 N.E.2d 246 (1967). See, "Agency—Ratification—Statute of Limitations No Bar to Ratification of Unauthorized Suit," *Rutgers Law Review,* 14:445, Winter 1960.
31. See, Floyd R. Mechem, "The Effect Of Ratification As Between The Principal And The Other Party," *Michigan Law Review* 4:269-283 (1906) and especially his analysis that ratification to be enforceable against the third party must be within a reasonable time and before the third party has signified his withdrawal from the contract.
32. Eliott v. Barell, 232 App. Div. 182, 249 N.Y.S. 580 (1931); Kneeland v. Shroyer, 214 Oreg. 67, 328 P.2d 753 (1958).
33. Higgins v. D. & F. Elec. Co., 110 Ga. App. 790, 140 S.E.2d 99 (1964); Gulf Refining Co. v. Travis, 201 Miss. 336, 30 So.2d 398 (1947). See, "What Is The Effect Of A Ratification Of An Agent's Unauthorized Contract?," *Louisiana Law Review,* 5:308-315, May 1943.
34. Pickel v. Conn., 209 App. Div. 410, 204 N.Y.S. 448 (1924); Stanton v. Granger, 125 App. Div. 174, 109 N.Y.S. 134 (1908). If an individual does not pose as or allege himself to be an agent for another but acts strictly on his own behalf and for his own benefit, a subsequent effort by the other to ratify will not bind him as a principal. See, Fellows v. Commissioners for Loaning United States Moneys, 36 Barb. 655 (1862). Moreover, the existence of a principal, when the act is performed, is an essential element of a ratification. See, Stainsby v. Frazer's Mettalic Life Boat Co., 3 Daly 98 (1869). Similarly, there may be no ratification by a principal who has not been disclosed to a third party. See, Huginnie v. Loyd, 483 S.W.2d 696 (Tex. Civ. App. 1972); Greene v. Golucke, 202 Ga. 494, 43 S.E.2d 497 (1947).
35. Grandi v. Le Sage, 74 N.M. 799, 399 P.2d 285 (1965); Lewis v. Martin, 30 Colo. App. 342, 492 P.2d 877 (1971).
36. See, Arthur Corbin, "Ratification In Agency Without Knowledge Of Material Facts," *Yale Law Journal,* 15:331 (1906); and Mott v. Scholes, 147 App. Div. 82, 131 N.Y.S. 811 (1911); Knapp v. Rochester Dog Protection Ass'n 235 App. Div. 436, 257 N.Y.S. 356 (1932); See-Tee Mining Corp. v. National Sales, Inc. 76 N.M. 677, 417 P. 2d 810 (1966).
37. Schwarz v. Weber, 43 Hun. 638, affid, 13 N.E. 943 (1887); Templeton Const. Co. v. Kelly, 130 Vt. 420, 296 A. 2d 242 (1972).
38. Riley v. Larocque, 163 Misc. 423, 297 N.Y.S. 756 (1937); NMS Indus., Inc. v. Premium Corp. 451 F. 2d 542 (5th Cir. 1971); Cannon v. Blake 353 Mo. 294, 182 S.W. 2d 303 (1944).
39. Different means of voluntary and involuntary ratification are analyzed in Philip Mechem, "The Rationale of Ratifi-

cation", *Univ. of Pennsylvania Law Review,* 100:649-677, March 1952. See, also, the distinction between express and implied ratification analyzed in "Agency-Ratification Of An Unauthorized Act", *South Carolina Law Review,* 19:788-797, 1967. See, Angerosa v. White Co., 248 App. Div. 425, 290 N.Y.S. 204 (1936); Flagg v. Nichols, 202 Misc. 1096, 115 N.Y.S. 2d 7 (1952); In Re Kroll's Estate, 8 Misc. 2d 133, 169 N.Y.S. 2d 495 (1957); Fatta v. Edgerton, 137 N.Y.S. 226 (1912); Coykendall v. Constable, 99 N.Y. 309, 1 N.E. 884 (1885); Harriss v. Tams, 258 N.Y. 229, 179 N.E. 476 (1932); Abraham v. American Exch. Nat. Bank. 191 App. Div. 594, 181 N.Y.S. 663 (1920); Gregory v. Fassett, 178 Pa. Super. 599, 116 A. 2d 304 (1955); NAACP v. Overstreet, 221 Ga. 16, 142 S.E. 2d 816 (1965).

40. Gray v. Prudential Ins. Co. of America, 46 N.Y.S. 2d 850 (1943), reversed on other grounds, 267 App. Div. 688, 48 N.Y.S. 2d 82 (1944); Harvey v. J. P. Morgan and Co., 116 Misc. 455, 2 N.Y.S. 2d 520 (1937); The Restatement, Second, Agency, Sect 89 (a). The Restatement, Second, Agency, Sect. 89 (c) (1958) also holds that if there is a material change of circumstances of the third party between time of the contract and time of ratification, such ratification will not be effective. Sect. 89(d) holds that a change in circumstances after ratification is immaterial except that if the ratification is not communicated to the third party and the third party changes his position in the belief that there has been no ratification, he can avoid the contract. However, if the third party elects nevertheless to enforce the contract, Sect. 95(b) holds that the principal is bound by said contract.
41. Ramsay v. Miller, 202 N.Y. 72, 95 N.E. 35 (1911); Evans v. Ruth, 129 Pa. Super. 192, 195 A. 163 (1937), where an unauthorized act of a construction foreman on behalf of his contractor was ratified by the contractor when he acknowledged that the act was done for him; Mardan Const. Corp. v. Rogers Auto Sales Corp., 13 Misc. 2d 196, 176 N.Y.S. 2d 439 (1958).
42. McCrillis v. A. & W. Enterprises, Inc., 270 N.C. 637, 155 S.E. 2d 281 (1967). While an agent by ratification need not profess actual authority, Public Sav. Ins. Co. of America v. Greenwald, 68 Ind. App. 609, 121 N.E. 47 (1918), he must at least purport to be acting on behalf of a principal. See, Pettit v. Vogt, 495 P.2d 395 (Okla. 1972).
43. Amalgamated Clothing Workers of America v. Kiser, 174 Va. 229, 6 S.E.2d 562, 125 A.L.R. 1251 (1940).
44. Kraft v. Spencer Tucker Sales, Inc., 39 Wash.2d 943, 239 P.2d 563 (1952); Alldrin v. Lucas, 260 Oreg. 373, 490 P.2d 141 (1971).
45. See, Berk v. Laird, 317 F. Supp. 715 (E.D.N.Y. 1970).
46. Andrews v. Claiborne Parish School Bd., 189 So. 355 (La. App. 1939), where the court found that since the act to be done was illegal and could not be duly authorized, it could not be ratified.
47. See, Henry W. Savage, Inc. v. Freidberg, 322 Mass. 321, 77 N.E.2d 213 (1948); Verschures Creameries, Ltd. v. Hull & Neth. S.S. Co., 2 K.B. 608 (1921); Rakestraw v. Rodrigues, 8 Cal.3d 67, 500 P.2d 1401, 104 Cal. Rptr. 57 (1972).
48. Carrel v. Lux, 101 Ariz. 430, 420 P.2d 564 (1966).
49. An agent's liability rests normally on the implied warranty which he makes to a third party regarding his agency and not on the contract he assumes to make for his principal. See, "Agency—Implied Warranty Of Authority—Accrual Of Cause Of Action—Statute of Limitations," *Virginia Law Review,* 16:164-169, December 1929. When an agent misrepresents his authority to act for a named principal, he may be held liable on a theory of either breach of warranty or of the tort of deceit. For an analysis of cases in support of each theory, see Albert S. Abel, "Some Spadework On The Implied Warranty Of Authority," *West Virginia Law Quarterly,* 48:96-129, February 1942. See, also, Restatement, Second, Agency, Sects. 329-331 (1958).

Case 3

Silverstein v. R. H. Macy & Co.

49 N.Y.S.2d 916 (1943)

Introduction

An agent has actual authority which is express or implied. The nature and extent of his implied authority must often be determined by a court to resolve the issue whether a principal is liable on the contract made by the agent in the principal's name. The following case illustrates the significant problem of whether and when an agent has implied authority to make warranties with regard to goods he sells for his principal.

Callahan, Justice

This is an action to recover damages for personal injuries suffered by the plaintiff while using a gymnastic device known as a "chinning bar" which he had purchased in defendant's department store. The complaint rested solely upon allegations of breach of warranty.

The device consisted of two metal tubes, one fitting within the other, with flattened ends in the nature of cups containing rubber rings, or washers. The device was to be fastened in a doorway of the user's home. It was to be tightened to fit the width of the doorway by turning the outer bar in one direction, which caused an internal screw to expand, thereby forcing the rubber-faced ends apart and against the door-frame. Pressure, not suction, was claimed to be responsible for its firmness.

There was proof that in directions stamped on the bar, and contained in advertising matter which was distributed with the bar, a purchaser was advised that a few turns of the outer tube with the hands would securely fasten the bar against the door-frame and supply sufficient holding power to safely sustain 250 pounds without any danger of injuring the woodwork. Users were directed to use no nails, screws or other fasteners. The directions further provided that the user was to be sure that the bar was up tight, and in a level position, and to test it with a strong tug before using it.

In addition to the foregoing directions stamped on the bar, and found in the pamphlet, the plaintiff testified that he was told by the salesman that the bar was a safe article to use for the purpose for which it was sold. Plaintiff further stated that the salesman directed him to use the bar in the manner specified in the pamphlets.

Plaintiff, who had purchased the bar in May, 1940, had used it in his home on numerous occasions during a period of about five months, or until October 5, 1940, without untoward result. On that day he had placed the bar in position in a doorway, tightened it as directed, and after seizing hold of it, swung his feet in pendulum fashion out and away from a point beneath the bar. Thereupon the bar fell from position, causing plaintiff to fall to the floor. He suffered serious injuries, for which he claims the right to recover damages.

Plaintiff weighed 170 pounds. He produced expert opinion evidence that the device was faulty in construction in that it provided no mechanism to check loosening of pressure when the outside bar was caused to turn by a person swinging on it.

The trial court dismissed the complaint upon the ground that the salesman was without authority to warrant the property sold, there being no evidence adduced on the part of the plaintiff that an article of the nature here involved was ordinarily sold with a warranty.

The trial court also held that the defendant, as seller, did not adopt the warranties contained in the pamphlets which had been furnished by the manufacturer, and, further, that there was no proof of breach of warranty.

We hold that these rulings were erroneous, and that it was improper to dismiss the complaint, for the reason that plaintiff's proof established, prima facie, defendant's warranties and the breach thereof.

In so far as we may glean from the record, the trial court treated this sale as one under Personal Property Law, § 96, subd. 4, that is a sale of a specific article under its trade name, and held there was no implied warranty of fitness for any particular purpose.

We need not determine whether under the present circumstances there was evidence to support an implied warranty, under any of the subdivisions of § 96 of the Personal Property Law. Here the plaintiff claimed an express warranty. If the testimony to support the express warranty was properly received, and was believed by the jury, and if breach thereof was established with resulting injury, plaintiff was entitled to prevail.

The rule concerning the authority of a salesman in connection with a sale is stated in Burke v. Bonat, 255 N.Y. 226, 230, 174 N.E. 635, 636, as follows: "A salesman has implied authority in effectuating a sale to do whatever is necessary according to the usual course of procedure prevailing in the business. . . . What that procedure is will commonly be a question of fact to be answered by a jury . . . unless the course of business is so notorious as to become a subject for judicial notice . . . sometimes the jury's answer may be given in the light of every day experience. This will be so when the transaction is of a type so ordinary and simple that everyday experience may reasonably and safely be accepted as a guide. . . . Sometimes the quality of the act or the setting of the circumstances may call for proof of what is usual before everyday experience may leap to a conclusion. If there is no proof of what is usual, a substitute may be found in evidence, direct or circumstantial, of expectation or desire".

Defendant points out that the rule as above quoted was enunciated concerning what a salesman is entitled to do in connection with a sale, rather than as to his right to make oral warranties.

An examination of the earlier cases . . . cited in Burke v. Bonat, supra, will show that the rule stated applies with equal force to the right of a salesman to make warranties usual in a sale of the nature involved. The question of the right of defendant's salesman to warrant the safety of the chinning bar was for the jury, in view of the fact that the present sale was one of such an ordinary nature.

The pamphlets above referred to were examined at the time of sale, and specifically discussed between plaintiff and the salesman. Respondent contends that any statements contained in the pamphlets as to the quality or fitness of the articles sold were representations of the manufacturers of the bar, and not binding on the defendant. We hold that the evidence would have warranted a finding that the defendant adopted the statements contained in these circulars.

Mechem in his work on Agency, 2d Ed. § 884, states the rule as follows: "§ 884. Authority to warrant in accordance with descriptions furnished by principal. Where the principal furnishes the agent with written or printed circulars, or other descriptive matter relating to the goods to be sold, for the purpose of having these delivered or exhibited to prospective buyers, or otherwise used as a means of inducing sales, the agent would doubtless have implied authority to warrant the goods in accordance with any statements of fact contained in such circulars, provided such statements, if made under the same circumstances by the principal in person, would constitute warranties." . . .

An inference was clearly warranted from the present circumstances that defendant had authorized the distribution of the pamphlets with the bar when sold. These pamphlets appear to contain representations as to the safety of the device which amounted to warranties.

The judgment should, therefore, be reversed, and a new trial ordered, with costs to the appellant to abide the event.

Judgment unanimously reversed and a new trial ordered with costs to the appellant to abide the event. Order filed. All concur.

Discussion questions

1. How could a principal give effective notice to his customer that his agents have no authority to make any oral or written warranties?
2. Does a court or jury determine whether an agent has implied authority to do a particular act or make a particular warranty?
3. Will a principal be bound by his agent's warranties if they were greater or different than the warranties made by the manufacturer of the product?

Case 4

Loma Vista Development Co. v. Johnson

Texas Supreme Court,
142 Tex. 686, 180 S.W.2d 922 (1944)

Introduction

Agents frequently make representations to prospective buyers without express authority from their principal. The following case illustrates the liability of the agent for doing so and to what extent a third party may rely on the agent's representations.

Mr. Judge Brewster of the Commission of Appeals delivered the opinion for the Court.

Thomas W. Johnson and his wife sued Loma Vista Development Company for damage for fraud in the sale of a dwelling house to them by the company. The trial court rendered judgment for the Johnsons on a jury verdict favorable to them. The Court of Civil Appeals at San Antonio reversed that judgment and remanded the cause on the ground that "there was no evidence establishing a legal measure of damages". . . . We shall refer to the company as "petitioner" and to the Johnsons as "respondents."

Petitioner was engaged in the construction and sale of dwelling houses in the Loma Vista Addition to the City of San Antonio. When the house in question was about finished, petitioner listed it with Wm. P. McNeley Company, real estate brokers, for sale. Roy Jones was a salesman for these brokers. On January 28, 1940, respondents were in the Loma Vista area looking for a house to rent, when they noticed an "Open for Inspection" sign in front of the property in question. They decided to look at the house, and when they went in Jones introduced himself as the salesman in charge. Then it was, they allege, that Jones made false representations as to the manner of construction of the house and the materials used in it, upon which they claim they relied and which induced them to buy it. At the request of Jones, petitioner then gave the McNeley Company an exclusive listing of the property for a few days to give him full opportunity to negotiate with respondents, whom he regarded as likely prospects. Jones continued his efforts by going the next evening to the home of respondents where, they say, he repeated the representations made to them the previous afternoon. On February 1 respondents signed an "earnest money agreement" to purchase the property, which showed the McNeley Company as agent and Jones as salesman. It was presented to petitioner, which signed and accepted it. The deed to respondents was delivered on March 19, and they moved in the next day.

Both Jones and one Saur, secretary of the petitioner, testified that petitioner did not authorize Jones to make any representations concerning the house, and Saur swore that he gave no such authorization to the McNeley Company. He also testified that he knew nothing about the alleged representations until after this suit was filed. Respondents in no manner controverted this testimony. . . .

During the trial and while Johnson was testifying in his own behalf, he declined petitioner's offer to rescind the conveyance. . . .

At the outset we are confronted by respondents' contention that Jones was established as a general agent by the jury finding that he was an agent, under the trial court's definition of an agent as "one who undertakes to transact some business or to manage some affair for another, by the authority and on account of the latter, and to render an account of it." We see nothing in that definition inconsistent with special agency, therefore we fail to see how the jury finding can enlarge Jones' power as they existed under the undisputed facts. It is a question of law, under what the facts show respecting the scope of the authority conferred upon him by petitioner, as to whether his agency was general or special. See Continental Oil Co. v. Baxter (Civ. App.), 59 S.W.2d 463, cited in 2 C.J.S., Agency, Sec. 101, p. 1238, note 29. It is clear to us that he was a special agent whose authority was limited to showing the property and finding a purchaser, and that he had no authority to consummate the sale. See Donigan v. Policek (Civ.App.), 34 S.W.2d 375 (er.dism.). That he claimed no power to bind petitioner, even by the earnest money contract, is shown by the fact that, after that instrument was executed by respondents, it was presented to, and accepted by, the petitioner. That a real estate broker ordinarily is only a special agent is the reason for the uniform decisions of this court that, in the absence of special agreement, he is entitled to his commission when he finds one who is ready, able, and willing to buy on his principal's terms because he has done all that his employment required or authorizes him to do.

In finding one who is so ready, able and willing to buy, does the agent have implied authority to make representations as to the quality of the real estate? In discussing this proposition, one authority has said: "The question as to the authority of a broker to bind the owner of land as to representations which affect the value of the land, where it is sought to hold the innocent owner for damages on the ground of imputed fraud, is involved in much difficulty. The result of sustaining the authority often is to impose upon the owner a burden clearly beyond that which the agent had either actual or ostensible authority to impose by an contract with the purchaser of the land. For example, the vendor may be held liable for damages based upon the differences between the actual value of the land and its value if it had been as the agent represented it, and certainly there can be no ground for saying that the agent had implied or ostensible authority thus to bind his principal." 57 A.L.R., Anno. 1, p. 112. . . . Moreover, since the buyer must deal directly with the seller in closing the transaction, he has an opportunity, before he accepts the deed, to inquire of the seller as to the truth of any representations made by the broker. As said in Lansing v. Coleman (N.Y.), 58 Barb., 611, 619, "Common prudence and justice to the vendor would seem to demand that the purchaser should go to him for the facts which are to influence the purchaser."

Therefore, we hold that Jones had no implied authority to make representations with respect to the quality of the property sold; and that the petitioner is not liable under Art. 4004, supra, for damages for his misrepresentations, since they were not expressly authorized by petitioner and were not known to it before its deed was delivered to respondents. See Lay v. Midland Farms Co. (Civ.App.), 8 S.W.2d 230 (er.ref.). While we find no Texas case exactly in point, we do find that our holding is supported by a wealth of authority from other jurisdictions. (Citing cases) We believe these authorities present the sounder view, although there is authority to the contrary.

This holding is neither unjust nor harsh from the standpoint of the defrauded buyer. In the first place, he has a cause of action for damages for fraud against the agent who makes the fraudulent representations. And he has at least two remedies against the seller: (1) he may sue to rescind the contract, or (2) he may recoup his damages or prevent a recovery by the vendor of the purchase price, on the ground of failure of consideration. In both instances the principle applied is that the seller will not be permitted to retain the fruits of the fraud of his agent on the ground that he did not know of, or authorize, the making of the fraudulent representations. 57 A.L.R., Anno. 1, p. 111. . . . Here the petitioner did not resist restitution; on the contrary, it offered a rescission, which respondents declined.

The judgments of both courts below are reversed, and judgment is here rendered for the petitioner, Loma Vista Development Company. . . .

Discussion questions

1. What could the buyers have done to protect themselves? Why?
2. What could the principal have done to protect itself? Why?

Case 5

Gunn v. Schaeffer

567 S.W.2d 30 (Texas 1978)

Introduction

It is a fundamental rule of agency law that a third party cannot enforce a contract against the disclosed principal unless the agent was acting within the scope of his actual or apparent authority. In an action based upon apparent authority, the third party has the burden of proof. Whether or not the agent has apparent authority to bind his principal, in whose name the agent contracts, will be determined by a number of factors. The following case illustrates the applicable rule of law when an agent borrows money from third parties in his principal's name.

Osborn, Justice

This summary judgment case involves the authority of an apartment house manager to act for the owners of the apartments in borrowing money and issuing short term certificates to evidence such indebtedness. The trial Court concluded that the owners were not liable and granted the motion for summary judgment. We affirm.

The Appellants were residents of an apartment complex known as Sagewood Apartments. The complex is owned by Sagewood Associates, Ltd., a Texas limited partnership, whose general partners are Mason & Schaeffer, Inc., Ruben Schaeffer and John D. Mason. From September, 1972, until June, 1976, Mr. and Mrs. Nick Bikos were managers of the apartments. Shortly before taking this position, they had moved to El Paso from Indiana where Mr. Bikos had operated a bar and spent considerable time gambling. He still owed about $18,000.00 in gambling debts when they left Indiana and was under considerable pressure to pay off these debts. As a result of heart problems which had disabled him, Mr. Bikos received social security disability payments. It was agreed that his wife would be hired as manager of the apartments and the entire salary paid to her, so as not to affect his social security income. Nevertheless, both Mr. and Mrs. Bikos actually served as apartment managers. They rented apartments, collected rent, made deposits and provided for necessary maintenance. They had no authority to write checks on the account where the rent money was deposited.

Beginning in December, 1972, Mr. Bikos permitted some tenants who desired to do so to pay a year's rent in advance and receive a small discount on their normal monthly payments. Rather than depositing the year's rent, he deposited one month's rent and kept the remainder which he used to pay on his gambling bill back in Indiana, or to pay personal living expenses in El Paso, or to provide funds for his current gambling operations. As the advance rental plan spread among the tenants, he had more advance money to use to pay the monthly rent of those whose money he had pocketed for himself in prior months.

Seeing how easy it was to obtain advance rentals, and as his need for more funds increased to meet the rental payments of those who had already paid in advance, Mr. Bikos devised a plan to sell short term savings certificates to the tenants. These certificates were issued in the name of Sagewood Apartments, Inc., and bore the name of Nick Bikos as manager and a ficticious name signed by Mr. Bikos as treasurer. The certificates provided for interest in excess of that paid by any bank or savings association.

Like most such plans, this one concluded with Nick Bikos being indicted for felony theft and the owners of the apartments being sued by the three Appellants in this case for $20,200.00 which they had paid for the worthless certificates. They alleged a conspiracy "by fraud and deceit to swindle, cheat, embezzle and convert from the Plaintiffs" the amounts paid for the purchase of the certificates of indebtedness. They also alleged that Nick Bikos was the agent, servant and employee of Defendants, who were responsible for his sale of the certificates held by Appellants.

The Appellees moved for summary judgment on the grounds that the wrongful and illegal acts of Nick Bikos were solely for himself, without authority from or knowledge of the Appellees who contended that they were not responsible for his unauthorized acts. They filed as supporting proof the deposition of Mr. Bikos in which he acknowledged the illegal scheme, but testified quite frankly that it was all his idea to try to raise money to pay gambling debts. When asked if he was not concerned about the fact that word of the scheme might get to Mr. Schaeffer or his corporation, he said: "Very concerned. Very concerned. But the other trouble I was in was way bigger than that concern." He testified that he had no authority to issue the certificates, that the owners never knew about his scheme, and that they never received any of the funds. He said that he acted on his own and no one else was involved, although he admitted that when he sold the certificates, he represented to the purchasers that the management of the apartments originated and were behind this plan to raise additional capital.

The Appellees also filed the affidavit of Ruben Schaeffer. He stated that none of the owners ever discussed the issuance and sale of certificates of indebtedness to any persons. He said none of the owners ever authorized Nick Bikos to issue and sell certificates of indebtedness to any person. He also said the conduct of Nick Bikos in selling certificates of indebtedness was without the knowledge of, or authority, consent or direction from the apartment owners.

The reply affidavit of Appellants states that they were told by Nick Bikos at the time of sale of the certificates that Ruben Schaeffer, Mason & Schaeffer, Inc., and Sagewood Apartments, Ltd., were sponsoring the sale of the certificates of indebtedness, and that they guaranteed them.

"An actionable civil conspiracy is a combination by two or more persons to accomplish an unlawful purpose, or to accomplish a lawful purpose by unlawful means." 12Tex.Jur.2d Conspiracy, Sec. 14. A principal is bound by all acts of a general agent whenever the acts are within the ordinary and usual course of the business entrusted to the agent. However, the principal is not bound by the agent's acts if they are done in excess of his authority. . . . This includes both actual and apparent authority.

The Appellants present five points of error contending that fact issues exist as to both the conspiracy theory and the agency theory of the case, and that because of the issue of credibility of both Ruben Schaeffer and Nick Bikos a summary judgment was not proper in this case. The points are all closely related and argued together and will be considered together to determine if a fact issue exists.

The affidavit of Ruben Schaeffer and the deposition of Nick Bikos show without doubt that Nick Bikos acted alone in devising the fraudulent scheme and carrying it out, and that he alone profited from its operation without any knowledge by the apartment house owners of his sinister scheme. The affidavit of Appellants does not show otherwise. We can only conclude that no conspiracy existed. . . .

On the issue of agency, the affidavit and deposition show that Nick Bikos had no actual authority to issue the certificates of indebtedness. Nevertheless, the issue as to the apparent authority must also be considered. We conclude that one employed to manage an apartment complex, with actual authority to collect and deposit rent, does not have any apparent authority to borrow money from the tenants and issue certificates of indebtedness in the name of the apartment complex. In Bolin v. Pacific Finance Corporation, 278S.W.2d879 (Tex.Civ.App.Amarillo 1954, no writ), the Court stated the controlling rules with regard to determining an agent's authority as follows:

> 'When an apparent authority is claimed to arise from representations or conduct, the acts and statements of the principal must be looked to for the requisite foundation and not those of the agent; the former alone can give rise to authority of this character; the latter are never in themselves sufficient for that purpose. The principal must have affirmatively held the agent out as possessing sufficient authority to embrace the particular act in question, or else have voluntarily and in due awareness, actual or constructive, of the agent's assumption of power permitted him to act as if he had the requisite authority. The powers which the agent pretends to have, or assumes to exercise, are inoperative as a basis for ostensible authority when the principal authority when the principal is not affected by knowledge of them and does not validate them by acquiescence or assent; and no mere combination of circumstances which may, without the principal's participation, mislead third persons, however reasonably, into a false inference of authority affords a sufficient predicate for apparent authority.' . . .

Following that quote, the Court went further and said:

> One who deals with an agent of a corporation must exercise proper diligence to ascertain the authority with which the agent has been clothed and cannot rely on the acts and declarations of the agent alone. . . .

With regard to the specific authority of an agent to borrow money in the name of the principal, the rule is set forth in Guaranty Bank & Trust Co. v. Beaumont Cadillac Co., 218S.W.638 (Tex.Civ. App.-Beaumont 1920, writ dism'd), as follows:

> 'Power to borrow money is not to be inferred without clear evidence of such grant. Such authority must be expressly conferred or necessarily implied from the authority granted, and will not be inferred from a mere general authority, unless the character of the

business or the duties of the agent are of such a nature that he is bound to borrow money . . . in order to carry out his instructions or the duties of his office.'

It is pointed out in the comment under Restatement of Agency 2d, Sec.73, that a manager has no power to borrow money in connection with the operation of the business or to issue negotiable instruments in the name of the principal, unless the business conducted is one involving the borrowing of money or the issuing of negotiable instruments such as banking and other financial business. Under the heading of "Authorization to Borrow." Section 74 says:

Unless otherwise agreed, an agent is not authorized to borrow unless such borrowing is usually incident to the performance of acts which he is authorized to perform for the principal.

The comment under this section notes that the authority to borrow is not inferred unless it is practically indispensable to the continuance of the principal's business or to prevent a very considerable loss to the principal and where it is impossible to communicate with the principal. There is no suggestion in the record in this case that the principals were in the business of borrowing money, nor is there a suggestion that it was indispensable to the continuance of their business or to prevent a loss that made the borrowing by the manager necessary in this case.

In Mattice v. Equitable Life Assurance Society, 270Wis.504,71N.W.2d 262, 55 A.L.R.2d 1206 (1955), and Lamb v. General Associates, Inc., 60 Wash.2d 623, 374 P.2d 677 (1962), the Courts reviewed the rules with regard to the authority of an agent to borrow money in the name of the principal. In each case, the Court concluded that since the principal was not in the business of borrowing money, the agent had neither actual nor apparent authority to borrow in the name of the principal. We reach the same result in this case.

The one remaining issue is whether in this summary judgment case there is a fact issue because of questions of credibility. We conclude that there is not. Although Ruben Schaeffer is an interested party, his affidavit is clear, direct and positive, and there are no circumstances in evidence tending to discredit or impeach such testimony. . . . The general rule set forth in those cases was followed in Voudouris v. Walter E. Heller & Company, 560 S.W.2d 202 (Tex.Civ.App. Houston (1st Dist.) 1977, no writ), where the Court held as a matter of law that one alleged to be a general partner had established by his own testimony, which was clear, direct and positive and without circumstances tending to discredit or impeach such testimony, that a general partnership did not exist and that there was no liability on his part for the debts of the partnership.

The deposition of Nick Bikos reflects that he is a longtime gambler, and that he admittedly lied to all of those to whom he sold these certificates. And, in his deposition, he did on one or two occasions take the Fifth Amendment with regard to identifying his signature on checks and certificates of indebtedness. Yet, all of his testimony is clear, direct, and positive, and there are no circumstances in the evidence tending to discredit or impeach such testimony that he acted alone in this fraudulent scheme which he conceived and operated without knowledge upon the part of the apartment owners. If others were involved, surely some proof could have been obtained to at least cast doubt on his testimony, particularly in view of the number of people and the amount of money involved in this particular operation. But there is none. Accepting Appellees' affidavit as true and giving them the benefit of every reasonable inference which properly can be drawn in favor of their position, we conclude that there is no fact issue in dispute. . . .

The Appellants' points of error are overruled. The judgment of the trial Court is affirmed.

Discussion questions

1. The court listed two instances when an agent has authority to borrow money in the name of his principal. What are they?
2. Could the injured third parties recover from the principal for the agent's tort of fraud in this case under the doctrine of respondeat superior where the tort was committed in the furtherance of the agent's interest and not the principal's interest? Why?

Case 6

Crane v. Gruenewald et al

120 N.Y. 274 (1890)

Introduction

In order for a third party to enforce a contract against a principal based upon the agent's apparent authority, the third party must prove that (1) the principal held out his agent as possessing greater authority than he actually had and (2) the third party acted reasonably in relying on such apparent authority. The following case analyzes whether the third party acted reasonably in relying on the agent's apparent authority where the agent did not have possession of the principal's mortgage at the time the agent received a payment from the third party that was due on the mortgage.

Parker, J.

A mortgagor who makes a payment to one, other than the mortgagee, does so at his peril. If the payment be denied, upon him rests the burden of proving that it was paid to one clothed with authority to receive it. There is, however, one exception to this general rule. If payment be made to one having apparent authority to receive the money, it will be treated as if actual authority had been given for its receipt. (Paley on Agency (3d ed.), 275; Story on Agency, § 98; Williams v. Walker, 2 Sandf. Ch. 325; Smith v. Kidd, 68 N.Y. 130; Brewster v. Carnes, 103 id. 556-564.)

So, if a mortgagee permits an attorney, who negotiates a loan, to retain in his possession the bond and mortgage after the principal is due, and the mortgagor, with knowledge of that fact, and relying upon the apparent authority thus afforded, shall make a payment to him, the owner will not be permitted to deny that the attorney possessed the authority which the presence of the securities indicated that he had. This rule comprises two elements: First, possession of the securities by the attorney with the consent of the mortgagee; and second, knowledge of such possession on the part of the mortgagor. The mere possession of the securities by the attorney is not sufficient. The mortgagor must have knowledge of the fact. It would not avail him to prove that subsequent to a payment he discovered that the securities were in the actual custody of the attorney when it was made. For he could not have been misled or deceived by a fact, the existence of which was unknown to him. It is the information which he acquires of the possession which apprises him that the attorney has apparent authority to act for the principal. It is the appearance of authority to collect, furnished by the custody of the securities, which justifies him in making payment. And it is because the mortgagor acts in reliance upon such appearance, an appearance made possible only by the act of the mortgagee in leaving the securities in the hands of an attorney that stops the owner from denying the existence of authority in the attorney which such possession indicates.

Now, applying that rule to the facts found by the learned trial court in this case, the attorney Baker negotiated the loan of $8,000, which was made to this defendant on his bond secured by a mortgage on real estate. The mortgagor and mortgagee never saw each other. The securities were permitted to remain in the possession of the attorney. He had authority to collect the interest, but was not authorized to collect the principal or any part of it. After the principal became due he received from the mortgagor two payments of $1,000 each, on each occasion exhibiting the bond and mortgage to the mortgagor. Clearly as to these two items the attorney had apparent authority to receive the principal and the mortgagor could not deny to them the effect of payment pro tanto by proof that he did not have actual authority. Subsequently, and while the bond and mortgage still remained in the possession of the attorney, this defendant paid to him a further sum of $1,000, to be applied as a payment on account of the principal due. True, he did not at this time see the bond and mortgage but it was actually in the possession of the attorney and the attorney so informed him. There then was possession and information of possession. It was information upon which he acted, and inasmuch as it was true, it constituted apparent authority. If it had turned out to be untrue it could not have avai'ed the defendant. We see no ground for insisting that a party must actually see and examine the securities in order to entitle him to the protection of the doctrine of apparent authority, if he has trustworthy information of the fact which he believes and relies upon and it shall prove to be true there seems to be no reason why it should not avail him as well as a personal examination of the securities. It follows, that the defendant should have been credited with the third payment of $1,000. The remaining $5,000, was paid to Baker after he had parted with the possession of the bond and mortgage and the question presented is, whether the defendant is entitled to be credited with the payments made by him while the attorney Baker did not have actual possession of the securities. It will be observed that Baker was not deprived of the possession by any act of Mrs. Crane. She believed that they were still in the custody of Baker. So far as she is concerned, therefore, or the plaintiff in this action who occupies no better or other attitude, she is not in position to deny such responsibility as her conduct imposes. She cannot say that by any act of hers she is relieved from the operation of the estoppel which prevents her from denying that the first three payments of $1,000 each were effectual as such. If then the defendant is not entitled to be credited with the payments aggregating $5,000, it is because he is not in a situation to insist upon the estoppel. We are of the opinion that a proper application of this doctrine of apparent authority, requires us to hold that the defendant's failure to take the precaution of ascertaining whether the attorney was actually in the possession of the securities when he paid the several sums aggregating $5,000, deprives him of the right to assert that he was induced to make the payments because it appeared to him that the attorney had the right to receive the money. For, as we have already observed, it cannot appear to the mortgagor than an attorney has authority to receive the principal, save where he has present possession of the securities.

Information of the physical fact of possession by the attorney is alone effectual for protection. And he must have such knowledge when every payment is made, for no presumption of a continuance of possession can be indulged in for the purpose of giving support to an apparent authority on the part of an attorney to act, where no actual authority exists. This knowledge he did not have, for it was not the fact. By his own wrongful act, the attorney had parted with possession, and as a necessary consequence has deprived himself of the power to longer misrepresent his authority in respect thereto the detriment of the mortgagee. The mortgagor thereafter placed his trust solely in the assertations of the attorney and was deceived. In so doing he was legally as much at fault as the mortgagee, who also relied upon the attorney's trustworthiness. Therefore, he cannot invoke in support of his contention the doctrine of apparent authority. A rule which undoubtedly had its foundation in the equitable principal, that if one of two innocent persons must suffer, he ought to suffer in preference whose conduct has misled the confidence of the other into an unwary act.

The judgment should be reversed and a new trial granted with costs to the appellant; unless within thirty days the plaintiff stipulates to modify the judgment by deducting therefrom, $104.50, that being the amount of the costs of General Term, and the further sum of $1,000, with interest thereon from July 1, 1882, to the date of entry of the judgment together with any other sum paid by Gruenewald to Baker whether for principal or interest prior to July 20, 1883, for which he was not credited by the trial court; in which event the judgment as modified is affirmed with costs of this court to the appellant.

Discussion questions

1. Would the court's decision be the same if the agent exhibited a "counterfeit" mortgage to the mortgagor and the mortgagor did not detect the forgery? Why?
2. Would the court's decision be the same if the agent never had possession of the mortgage? Why?

Case 7

Harnischfeger Sales Corporation v. Coats

48P.2d 662 (Cal.1935)

Introduction

Principals usually include provisions in their written contracts made by their agents on their behalf with third parties to the effect that "there are no prior writings, verbal negotiations, understanding, representations or agreements between the parties, nor herein expressed". Such provisions are included for the purpose of putting third parties on notice that the agent has no authority to alter any of the terms and conditions expressly provided in the written contract and that therefore the principal has no liability for any tort based upon the agent's fraud and deceit in connection with the execution of the contract by the third party. The question then arises as to what rights the victim of the agent's fraud has on the contract in view of the typical provision referred to? The following case illustrates the victim's rights in such a case.

Langdon, Justice

This is an action by plaintiff to recover the balance due on a conditional sale contract for the sale of a power shovel. Defendant answered and counterclaimed, setting up the defense of fraud. The jury brought in a verdict in favor of defendant on his counterclaim, in the sum of $2,500. The court, however, gave judgment for plaintiff notwithstanding the verdict, for the entire balance due on the contract. Defendant appealed.

The contract in this case was entered into after negotiations by defendant with plaintiff's agent, and it is the false representations of this agent which constitute the defense of fraud. After being signed by defendant and plaintiff's agent, the contract was sent to the eastern office of plaintiff, where it was approved, executed, and a copy returned to defendant. The contract contained the following provision: "This agreement shall not be considered as executed, and shall not become effective until accepted by the vendee, and executed and approved by the president, or vice-president, or secretary of the vendor, and it is hereby further declared, agreed and understood that there are no prior writing, verbal negotiations, understandings, representations or agreements between the parties, not herein expressed."

It seems clear that this stipulation limits the authority of the agent to make representations, and purports to absolve the principal from all responsibility therefore. The question is whether such a stipulation may be given effect.

This problem was the subject of conflicting decisions in California until recently, when this court, in Speck v. Wylie, 1 Cal. (2d) 625, 36 P. (2d) 618, 95 A. L. R 760, announced the governing rule. It was there held that an innocent principal might by such a stipulation protect himself from liability in a tort action for damages for fraud and deceit, but that the third party would nevertheless be entitled to rescind the contract. This is the rule declared in the Restatement of the Law of Agency, § 250 and 260. . . . The distinction between the two situations is a sound one. The principal would normally be liable in tort for misrepresentations by an agent acting within the scope of his actual or ostensible authority, and by stipulating in the contract that the agent has no such authority, the principal has done all that is reasonably possible to give notice thereof to the third party. Under such circumstances the innocent principal may justly be relieved of liability for the agent's wrong. But where the principal sues to recover on the contract, he is seeking to benefit through the agent's fraud. This he cannot be permitted to do. His personal liability may be avoided, but the fraudulently procured contract is subject to rescission.

In the instant case, the counterclaim, which seeks the affirmative relief of damages, is objectionable for the same reason that an independent tort action would be. However, the principle followed in Speck v. Wylie, supra, warrants relief for fraud whether the injured party sets it up in an affirmative action for rescission, or as defensive relief in an action by the other party to enforce the contract; that is to say, the right of the aggrieved buyer to rescission exists regardless of which party initiates the proceeding on the contract. That the buyer may set up a claim for rescission in the seller's action has recently been held by the District Court of Appeal. . . . The defensive relief must not be such as to subject the plaintiff to affirmative liability for damages; nor would it be proper, under the rule just discussed, to permit an award of damages to offset liability for the balance of the purchase price. The defendant's relief is limited to rescission of the contract. Hence the affirmative verdict in favor of the defendant on his counterclaim for damages is improper; but defendant may be entitled, because of the fraud, to be placed in statu quo, by restoration of the consideration or its equivalent by both parties. . . . The failure to demand the specific remedy of rescission is not, of course, fatal to the right, where the facts pleaded justify it. The fraud, and not the remedy therefore, constitutes the cause of action. The present judgment must be reversed and the case retried, with amended pleadings if defendant desires to offer them, to set forth such facts as may warrant rescission. If, upon a retrial of the cause, it appears that the requirements of rescission are satisfied, defendant should have judgment.

The judgment is reversed.

Discussion questions

1. Could the third party hold the agent personally liable for the tort of fraud and deceit since the agent committed the tort while in the scope of his employment? Why?
2. Assuming the agent was held liable to the third party for his tort, would the agent be entitled to reimbursement or indemnity since he committed the tort for the sole purpose of furthering his principal's interest? Why?
3. Would a provision in the contract to the effect that the third party could not rescind the contract under any circumstances and that his sole remedy would be against the agent be enforceable? Why?

Case 8

Farm Bureau Mutual Insurance Company v. Coffin

186 N.E.2d 180 (1962)

Introduction

In order for a third party to be able to enforce a contract against the principal, he must prove that the agent had actual authority or apparent authority. Many times, parties deal with an agent by telephone and rely on the spoken word. The question arises to what extent the third party may properly rely upon "the person on the other end of the telephone"? The following case illustrates the usual problems encountered in telephone dealings between third parties and agents and how the court resolves them.

Pfaff, Judge

This action was begun by the appellee, Bonnie Eugene Coffin, to recover on an alleged oral contract of insurance between the appellee and the appellant through its employee, James R. Pierson, in which contract appellee's liability and property damage insurance was transferred to a new car and comprehensive and collision coverages were added to the policy. The appellant's answer denied that appellee had his automobile insured with the appellant except for bodily injury and property damage.

The issues having been formed, a trial was held and evidence was heard before the court without a jury, which resulted in a finding and judgment for the appellee in the sum of $1760.00, plus costs. A motion for a new trial and later an amended motion for a new trial were filed and overruled. The assignment of errors contains four specifications. Two are combined for discussion in the appellant's brief and one is waived. Thus the appellant has relied on two grounds for reversal.

The evidence discloses that the appellee, Bonnie Eugene Coffin, who was an assigned risk to the appellant, Farm Bureau Mutual Insurance Company, called the appellant's home office on December 13, 1955. When a girl answered the telephone, appellee stated that he wanted to transfer the insurance on his car. The call was switched to a second girl who in turn stated that she would connect appellee with Dick Pierson (James R. Pierson). When the appellee told James R. Pierson that he wanted to transfer the liability and property damage insurance on his 1953 Chevrolet to a new 1956 Buick and get additional collision and comprehensive insurance, the reply was "O.K. you are covered." Pierson has a different version of this conversation, but in view of the fact that the appellee was successful he is entitled to the testimony most favorable to him.

Pierson also told the appellee that his application papers would be in the morning mail and the appellee should fill them out and return them. In completing these forms, appellee, Coffin, did not properly mark the application to indicate that he desired the comprehensive and collision coverages.

The testimony indicates that James R. Pierson was not an insurance agent. At the time in question, he was Typing Supervisor in the Auto Underwriters Department. Transfers of insurance were routine matters; however evidence revealed the home office would only give additional coverage on written directives. The usual practice was to deal through an agent. There is no contrary testimony to the statements that Pierson had no authority to give collision coverage to an assigned risk.

The appellee had an accident one day after he talked to Pierson, that is, on December 14, 1955. This action was begun to recover for damage to the appellee's car which damage was caused by that accident.

The Pittsboro Branch, Lizton State Bank, Pittsboro, was a party to the original action because they held a mortgage on the appellee's 1956 Buick. They requested that the appellee obtain the comprehensive and collision coverage. The bank, however, is no longer concerned in the outcome as the loan has been repaid.

The briefs of the appellant and the appellee do not argue conflicting cases but rather each earnestly and somewhat accurately presents a different position. The appellant alleges that Pierson is a special agent; therefore appellee, Coffin, had a duty to inquire as to the extent of his authority. The appellee contends that regardless of the actual authority of Pierson he had the appearance of a general agent; therefore it was unnecessary for the appellee to inquire as to his specific authority.

The problem is whether the law applicable to special agents or that applicable to general agents should be followed in this case.

> The distinction between a general and special agent is very accurately and correctly stated by Mr. Wait, in his work on Law and Practice, vol. 1, p. 215, where it is said: 'A general agent is one who is authorized to transact all the business of his principal, or all his

business of some particular kind, or at some particular place. The principal will be bound by the acts of a general agent, if the latter acted within the usual and ordinary scope of the business in which he was employed, notwithstanding he may have violated the private instructions which the principal may have given him, provided the person dealing with such agent was ignorant of such violation and that the agent exceeded his authority. The authority of an agent being limited to a particular business does not make it special; it may be as general in regard to that, as though its range were unlimited. A special agent is one who is authorized to do one or more specific acts, in pursuance of particular instructions or within restrictions necessarily implied from the act to be done. The principal is not bound by the acts of a special agent, if he exceeds the limits of his authority. And it is the duty of every person who deals with a special agent to ascertain the extent of the agent's authority before dealing with him. If this is neglected, such person will deal at his peril, and the principal will not be bound by any act which exceeds the particular authority given.'

In Buchanan v. Caine (1914), 57 Ind. App.274, 282,106 N.E. 885, 888, the trial court gave the following jury instruction:

> '(9) Under the law a special agent can bind his principal only to the extent that he has authority from such principal, unless such principal should ratify the unauthorized acts of such agent, which matter I shall speak of further on. It, therefore, follows in this case that if you should find that the defendant and John G. Ingalls entered into the contract at Indianapolis, as claimed by the defendant, before you can charge the plaintiff in any way with such agreement, you must find that John C. Ingalls had authority from the plaintiff to make such contract, or if he did not in fact have such authority, then that the plaintiff subsequently ratified the action of said Ingalls in entering into such new contract, if you should find the same was entered into.'

Before the Appellate Court error was charged on the basis that this instruction ignored the possibility that a special agent might act within his apparent authority. The court held that the instruction assumed that the appellee was a special agent, and this was error because the question as to whether Ingalls was a special agent or a general agent is a fact determination.

In Jasper County Farms Co. v. Holden (1923), 79 Ind.App. 214,216,137 N.E.618, it is stated:

> The character of said agency, whether general or special, was also a question of fact and for the purpose of determining this fact all the acts and dealings of the said agent were competent. This necessarily follows, because the ostensible powers of an agent are his real powers; and so the vital question was one of apparent authority of the agent.

Since the trial judge below found for the appellee and entered judgment, he must have concluded that Pierson was clothed with such authority that the appellee was justified in assuming that Pierson was a general agent. The question then is whether sufficient evidence was presented from which the trial judge could find that James R. Pierson had apparent authority to enter into an oral contract for the transfer of the appellee's liability insurance and the addition of comprehensive and collision insurance to the policy. The appellee called the appellant's home office and stated that he desired to transfer his insurance. He talked to two different girls who did not have authority to make such a transfer. Finally he was connected with James R. Pierson, who told the appellee that he had collision coverage as of that moment. We think that these facts are sufficient to sustain a finding that James R. Pierson had apparent authority to transfer the appellee's liability and property damage insurance and to add collision coverage.

When one has the appearance of a general agent the law is clear that a third person dealing with him is not bound to inquire into his specific authority, nor is the principal protected by secret limitations upon the authority of such an agent. The reason for the rule is that where one of two innocent persons must suffer because of the betrayal of a trust reposed in a third, the one who is most at fault should bear the loss. Since the principal put the agent in the position of trust, he is the one who should suffer the detriment.

The appellant has relied almost exclusively upon State Life Ins. Co. v. Thiel (1939), 107 Ind.App. 75, 20 N.E.2d 693. However, that case can be distinguished from the issue before us, because Besing, the local representative in that case, was a special agent. The court said that there was no evidence that Besing had actual or apparent authority. On the other hand, appellant herein clothed Pierson with apparent authority. The appellee called the appellant's home office and stated that he wanted to transfer his insurance. Employees of the appellant (principal) then connected appellee (third party) with Pierson (apparent general agent).

The remaining assignment of error was the overruling of appellant's contention in the Amended Motion for New Trial to the effect that the trial court erred in admitting in evidence, over the objection of the appellant, the evidence on direct examination of the appellee, Bonnie Eugene Coffin, of his telephone conversation with Pierson. The appellant asserts that the application filed by the appellee subsequent to his telephone conversation with Pierson embraced any previous oral contract with the appellees, because this application for transfer was in writing.

Appellant cites general authority for parts of his argument. However he fails to present cases or a cogent argument why the written application here should be treated as a written contract. The application in this case does not on its face contain any provisions of a policy, oral or written, issued or agreed to by appellant. The record does not indicate nor does appellant contend that any policy of insurance, written or oral, was issued or agreed to by appellant in reliance upon any statement or representations contained in the written application.

In Wright v. State (1958), 237 Ind. 593,595, 147 N.E.2d551,552, the Supreme Court said:

Appellant asserts here as cause for appeal grounds numbered 1 to 11 as stated in the motion for new trial. However, grounds numbered 6 through 11 are not supported by any cogent argument or citation of authorities. It is encumbent upon appellant on appeal, whether the cause be civil or criminal, to affirmatively show harmful error by argument and citation of authorities. Rule 2-17(e). Errors assigned and causes for new trial not so treated are deemed to be waived. Rule 2-17(f).

In this case appellant has failed to make such a cogent argument or presentation of authorities in its brief as to merit further consideration of this contention.

Even if the trial court concluded that said James R. Pierson was a special agent, it appears, nevertheless, upon the record herein, that the evidence was amply sufficient to support the finding that he was clothed with the apparent authority of a general agent authorized to enter into the contract now in question on behalf of the appellant. The appellant has failed to show error by the record; therefore the judgment must be affirmed.

Judgment affirmed.

Gonas, P.J., and Bierly and Kelley, JJ., concur.

Discussion questions

1. How could the principal have avoided the result in this case? Why?
2. What rights, if any, does the principal-employer have against his agent-employee? Why?

Case 9

Legal Aid v. Economic

132AD2d113 (1987)

Introduction

This case illustrates what a plaintiff must prove when it claims that an agent had apparent authority to contract on behalf of the principal.

Opinion of the court

Mahoney, P. J.

In January 1981, defendant Economic Opportunity Commission of Nassau County, Inc. (hereinafter EOC) entered into a grant agreement with the United States Community Services Administration (hereinafter CSA) whereby CSA agreed to provide EOC with $100,000 for the operation of a one-year "Energy Support Program" to protect the interests of New York's low-income energy consumers in proceedings before the State Public Service Commission and the Power Authority of the State of New York. The agreement stated that defendant New York State Alliance of Community Action Programs, Inc. (hereinafter Alliance) would be responsible for implementing the $100,000 program.

Pursuant to the grant agreement, EOC and Alliance agreed to enter into a contract with a legal services institution to provide no less than 375 hours of "energy reform and advocacy" to low-income residents of New York; $20,000 of the $100,000 grant was allocated for this purpose. Plaintiff legal Aid Society of Northeastern New York, Inc. (hereinafter Legal Aid) alleges that Alliance entered into an oral contract with plaintiff Public Utility Law Project (hereinafter PULP), a project within the corporate body of Legal Aid, as the legal services agency to provide the services described in the grant agreement. Plaintiffs state that, in reliance on the oral contract, PULP performed legal services. Plaintiffs thus demanded payment of $20,000 from Alliance, but no payment was received.

Plaintiffs commenced this action against defendants, setting forth causes of action alleging breach of contract, account stated, quantum meruit, third-party beneficiary and intentional misallocation of Federal funds. A jury trial was held. At the close of plaintiffs's evidence, Supreme Court granted defendants motion dismission all five causes of action pursuant to CPLR 4401. This appeal ensued.

While Supreme Court dismissed plaintiffs entire complaint, plaintiffs brief on appeal only addresses 3 of the 5 causes of action which were dismissed. Their first argument concerns the dismissal of the breach of contract cause of action. Plaintiffs contend that Supreme Court erred when it found a lack of proof on the issue of whether the Alliance representative who allegedly dealt with PULP had the authority to contract on defendants behalf. We disagree. The record shows that in February 1981, Rose Brown, Alliance's representative, had several conversations with PULP's director and general counsel. At trial, however, plaintiffs failed to introduce any proof of Brown's authority to contract on Alliance's behalf. Brown was unavailable to testify. Therefore, while testimony was received concerning Brown's negotiations with PULP, plaintiffs failed to produce any connecting evidence of Brown's authority. Further, plaintiffs reliance on what they characterize as Brown's "apparent authority" to contract for Alliance is misplaced. When a party deals with an agent he does so at his peril, and must make the necessary effort to discover the actual scope of authority (*Ford v Unity Hosp.*, 32 NY2d 464, 472; see, *Warson Constr. Co. v Schlussel,* 68 AD2d 947, 948). In any event, a third party can invoke the doctrine of apparent authority only when the words or conduct of the *principal,* communicated to the third party, have caused the third party to believe that an agent has authority to contract on the principal's behalf (*Melstein v Schmid Labs.*, 116 AD2d 632, 634). Here, there was no evidence that Alliance caused plaintiffs to rely upon Brown's "apparent authority". Moreover, B. Robert Piller, PULP's director and general counsel and the individual with whom Brown had several conversations concerning a possible contract, admitted that he never inquired about the scope of Brown's authority. Finally, even assuming that Brown had authority, the record is void of any competent evidence of offeror acceptance. This court recently stated that a breach of contract cause of action is properly dismissed under CPLR 4401 when there is no proof of the terms of any agreement between the parties (*Salzman v Rosell,* 129 AD2d 833).

Discussion Question

1. What should the plaintiff have asked the agent to produce as evidence of the agent's authority to act for its employer-principal?

Case 10

Penn Ins. v. Irving Trust Co.

145AD2d174 (1st Dept., 1989)

Introduction

This case examines the legal issue of whether the third party who deals with an agent has any duty to verify the agent's authority. The case also examines the legal issue of whether his failure to do so imposes any liability to the principal when the third party pays the agent money intended for the principal but the disloyal agent steals such funds.

Opinion of the Court

Wallach, J.

"One who deals with an agent does so at his peril, and must make the necessary effort to discover the actual scope of authority" (*Ford v Unity Hosp.*, 32 NY2d 464, 472). Plaintiff relies on this comment by the Court of Appeals and other statements to like effect as justification for an action based on the theory that a third person who deals with an agent but fails to make reasonable inquiry into the agent's authority becomes liable to the principal in tort for defalcations of the agent that could have been prevented had such an inquiry been made. The comment, however, must be kept in its context, which was an action not by a principal against a third person who dealt with a disloyal agent, but by a third person against a principal that was held to be without merit because of the agent's lack of apparent authority to enter into the contract sought to be enforced. The point of the comment was that since the doctrine of apparent authority does not automatically bind the principal to every transaction entered into by his agent purportedly on his behalf, prudence, if nothing else, dictates that when an agent's authority to enter into a particular transaction is less than certain, an inquiry be made of the principal to confirm the actual scope of the agent's authority. In other words, a duty of inquiry, if such it be, is owed by the third person not to the principal but to himself. Thus this action, based as it is on the theory that the failure to so inquire constitutes negligence, should have been dismissed for failure to state a cause of action.

Insofar as pertinent to this appeal, the complaint alleges that plaintiff, William Penn Life Insurance Company (Penn), was a stakeholder in a lawsuit concerning certain life insurance proceeds in which a judgment of approximately $114,000, representing the full amount of the policy plus interest, was entered against it. Asserting that the last premium due under the policy had never been paid, and that the amount thereof, approximately $8,000, should have been set off against the proceeds of the policy, Penn issued its check for approximately $107,000, representing the proceeds of the policy less the amount of the unpaid premium plus interest, and gave it to its attorney, one Richard Pikna, with instructions to deliver it to the prevailing claimant's attorney, to whom it was made payable, and with further instructions to take an appeal seeking to reduce the amount of the judgment by the amount of the unpaid premium. It is then alleged that Pikna forged the signature of the prevailing claimant's attorney and deposited the check in an account he had with defendant Citibank. N. A. Citibank accepted the check and forwarded it for payment to the drawee bank, defendant Irving Trust Company, who completed the collection process by accepting the check and debiting Penn's account. In the meantime, Pikna, according to the complaint, "in order to avoid detection", noticed an appeal for the entire amount of the judgment entered against Penn, not just the unpaid premium as he had been instructed, and "arranged" with defendant General Insurance Company of America (General), a surety bonding company to have an appeal bond in the amount of $120,000 issued in Penn's name. Issuance of this bond automatically stayed enforcement of the entire judgment against Penn, effectively "precluding the possibility that the prevailing claimant's attorney would seek to enforce the judgment—a possibility that would have "revealed" such attorney's nonreceipt of Penn's check. Not until almost a year later, when the dismissal of Penn's appeal prompted the prevailing claimant's attorney to contact General, and General in turn contacted Penn, did Penn learn that the prevailing claimant's attorney had never received its check for $107,000. What became of Pikna the complaint does not say, although the argument proceeds on the assumption that he is not amenable to suit. It is a matter of some emphasis in the complaint, and especially in Penn's argument, that Penn itself never executed an application for an appeal bond, and that General never demanded such or otherwise sought instructions directly from Penn.

The complaint seeks to hold General liable in the amount of Penn's check on the ground that "General Insurance had a duty to notify William Penn within a reasonable time that General Insurance had issued the Bond in william Penn's name", and that the failure to so notify constitutes actionable negligence since it resulted in the loss of the check. We understand this to mean that had Penn been informed of the nature of Pikna's dealings with General when such dealings were current, it would have questioned him as to why he was taking out a bond for the full amount of the judgment, when he was authorized to bond only the unpaid premium, and learned that he was doing so for dishonest purposes. With such knowledge, Penn would have stopped bank collection of its check, or, if that process had already been completed, at least might have been able to recover the proceeds from Pikna before he was able to dispose of them.

The duty that Penn asserts General had to notify it of the issuance of the bond is not claimed to exist by reason of any statute, rule or custom of the surety bonding industry. Rather, it is Penn's contention that under common-law principles of agency, General should have suspected Pikna's authority to procure the bond, and thus made inquiry of Penn concerning it, if not immediately, then certainly when General did not receive a written bond application from Penn itself within a reasonable, but otherwise unspecified, period of time. To put it in black-letter terms, Penn is arguing that when a third person is approached by a second person who proclaims himself to be an agent for a first person, but who lacks any indicia of authority other than his own self-proclamation, the third person owes a duty to the first person, the putative principal, to make a reasonable inquiry into the authority of the second person, the putative agent, which, if breached, makes the third person liable for any losses sustained by the putative principal attributable to the unauthorized acts of the putative agent that could have been prevented had the putative agent's lack of authority been exposed at or about the time of his dealings with the third person. According to Penn, this "duty of inquiry and verification" could have been satisfied in this case had General taken the minimal step of contacting Penn to confirm the fact and scope of Pikna's supposed authority.

We reject Penn's contention that General owed it a duty of inquiry. Again, the source of this duty is claimed to be found not in any statute, rule or custom, but in case law. But the cases cited by Penn—because they speak of a third person dealing with an agent at his peril if reasonable inquiry is not made into the agent's authority—all involve an attempt by the third person to hold the putative principal liable on the contract executed by the putative agent (*Ford v Unity Hosp.*, 32 NY2d 464, supra; *Strip Clean Floor Refinishing v New York Dist. Council No. 9 Bhd. of Painters,* 333 F Supp 385; *Matter of Lester*, 87 Misc 2d 717; *Schenck v Bear, Stearns & Co.*, 484 F Supp 937; *Matter of Karavos Campania Naviera v Atlantica Export Corp.*, 588 F2d 1). None of these cases, nor any others of which we are aware, stand for the proposition that a third person can be held liable in tort to a putative principal for dealing with someone who claims to be an agent but is not, or who is, but exceeds his authority. Rather, they simply stand for the principle that if such dealings are undertaken without the third person making reasonable inquiry into the putative agent's authority, then the third person may not look to the putative principal to make good any damages that he, the third person, sustains. Or, as General aptly puts it, the duty of reasonable inquiry is owed by the third person to himself, not the putative principal. The situation, as General readily acknowledges for the sake of argument, would be altogether different were this an action by general against Penn to recover, for example, a premium payment, or otherwise seeking to hold Penn liable on the suretyship agreement that Pikna presumed to enter into on Penn's behalf.

General argues that the duty of inquiry urged by Penn is not only novel but also at odds with analogous case law in that it would impose upon a third person dealing with an agent an affirmative duty to protect the principal from the defalcations of his own selected agent (citing *Hutzler v Hertz Corp.*, 39 NY2d 209, 215 [principal sought to hold third person liable for loss sustained by principal when agent appropriated the proceeds of a check made payable by third person to principal and agent jointly; *held:* "It is the (principal), after all, who selected a dishonest person to represent him, and he, not the (third person), should bear the risk of his unauthorized acts, having placed him in a position to perpetrate the wrong."]). Against this, Penn points out that the agent in *Hutzler*, also an attorney, was known to be such for reasons much more reliable than his own representations, thus making the third person's dealings with him clearly justifiable, and argues that the threshold question is not, as General would have it, whether Pikna was, as it happened, "vested with some modicum of authority" to act on Penn's behalf, but whether General did enough "to learn about that purported 'agency when Pikna proclaimed its existence" such as would have given it reason to believe that he was in fact what he represented himself to be, Penn's agent, and justified its dealing with him in that capacity. Unless the issue is so defined, Penn argues, "there would be no protection against even the most transparent of pretenders." We are not persuaded. Protection is needed not against pretenders or, as Penn elsewhere puts it, "strangers", but against unfaithful agents. A stranger, after all, would not have had the opportunity to steal Penn's money since he would not have been entrusted with it in the first place. Notwithstanding that Pikna's authority could, in contrast to Hutzler, be deemed not apparent, as between General, who merely took Pikna at his word, and Penn, who placed Pikna in a position of trust enabling him to perpetrate the wrong, it is Penn who should bear the loss it sustained as a result of Pikna's swindle.

If the fact of Pikna's employment by Penn to act as its attorney does not itself estop Penn from asserting as against General that Pikna lacked authority to procure the appeal bond, and if it is true, as Penn contends, that it was unreasonable for General to issue that bond without inquiring into Pikna's authority, then, just as General would not have a cause of action against Penn in contract on the suretyship agreement, neither should Penn have a cause of action against General in tort. Both should bear their own loss; neither should have to bear the other's.

Accordingly, the order of the Supreme Court, New York County (David H. Edwards, Jr., J.), entered on or about October 13, 1987, which denied General's motion to dismiss the complaint for failure to state a cause of action, should be reversed, on the law, without costs, and the motion granted.

KUPFERMAN, J. (dissenting). I would affirm. A claim for negligence is adequately stated in connection with the failure timely to notify the plaintiff-respondent. While the bond may have been issued at the request of an attorney who had apparent authority, there should, within a reasonable time, have been a verification of the agency relationship by the receipt of an executed bond application, which was not done. It is in this that there may have been negligence, and so a cause of action is stated.

MURPHY, P.J., ASCH and KASSAL, JJ., concur with WALLACH, J.; KUPFERMAN, J., dissents in a separate opinion.

Order, Supreme Court, New York County, entered on or about October 13, 1987, reversed, on the law, without costs and without disbursements, and the motion to dismiss the amended complaint granted.

Discussion question

1. How could the plaintiff have avoided the result of this case when it gave the check to its agent?

Name: ______________________

PROBLEMS

Date: ______________________

Section Number: ______________________

1. An agency relationship

______ a. Must be in writing if it is to be legally enforceable.

______ b. Creates a fiduciary duty on the principal's part.

______ c. Can be created by estoppel, i.e., implied as a matter of law.

______ d. Is normally delegable as a matter of law.

2. P engaged A as its agent to purchase original oil paintings for resale by P. A's express authority was specifically limited to a maximum purchase price of $25,000 for any collection provided it contained a minimum of five oil paintings. A purchased a seven-picture collection on P's behalf for $30,000. Based upon these facts, which of the following is a correct legal conclusion?

______ a. The express limitation on A's authority negates any apparent authority.

______ b. P can not ratify the contract since A's actions were clearly in violation of his contract.

______ c. If P rightfully disaffirms the unauthorized contract, A is personally liable to the seller.

______ d. Neither P nor A is liable on the contract since the seller was obligated to ascertain A's authority.

3. P operated a cotton factory and employed A as a general purchasing agent to travel through the southern states to purchase cotton. P telegraphed A instructions from day to day as to the price to be paid for cotton. A entered a cotton district in which she had not previously done business and represented that she was purchasing cotton for P. Although directed by P to pay no more than 25 cents a pound, A bought cotton from T at 30 cents a pound, which was the prevailing offering price at that time. P refused to take the cotton. Under these circumstances, which of the following is correct?

______ a. The negation of actual authority to make the purchase effectively eliminates any liability for P.

______ b. P is not liable on the contract.

______ c. A has no potential liability.

______ d. P is liable on the contract.

4. P shipped 100 bales of hops to T. The agreement specified that the hops were to be of a certain grade. Upon examining the hops, T claimed that they were not of that grade. P's general sales agent who made the sale to T agreed to relieve T of liability and to have the hops shipped elsewhere. This was done, and the hops were sold at a price less than T was to have paid. P refused to accede to the agent's acts and sued T for the amount of its loss. Under these circumstances

______ a. P will prevail only if the action by its agent was expressly authorized.

______ b. Even if P's agent had authority to make such an adjustment, it would not be enforceable against P unless ratified in writing by P.

______ c. Because the hops were sold at a loss in respect to the price T had agreed to pay, T would be liable for the loss involved.

______ d. P is bound because its agent expressly, impliedly, or apparently had the authority to make such an adjustment.

5. Agents sometimes have liability to third parties for their actions taken for and on behalf of the principal. An agent will not be personally liable in which of the following circumstances?

______ a. If he makes a contract which he had no authority to make but which the principal ratifies.

______ b. If he commits a tort while engaged in the principal's business.

_____ c. If he acts for a principal which he knows is nonexistent and the third party is unaware of this.

_____ d. If he acts for an undisclosed principal as long as the principal is subsequently disclosed.

6. A made a contract with T which exceeded A's authority. If P wishes to hold T to the contract, P must prove that

_____ a. P ratified the contract before withdrawal from the contract by T.

_____ b. A was acting in the capacity of an agent for an undisclosed principal.

_____ c. A believed he was acting within the scope of his authority.

_____ d. A was P's general agent even though A exceeded his authority.

7. A is a car salesman employed by P. P instructed A not to sell a specially equipped and modified car owned by the company. P had decided to use this car as a "super" demonstrator to impress potential purchasers. The car just arrived from Detroit, had been serviced, and was parked alongside other similar models. T "fell in love" with the car and, after some negotiations with A, signed a contract to purchase the car. T gave A a check for 20% of the purchase price and executed a note and a purchase money security agreement. A forged P's name on the check and disappeared. P seeks to repossess the car from T. What is the probable outcome based on the above facts?

_____ a. P will be permitted to repossess the car but must compensate T for any inconvenience.

_____ b. T will be permitted to keep the car if T assumes the loss on the check given to A.

_____ c. P will be permitted to repossess the car because there was an express prohibition against the sale of this car.

_____ d. T will be permitted to keep the car because A had the apparent authority to bind P to the contract of sale.

8. P engaged A as one of its sale representatives to sell automotive parts. A signed an employment contract which required him to obtain home-office approval on any contract in excess of $500 entered into by A on P's behalf. The industry custom and most of P's agents had authority to make such contracts if they did not exceed $1,000. A signed a contract on P's behalf with T for $850. P rejected the contract and promptly notified T of its decision. Under these circumstances

_____ a. A is a del credere agent.

_____ b. A did not have express authority to make the contract with T.

_____ c. A had the implied authority to make the contract.

_____ d. P's prompt disaffirmance of A's action retroactively terminated any liability it might have had.

9. In order to hold the principal liable under the ratification doctrine for the unauthorized act of a party purporting to act as his agent

_____ a. The principal need not have been in existence at the time the contract was made.

_____ b. The purported agent must have been acting for an undisclosed principal.

_____ c. The principal must have full knowledge of the facts regarding the action taken on his behalf.

_____ d. The ratification must be in writing and made within a reasonable time after the unauthorized action was taken on his behalf.

10. The ratification doctrine with respect to principal and agent

_____ a. Does not apply to real estate contracts.

_____ b. Requires that a written notice of ratification be sent to the third party and the agent in order to create an enforceable contract.

_____ c. Does not apply to torts committed by the agent.

_____ d. Requires that the agent or purported agent indicates to the third party that he is acting for and on behalf of the person subsequently ratifying.

11. The ratification doctrine

______ a. Is not applicable to situations where the party claiming to act as the agent for another party claiming to act as the agent for another has no express or implied authority to do so.

______ b. Is designed to apply to situations where the principal was originally incompetent to have made the contract himself, but who, upon becoming competent, ratifies.

______ c. Requires the principal to ratify the entire act of the agent and the ratification is retroactive.

______ d. Applies only if the principal expressly ratifies in writing the contract made on his behalf within a reasonable time.

12. A made a contract for and on behalf of his principal which was legally unauthorized. What is the status of this contract?

______ a. It is illegal.

______ b. It can be ratified only by a written affirmation of the contract.

______ c. It can not bind the third party regardless of the principal's subsequent action.

______ d. It can be ratified by the principal by his silence and the receipt and retention of the benefits of the contract.

13. A was employed as an agent for P to purchase newer model used cars. His authority was limited by a $3,000 maximum price for any car. A wholesaler showed him a 1938 classic car which was selling for $5,000. The wholesaler knew that P only dealt in newer model used cars and that A has never paid more than $3,000 for any car. A bought the car for P, convinced that it was worth at least $7,000. When he reported this to P, P was furious but he nevertheless authorized processing of the automobile for resale. P also began pricing the car with antique car dealers who indicated that the current value of the car was $4,800. P called the wholesaler, told him that A has exceeded his authority, that he was returning the car, and that he was demanding repayment of the purchase price. What is the wholesaler's best defense in the event of a lawsuit?

______ a. A had apparent authority to purchase the car.

______ b. A's purchase was effectively ratified by P.

______ c. A had express authority to purchase the car.

______ d. A had implied authority to purchase the car.

14. To successfully invoke the doctrine of ratification

______ a. The agent must have had the legal capacity to have so acted.

______ b. The agent must in fact be the agent of the principal although the action taken was totally without authority.

______ c. The ratification must have been stated expressly.

______ d. The ratification must be made with knowledge of the material facts of the transaction.

15. A is an agent for P with the express authority to solicit orders from customers in a geographic area assigned by P. A has no authority to grant discounts nor to collect payment on orders solicited. A secured an order from T for $1,000 less a 10% discount if T makes immediate payment. T had previously done business with P through A but this was the first time that a discount-payment offer had been made. T gave A a check for $900 and thereafter T turned in both the check and the order to P. The order clearly indicated that a 10% discount had been given by A. P shipped the order and cashed the check. Later P attempted to collect $100 as the balance owed on the order from T. Which of the following is correct?

______ a. P can collect $100 from T because A contracted outside the scope of his express or implied authority.

______ b. P can not collect the $100 from T because A as an agent with express authority to solicit orders had implied authority to give discounts and collect.

______ c. P can not collect the $100 from T as P has ratified the discount granted and payment made to A.

______ d. P can not collect the $100 from T because although A had no express or implied authority to grant a discount and collect, A had apparent authority to do so.

16. Under which of the following circumstances will an agent acting on behalf of a disclosed principal not be liable to a third party for his actions?

______ a. He signs a negotiable instrument in his own name and does not indicate his agency capacity.

______ b. He commits a tort in the course of discharging his duties.

______ c. He is acting for a nonexistent principal which subsequently comes into existence after the time of the agent's actions on the principal's behalf.

______ d. He lacks specific express authority but is acting within the scope of his implied authority.

17. Arlen is employed as an accountant and paymaster in the office of Purex Corp. An invoice is presented by a creditor for immediate payment at a time when there are insufficient funds to pay it. Without consulting anyone in a position of authority because they are all away at a business convention, Arlen borrows money in the name of Purex Corp. to avoid a threatened lawsuit.

a. Does Arlen have authority to borrow money by reason of his position? Why?

____

____

____

____

____

b. Does Arlen have authority to borrow money by reason of the circumstances? Why?

____

____

____

____

____

18. On February 1, Cook was hired as the purchasing manager of the CVX Company, which operated a chain of drug stores in a tri-state area. His employment contract was for three years. He was specifically instructed by the president, Portnoy, not to purchase any tobacco products. Contrary to this instruction, two days later Cook ordered $300,000 of cigarettes at a heavy discount from a distributor, Duncanson, who sold to other drug stores in the same area. Cook did so because he believed the wholesale price was so low that the cigarettes could be offered at such an attractive low retail price that it would increase customer traffic and business. Duncanson did not know that Cook was expressly prohibited from buying cigarettes. When Portnoy learned of the order, he promptly repudiated it.

a. In an action by Duncanson against CVX Company, judgment for whom? Why?

____

____

____

____

____

b. If CVX Company is liable to Duncanson, what rights does it have against Cook? Why?

19. Archer was duly appointed as manager of Marcy's department store. Marcy told Archer not to hire any salespersons because he, Marcy, preferred to do so himself. In violation of this restriction, Archer hired Sampson as a salesperson at a salary of $1,500 a month. Sampson assumed Archer had authority to hire her. Sampson worked for one month but Marcy refused to pay her salary.

a. In an action by Sampson against Marcy, judgment for whom? Why?

b. If judgment is recovered by Sampson against Marcy, what rights, if any, does Marcy have against Archer? Why?

20. Nikal appointed Adair as his general agent to sell wheat in Chicago. Nikal instructed Adair not to sell below the market price under any circumstances and not to give any of the usual warranties as to the quality of the wheat given by other such agents in the Chicago area. In violation of these two instructions, Adair sold $100,000 of wheat to Talbott at 5% below the market price with a warranty of quality similar to that given by other such agents. The wheat was delivered to Talbott who paid for it at the reduced price. It was not the quality represented.

a. Is Nikal bound by the sale? Why?

b. What rights, if any, does Nikal have against Adair? Why?

21. Peters owned a medium sized insurance agency which had ten inexpensive computers. Peters decided to replace them over a two year period with modern and sophisticated computers. He instructed Abbot, his office manager, to purchase one IBM Model 9000 computer. Abbot did so and Peters paid $25,000 for it. Three months later, Peters authorized Abbot to purchase another such computer from the same seller which Abbot did. Peters paid $25,000 for it. Two months later, Abbot on his own, without authority, ordered another such computer from the same seller at the special low price of $17,000 which expired on that day. Abbot did so because Peters was away on a business trip and could not be reached and Abbot knew about Peters' plan to replace the existing computers and believed in good faith that Peters would want to purchase the computer at such a good price. When Peters returned and learned what Abbot did, Peters promptly informed the seller that he was repudiating the contract because Abbot had no authority to make the particular purchase.

a. In an action by the seller against Peters, judgment for whom? Why?

b. In an action by the seller against Abbot, judgment for whom? Why?

22. Abbey was a salesman for Green Valley Nursery, Inc., a dealer in garden products. Abbey sold to Torrance 250 gallons of "Weed Killer #007". Torrance was a commercial grower of lily bulbs for about ten years. She knew generally that weed killers were in the experimental stage but had no specific knowledge about "Weed Killer #007". Torrance explained to Abbey that she wanted to use a weed killer on a field in which she planted lily bulbs. Abbey expressly warranted that "Weed Killer #007" could be used safely on ground in which lily bulbs were planted. Torrance used the product but it caused a toxic condition in the soil and the bulbs were destroyed.

a. In an action by Torrance against Green Valley Nursery, Inc., judgment for whom? Why?

b. In an action by Torrance against Abbey, judgment for whom? Why?

23. Acme Construction Equipment Corporation sued Sims to recover the price of $50,000 due on a contract for the sale of a bulldozer. Sims set up fraud as a defense. The seller agent entered into the contract, prepared by the seller, with Sims and Sims' defense of fraud is based upon false oral representations made by the seller's agent. After the contract was signed by Sims, it was sent to Acme who approved it, signed it, and returned a copy to Sims. The contract contained a clause in bold type reciting that "there are no prior writings, understandings, or representations not herein expressed."

a. Judgment for whom? Why?

b. Would your answer to a. be different if the clause appeared in the same size type as the rest of the contract? Why?

c. Would your answer to a. be different if the clause appeared in smaller type than used for the rest of the contract? Why?

24. The Metropolitan Club owned a large building and rented one floor to a restaurant doing business as "The Gardens". A salesman for Gourmet Foods, a food supplier, sold food to the restaurant and was told to send the bill to the Metropolitan Club. Thereafter, over a six month period the salesman made similar sales and bills were sent monthly to the Metropolitan Club. The Club bookkeeper who, in addition to her regular duties had the authority to open mail, received the bills and turned them over to the restaurant. All bills received indicated that orders for food were taken in the name of the Metropolitan Club. The bills for the first two months were paid by the restaurant, but those for the next four months were unpaid and the restaurant is not out of business.

a. In an action by Gourmet Foods against the Metropolitan Club, judgment for whom? Why?

b. Assuming the Metropolitan Club is liable to Gourmet Foods, what rights, if any, does it have against its bookkeeper? Why?

25. Stephen, a traveling salesman for Ace Television, sold Tim a color television set for $800. Stephen did not have the set in his possession but it was to be shipped in one week. The bill of sale clearly indicated that Stephen was authorized only to collect 10% of the purchase price as a down payment. A week later, after Tim had received the set from Ace Television, Stephen, without authority, obtained payment of the balance. He absconded with all the money.

In an action by Ace Television against Tim to recover $800, judgment for whom? Explain.

26. George Williamson was one of the purchasing agents of Super Wholesale Appliances Corporation. On August 11, the president of the corporation sent Williamson a lengthy memorandum indicating that storage space had become so costly that the corporation was no longer prepared to purchase and store a large inventory of appliances during the winter. The president stated that no further purchases were to be made. The corporation had previously made such purchases when it could buy manufacturer close-outs at bargain prices.

Williamson glanced hurriedly at the memo but did not pay serious attention to it at the time. Unfortunately, he called upon Modern Kitchens, Inc., one of the corporation's leading suppliers of appliances later on the same day and was offered 500 large kitchen appliances at a substantial reduction. Williamson promptly accepted and signed an order for the 500 kitchen appliances on behalf of the corporation. Williamson had made such purchases in prior years from the same supplier. When the president learned of the purchase the next morning, he promptly notified the manufacturer that it cancelled the order and denied liability because Williamson had no authority to make the purchase.

In an action by Modern Kitchens, Inc. against Super Wholesale Appliances Corporation, judgment for whom? Explain.

27. Vogel, an assistant buyer for the Granite City Department Store, purchased metal art objects from Duval Reproductions. Vogel was totally without express or apparent authority to do so, but believed that his purchase was a brilliant move likely to get him a promotion. The head buyer of Granite was livid when he learned of Vogel's activities. However, after examining the merchandise and listening to Vogel's pitch, he reluctantly placed the merchandise in the storeroom and put a couple of pieces on display for a few days to see whether it was a "hot item" and a "sure thing" as Vogel claimed. The item was neither "hot" nor "sure" and when it didn't move at all, the head buyer ordered the display merchandise re-packed and the entire order returned to Duval with a letter that stated the merchandise had been ordered by an assistant buyer who had absolutely no authority to make the purchase. Duval countered with a lawsuit for breach of contract.

    Judgment for whom? Explain.

28. Banks, one of the best salesmen of the Nikal Automobile Agency was approached by his good friend, Gordon, with news of a wonderful prospect who was coming to the showroom that evening to buy a new car. Since Banks had other appointments for the evening, he told Gordon to sign up the prospect, gave him the forms and instructions to follow, and told him that the company would give him the commission if he made the sale. Unfortunately, in order to close the deal, Gordon gave the buyer, Dannon, such a large discount that Nikal, the owner, wishes to avoid the sale. Nikal believes he is justified because Banks had no authority to hire salesmen. Dannon insists that the sale to him was binding on Nikal.

    1. Is the sale binding on Nikal? Explain.

    2. List four exceptions to the general rule that an agent cannot delegate his authority to another without the express or implied consent of his principal.

29. In 1983, Fantastic Fan and Air Conditioning Corporation retained Joe Wells, a free lance jobber, to sell certain of its products. During the last six months their relationship had deteriorated and during the last three months Wells had not been commissioned to make such sales. Nevertheless, Wells, representing himself as a sales agent for Fantastic Fan made a $15,000 sale of air conditioning equipment to Arista Apartments. Upon receiving the Arista order from Wells, Fantastic Fan promptly notified Arista that it accepted the order and would ship within 10 days.

Prior to delivery, Arista, learning of Wells' lack of authority and realizing that it had made a bad bargain, promptly repudiated its order by notifying Fantastic Fan that it was not bound on the purchase contract because of Wells' lack of authority.

In an action by Fantastic Fan against Arista Apartments, judgment for whom? Explain.

____

____

____

____

____

30. Red entered into a contract with Maple on behalf of Gem, a disclosed principal. Red exceeded his authority in entering into the contract. In order for Gem to successfully ratify the contract with Maple,

_____ a. Gem must expressly communicate his intention to be bound.

_____ b. Gem must have knowledge of the relevant material facts concerning the transaction.

_____ c. Red must **not** have been a minor.

_____ d. Red must have acted reasonably and in Gem's best interest.

Items 31 and 32 are based on the following information:

Able, on behalf of Pix Corp., entered into a contract with Sky Corp., by which Sky agreed to sell computer equipment to Pix. Able disclosed to Sky that she was acting on behalf of Pix. However, Able had exceeded her actual authority by entering into the contract with Sky.

31. If Pix does **not** want to honor the contract, it will nonetheless be held liable if Sky can prove that

_____ a. Able had apparent authority to bind Pix.

_____ b. Able believed she was acting within the scope of her authority.

_____ c. Able was an employee of Pix and not an independent contractor.

_____ d. The agency relationship between Pix and Able was formalized in a signed writing.

32. If Pix wishes to ratify the contract with Sky, which of the following statements is correct?

_____ a. Pix must notify Sky that Pix intends to ratify the contract.

_____ b. Able must have acted reasonable and in Pix's best interest.

_____ c. Able must be a general agent of Pix.

_____ d. Pix must have knowledge of all material facts relating to the contract at the time it is ratified.

33. Frost's accountant and business manager has the authority to

_____ a. Mortgage Frost's business property.

_____ b. Obtain bank loans for Frost.

_____ c. Insure Frost's property against fire loss.

_____ d. Sell Frost's business.

34. Borg is the vice-president of purchasing for Crater Corp. He has authority to enter into purchase contracts on behalf of Crater provided that the price under a contract does not exceed $2 million. Borg entered into a $2.5 million purchase contract with Shady Corp. without Dent's approval. Shady was unaware that Borg exceeded his authority. Neither party substantially changed its position in reliance on the contract. What is the most likely result of this transaction?

______ a. Crater will be bound because of Borg's apparent authority.

______ b. Crater will **not** be bound because Borg exceeded his authority.

______ c. Crater will only be bound up to $2 million, the amount of Borg's authority.

______ d. Crater may avoid the contract since Shady has **not** relied on the contact to its detriment.

35. Simmons, an agent for Jensen, has the express authority to sell Jensen's goods. Simmons also has the express authority to grant discounts of up to 5% of list price. Simmons sold Hemple goods with a list price of $1,000 and granted Hemple a 10% discount. Hemple had not previously dealt with either Simmons or Jensen. Which of the following courses of action may Jensen properly take?

______ a. Seek to void the sale to Hemple.

______ b. See recovery of $50 from Hemple only.

______ c. Seek recovery of $50 from Simmons only.

______ d. Seek recovery of $50 from either Hemple or Simmons.

36. Starr is an agent of a disclosed principal, Maple. On May 1, Starr entered into an agreement with King Corp. on behalf of Maple that exceeded Starr's authority as Maple's agent. On May 5, King learned of Starr's lack of authority and immediately notified Maple and Starr that it was withdrawing from the May 1 agreement. On May 7, Maple ratified the May 1 agreement in its entirety. If King refuses to honor the agreement and Maple brings an action for breach of contract, Maple will

______ a. Prevail since the agreement of May 1 was ratified in its entirety.

______ b. Prevail since Maple's capacity as a principal was known to Starr.

______ c. Lose since the May 1 agreement is void due to Starr's lack of authority.

______ d. Lose since King notified Starr and Maple of its withdrawal prior to Maple's ratification.

Chapter 6

The Undisclosed Principal and Partially Disclosed Principal

56. Introduction.

We have seen in the preceding chapter that where an agent contracts in the name of his principal with a third party pursuant to actual authority, express or implied, the principal and the third party will be liable to each other on the contract. Moreover, in such a case, the agent will have no personal liability on the contract to either the third party or to his principal. In the business world almost all contracts are made by an agent in the name of his principal. In such a case, the principal is called a disclosed principal, and the third party knows whom he is contracting with and is liable to, and may enforce the contract against the disclosed principal.

However, in the business world principals have learned that on certain occasions it is more advantageous to have their agent negotiate and ultimately contract with a third party in the agent's own name rather than in the name of the principal. The two most common occasions are where the principal believes that if his identity were known to the third party (1) the third party would charge him more or pay him less than the amount the third party would charge or pay to someone else or (2) the third party *might* not contract with him. Therefore, in such a case, the principal will usually instruct his agent to negotiate and contract in his own name with the third party and not disclose to the third party that he is acting for a principal or alternatively to disclose that he is acting for an undisclosed principal but not to disclose the name of the undisclosed principal. Where the agent does not disclose to the third party that he is acting for a principal, the latter is called an undisclosed principal. And where the agent discloses to the third party that he is acting for a principal but does not disclose his identity, the latter is called a partially disclosed principal.[1]

Three important legal questions arise when the agent contracts in his own name with a third party: (1) May the undisclosed principal enforce the contract against the third party? (2) May the third party enforce the contract against the undisclosed principal when he discovers his identity? (3) What are the agent's rights, duties, and liabilities with respect to the contract which he made in his own name with the third party before and after the third party discovers the undisclosed principal's identity? Each question will be discussed and answered separately in the following three sections.

57. Undisclosed principal's rights and liability on contracts made by agent in his own name with third party.

In the judicial development of the rules of agency law, the general rule was adopted, subject to four major exceptions discussed hereafter, that a principal may lawfully authorize his agent to contract in his own name with a third party for the undisclosed principal's benefit without revealing the existence or identity of his undisclosed principal and that the undisclosed principal may sue and be used on said contract, provided the agent acted within the scope of his actual authority.[2] The undisclosed principal may authorize his agent to do so orally because no statutes specifically require an undisclosed principal's authorization to be written. However, written authorization is generally required by statute where the agent is employed by his principal to buy or sell real property regardless of whether the principal is disclosed, partially disclosed, or undisclosed.

This general rule of agency law has troubled legal commentators because it violates one of the basic theories of contract law that only those who are in privity of contract may sue and be sued on the contract. Yet, there is no privity of contract between the undisclosed principal and the third party because the contract is in fact and in law between the agent (in his own name) and the third party. Moreover, when the third party contracted with the agent in his own name, he did not manifest his consent to be bound to the undisclosed principal. As Justice Oliver Wendell Holmes, Jr. once observed in discussing the anomaly of the general rule allowing an undisclosed principal to have the right to enforce the agent-third party contract even though he is not in privity of contract with the third party: "common sense is opposed to allowing a stranger to my overt acts and to my intentions, a man of whom I have never heard, to set up a contract against me which I had supposed I was making with my personal friend."[3]

Despite the long history of criticism of the general rule of law, it is universally recognized today, subject to the four major exceptions discussed hereafter. The rationale of the general rule of agency law which allows the undisclosed principal to enforce the agent-third party contract against the third party though he is not in privity of contract with him is that the third party may easily avoid the application of this rule and not be bound to the undisclosed principal by either (1) telling the party whom he contracted with (the agent) that he would not deal with a particular undisclosed principal or with any undisclosed principal, or (2) asking the party he contracted with whether he was representing an undisclosed principal, or (3) including a provision in the contract excluding or prohibiting any party other than the agent from having any rights on the contract. Where the third party does not do anything to avoid the effect of the general rule at the time he contracts with the agent, he may be considered to have waived his right to object to the legal presence of the agent's undisclosed principal at a later date.

The final question may arise as to what rights an undisclosed principal has against his agent where the agent claims he changed his mind and contracted in his own name with the third party for his own benefit and not on behalf of his undisclosed principal. In such a case, the agent may not properly change his mind and contract for his own benefit after he originally agreed to act as agent for an undisclosed principal. An agent who attempts to do so breaches the fiduciary duty of undivided loyalty that is imposed by law upon every agent. Therefore, the principal has the right in such a case to recover any property purchased by the agent from the third party in his own name. And where the agent wrongfully resells the purchased property at a profit rather than turn it over to his principal, the agent is liable to his principal for said profit. Moreover, where the agent-third party contract has not yet been performed, the undisclosed principal may enforce it as well as be liable thereon, notwithstanding the agent's claimed change-of-mind.

In summary, an undisclosed principal may sue and be sued on a contract made by his agent in his own name with a third party provided it was made in accordance with the actual authority, express or implied, conferred upon him, subject to four major exceptions.

58. Agent's rights and liability on contracts made in his own name on behalf of an undisclosed principal.

It is a fundamental rule of agency law that an agent who contracts in his own name with a third party for the benefit of his undisclosed or partially disclosed principal is always personally liable on the resulting contract.[4] This immutable rule applies even where the agent is acting pursuant to his principal's express instructions and would not otherwise enter into the contract and even though the agent subsequently discloses his principal's identity to the third party and states he does not want to have any liability on the contract. The agent cannot legally compel the third party to enforce the contract only against his principal and to discharge the agent from liability on the contract. Rather, it is the option of the third party to elect the party against whom he wishes to enforce the contract.[5] Thus, an agent who contracts in his own name with a third party on behalf of an undisclosed or partially disclosed principal does so at his peril.

However, an agent who is held liable on the contract he made in his own name with the third party has the right to obtain reimbursement or indemnification from his principal provided he acted within the scope of the actual authority, express or implied, conferred upon him. If he did not so act, he is not entitled to any reimbursement or indemnification from his principal even though he suffers a loss. Whether or not the principal is solvent, insolvent, bankrupt or outside the jurisdiction of the court, the rule remains the same: the agent is always personally liable on every contract he makes in his own name with the third party for the benefit of his undisclosed or partially disclosed principal.[6]

Since an agent is personally liable on such a contract, he has the right to enforce the contract in his own name against the third party even though he made the contract on behalf of and for the benefit of an undisclosed principal. Thus, an undisclosed principal may properly instruct his agent to enforce the contract by bringing suit in his own name against the third party and the agent may properly do so, as where the undisclosed principal does not wish to disclose his own identity during the ensuing litigation. Of course, in such a case the agent has a right to demand and receive reimbursement and indemnification from his principal for his legal fees and expenses.

The agent who acts or contracts for an undisclosed or partially disclosed principal does not commit any fraud by doing so nor is he legally required to disclose his principal's identity prior to performance. Moreover, if the third party discovers that the party he contracted with is acting as an agent for an undisclosed principal, he cannot unilaterally rescind the contract or avoid liability on the contract to the agent unless he can prove that one of the four exceptions to the general rule applies.

59. Third party's rights and liability on contracts made with agent for an undisclosed principal.

As a general rule, a third party can always enforce the contract against the agent personally because the agent contracted in his own name. This general rule applies whether or not the agent acted within or outside the actual authority, express or implied, conferred upon him by his principal. Similarly, the third party is personally liable on the contract to the agent unless he can prove that one of the four exceptions to the general rule applies.

Furthermore, when the third party learns the identity of the undisclosed or partially disclosed principal, he may elect to enforce the contract against the principal where the agent acted within the scope of his actual authority, express or implied. The application of this rule does not prejudice the principal because the authorized contract made by his agent in his own name is exactly what the principal wanted. Therefore, to hold the principal liable on such a contract imposes no hardship or surprise on him. Thus, upon discovery of the principal's identity, the third party may at his option elect to sue either the agent or the principal.[7] This rule applies even where the third party might have refused originally to contract with the undisclosed or partially disclosed principal who, believing this to be a possibility, used the covert agent to make a contract with the third party.[8] However, the third party cannot sue the agent and principal jointly on the contract but must make an election which in some states is irrevocable. However, in many states if the judgment he obtains against the party he elected to sue is not satisfied, he may thereafter sue the other party on the contract.[9] However, satisfaction of a judgment obtained from the agent will bar any subsequent action against the principal even though the third party was unaware of the existence or identity of the principal at the time he obtained satisfaction of the judgment from the agent.[10]

As noted earlier, the third party is liable on the contract he made with the agent in his own name both to the agent and to the undisclosed or partially disclosed principal who seeks to enforce it unless one of the four exceptions to the general rule applies. When the undisclosed principal sues to enforce the authorized contract, the third party may properly interpose against him any defense or set-off he has against the agent, whether arising out of the same transaction or any other transaction between the agent and third party.[11] Applying this rule, where the third party contracts to buy goods from the agent who is acting for an undisclosed principal, the third party may set-off any payment made to the agent prior to the date the undisclosed principal seeks to enforce the contract. Moreover, even after he learns the identity of the undisclosed principal, he may pay either the agent or now-disclosed principal.[12] However, where the now-disclosed principal instructs the third party how and to whom payment should be made, the third party must comply. If he does not, as where he pays the agent instead of the principal, he will be liable to the principal for the amount wrongfully paid to the agent.[13]

60. When an undisclosed principal cannot enforce an unauthorized contract made by an agent in his own name with a third party.

Although the general rule of agency law allows an undisclosed principal to enforce an authorized contract made by his agent in his own name with a third party, there are four major exceptions to this general rule when the undisclosed principal may not do so.

The first exception to the general rule is where a principal *knows* that the third party would not contract with him. In such a case, a court will not permit a principal to obtain indirectly, through a covert agent, what he could not obtain directly. Based upon this equitable rule of law, neither the agent nor undisclosed principal may enforce the contract. The third party may rescind the contract at any time before or after he performs provided he does so within a reasonable time after he discovers the existence of the undisclosed principal.

The principal's knowledge that the third party would not contract with him may be acquired by the principal personally or derivatively through his agent. The principal's personal knowledge may be based upon statements made directly to him by the third party or from statements made indirectly by the third party to others which subsequently come to the principal's attention. By contrast, the principal's knowledge that the third party would not contract with him is acquired derivatively through his agent when the third party informs the agent that he would not deal with the principal.[14] Such notice given to the agent is deemed by law to be automatic and instantaneous constructive notice to his principal so that the principal has such knowledge and therefore cannot enforce the contract.[15] Furthermore, in such a case, the agent who receives such notice is said to have an affirmative duty to disclose to the third party that he is acting for the undisclosed principal. The agent's silence under these circumstances is deemed a fraudulent concealment of a material fact which entitles the third party to rescind his contract with the agent.[16] By contrast, if the undisclosed principal or agent acquires knowledge that the third party would not have dealt with him *after* the agent contracted in his own name with the third party, the general rule would apply that the undisclosed principal and the agent can each enforce the contract.[17]

However, the mere suspicion by a principal that a third party might not contract with him does not constitute "knowledge". Accordingly, an undisclosed principal who merely suspects (but does not know) that a third party would not deal with him may enforce the authorized contract made by his agent in his own name with the third party in accordance with the general rule.

The second exception to the general rule is where the agent fraudulently induces the third party to contract with him by representing (orally or in writing) that he is acting only for himself and not for any undisclosed principal. The fraud of the agent committed within the scope of his employment is imputed to his principal by operation of law under the doctrine of respondeat superior which holds the principal liable for his agent's torts. Therefore, neither the undisclosed principal nor his agent can enforce the fraudulently induced contract made with the third party. This rule applies even where the undisclosed principal told his agent not to commit fraud upon the third party. In any such case where the agent commits such fraud, the third party may rescind the contract made with the agent in his own name at any time before or after it is performed provided he rescinds within a reasonable time after he discovers the fraud.

The third party who wishes to exclude an undisclosed principal from having any rights on his contract and who wants to have the benefit of this important exception to the general rule will always require the agent to make a written representation to him that he is contracting only for himself and not acting on behalf of anyone else. Where he does not receive this oral or written representation and where none of the other three exceptions apply, the third party will be liable to the undisclosed principal in accordance with the general rule. Accordingly, a provision in the agent-third party contract which prohibits assignment will not operate to bar an undisclosed principal from enforcing the contract because his rights are based upon the fact that the contract was made for him as an undisclosed principal and not upon any assignment of the contract.

The third exception to the general rule is where the oral or written contract between agent and third party expressly excludes or prohibits any undisclosed principal from having any rights under the contract. Where a third party includes a provision in his contract with the agent to the effect that the contract may be enforced only by the agent and no one else, the third party has effectively aborted any rights that the agent's undisclosed principal might otherwise have under the general rule. Such a provision is usually accompanied by another provision which prohibits the assignment of the contract by the agent. The cumulative effect of these two provisions is to effectively deny the undisclosed principal any rights on the agent-third party contract as a principal or as an assignee. However, in such a case there is no other legal rule which prohibits the agent performing the contract in his own name and thereafter transferring to his principal what he has acquired from the third party, provided the agent committed no fraud against the third party. Thus, in the final analysis the undisclosed principal attains his business objectives in such a case, but his right to do so is not based upon his rights as a principal against the third party on the agent-third party contract but rather only upon his rights against his agent based upon his own contract with his agent.

The fourth exception to the general rule is where the contract entered into by the agent in his own name with the third party requires the agent to perform services for the third party (rather than to sell or buy property). In such a case, the undisclosed principal may not enforce the personal service contract by offering to perform the services specified in the agent-third party contract. In a personal service contract, the third party may properly reject the tender of performance by the undisclosed principal, however competent he may be, and may properly demand performance by the agent. If the agent does not perform, he will be in breach of contract and liable to the third party even though he entered into the contract solely for the benefit of his undisclosed principal, would not have done so otherwise, and never had any intention to perform personally.

In addition to the above four major exceptions to the general rule, there are special rules of law applicable to the liability of an undisclosed principal in two cases: (1) where his agent issues negotiable instruments in his own name and (2) where he gives his agent funds to purchase property from the third party which his agent misappropriates. Each will be discussed separately in the next two sections.

61. Liability of undisclosed principal and agent on negotiable instruments.

It is a fundamental rule of statutory law, set forth in Article 3 of the Uniform Commercial Code, that the only party who is liable on a negotiable instrument (check, promissory note, or draft) is the party whose name or signature appears thereon.[18] The effect of this major rule is that only the agent and not the principal is liable on a negotiable instrument which the agent signs in his own name without disclosing both his principal's name and his own representative capacity. And even where the agent signs the negotiable instrument in his own name and states his representative capacity, such as "agent" or "vice president" without disclosing his principal's identity, he will still be personally liable on the negotiable instrument.[19] In neither case can the holder of the negotiable instrument enforce the negotiable instrument against the undisclosed or partially disclosed principal when he subsequently learns his identity. This rule applies even where the party receiving the negotiable instrument signed by the agent knew that it was intended to be the legal obligation of the principal only.[20]

Similarly, where a third party issues a negotiable instrument payable to the order of the agent only, the only person who is the "holder" of the instrument and who can enforce the instrument by suing on the instrument is the agent to whose order it is payable, and not the principal. This rule applies even though the agent received the negotiable instrument in his capacity as agent for an undisclosed principal. In such a case the only way the undisclosed principal could obtain the right to enforce the negotiable instrument against the third party, subject to the rules of Article 3 of the Uniform Commercial Code, is for the agent to endorse and deliver the negotiable instrument to his principal, who thereby becomes a "holder".[21]

Although the third party cannot enforce the negotiable instrument against the undisclosed or partially disclosed principal, he can enforce the underlying contract against him which was the basis for the issuance of the negotiable instrument. Moreover, the third party can enforce both the underlying contract and the negotiable instrument against the agent.

62. Liability of undisclosed principal to third party where agent misappropriates principal's funds intended for third party.

It is common practice for an undisclosed principal to give his agent funds to purchase property from the third party for cash before the agent contracts to do so with the third party because either the agent does not have sufficient funds or insists upon it. The important question then arises whether the undisclosed principal is liable to the third party where his dishonest agent, in violation of his principal's instructions, buys in his own name on credit, instead of for cash, takes the property with him and disappears with the property and his principal's funds? In such a case the third party sues the principal on the contract when he discovers his identity. The principal's defense is that his prior payment to his agent discharges him from liability even though the agent did not use the principal's funds as directed.

The leading New York case, Laing v. Butler,[22] resolved this important question by holding that an undisclosed principal was not liable to the third party where he gave his agent the funds to pay the purchase price prior to the time the agent contracted in his own name to purchase the property from the third party. The court reasoned that the third party who contracted with the agent in his own name, delivered the goods to the agent and extended personal credit to him, did so in reliance on the agent's credit and not on the credit of some undisclosed principal. The court concluded that the undisclosed principal acted properly when he gave his agent funds to make a purchase for cash and therefore was discharged from any liability on the agent-third party contract. Many states follow the New York rule, the effect of which is to place the loss on the third party and not the undisclosed principal who employed the dishonest agent.

More recent cases in other jurisdictions and the Restatement on Agency favor the opposite rule that an undisclosed principal is not discharged from liability to a third party on the agent-third party contract where the undisclosed principal gives his agent funds prior to the agent contracting with the third party and the agent misappropriates the funds.[23] The Restatement expresses the view that an undisclosed principal will not be discharged under the facts stated unless he paid or settled with his agent in reasonable reliance upon the conduct of the third party, which is not induced by the agent's misrepresentation and which indicates that the agent settled the account.

The Restatement view is predicated on the premise that the undisclosed principal who hires a dishonest agent should assume the loss where the agent misappropriates the funds and the third party is not paid unless the reason the principal gave his agent the funds was his reasonable reliance upon the conduct of the third party, as where it was widely known in the marketplace that the third party sells his goods only for cash and not on credit. However, where the third party has misled the principal into believing that he has already been paid, as where he delivers the purchased goods to the agent with an invoice marked "paid" even though sold on credit, the principal will be discharged from further liability on the agent-third party contract unless the third party's actions were induced by the misrepresentations of the agent.[24]

Current References

"The conditions and perils of agency, dual agency and undisclosed agency," by James A. Bryant and Donald R. Epley, 21 *Real Estate Law Journal,* 117-135, Fall 1992.

"Let the agent beware: undisclosed corporate status [Case Note] *Wilkinson v. Sweeney,* 532 So.2d 243 (La. App. Ct. 1988)," by John C. Geyer, 50 *Louisiana Law Review* 1183-1194, July 1990.

Notes

1. The theoretical foundations of the undisclosed principal doctrine are examined in Merton L. Gerson, "Undisclosed Principals," *University of Cincinnati Law Review,* 22:131-160, March 1953. For an analysis of the distinction between disclosed and undisclosed principals in the context of apparent authority vis-a-vis apparent ownership, see Floyd R. Mechem, "Ostensible Agency or Ownership," *Illinois Law Review* 22:652 (1928); J. Ewart, *Estoppel,* Chapt. XVII (1900). See, also, Restatement, Second, Agency, sects. 4 and 8 (1958). The difficulties and anomalies of the undisclosed principal are examined in W. Müller-Freienfels, "The Undisclosed Principal," *Modern Law Review,* 16:299-317, July 1953. See, also, Comment, "The Undisclosed Principle of Undisclosed Principals," *McGill Law Journal,* 21:298-306, Summer 1975; "The Equity Of The Undisclosed Principal," *Modern Law Review,* 28:167, March 1965; Ames, "Undisclosed Principal—His Rights and Liabilities," *Yale Law Journal,* 18:443 (1909); Lewis, "The Liability of an Undisclosed Principal," *Columbia Law Review,* 9:116

(1909); A.L. Goodhart and C.J. Hamson, "Undisclosed Principals In Contract," *The Cambridge Law Journal,* 4:320-356 (1932). German agency law does not recognize the concept of the undisclosed principal; see, W. Müller-Freinfels, "Law of Agency," *American Journal of Comparative Law,* 6:165 at 178 (1957).

2. Manchester Supply Co. v. Dearborn, 90 N.H. 447, 10 A.2d 658 (1940); Boettcher v. Goethe, 165 Neb. 363, 85 N.W.2d 884 (1957); Mintken v. Nebraska Sur. Co., 187 Neb. 215, 188 N.W.2d 819 (1971); Floyd R. Mechem, "The Liability of an Undisclosed Principal," *Harvard Law Review,* 23:513-530 (May 1910) and 590-602 (June 1910).
3. Holmes, "The History of Agency" in Association of American Law Schools, *Select Essays in Anglo-American Legal History* (Boston: Little Brown & Co., 1909), vol. 3, 368 (first published in Harvard Law Review 4:345 (1891)) and 390 (first published in Harvard Law Review 5:1 (1891)).
4. Kelly Asphalt Block Co. v. Barber Asphalt Paving Co., 211 N.Y. 68, 105 N.E. 88 (1914).
5. Woodruff v. McGehee, Sup. Ct. Ga., 30 Ga. 158 (1860) reported in Floyd R. Mechem, Selected Cases on the Law of Agency, 4th Edition by Philip Mechem (Chicago: Callaghan & Company, 1954), 262; Stanley Patch Lumber Corp. v. Barry, 148 Misc. 376, 265 N.Y.S. 879 (1933); Puleo v. Rua, 141 N.Y.S.2d 156 (1955); McGraw v. Godfrey, 56 N.Y. 610 (1874).
6. Mawer-Gulden-Annis, Inc. v. Brazilian & Colombian Coffee Co., 49 Ill. App.2d 400, 199 N.E.2d 222 (1964); Bank of America National Trust & Savings Association v. State Board of Equalization, 209 Cal. App.2d 780, 26 Cal. Rptr. 348 (1962).
7. The legal difficulties inherent in election by a third party to sue either the agent or the undisclosed principal is discussed in "Agency-Election Of Third Party's Rights Against Undisclosed Principal And Agent," *New York University Law Quarterly Review,* 7:957-961, June 1930.
8. Kayton v. Barnett, 116 N.Y. 625, 23 N.E. 24 (1889).
9. Dages v. Melrose Iron Co., 140 N.Y.S. 392 (1913).
10. Restatement, Second, Agency, Sect. 211 (1958).
11. Summerlin v. S. & K., Inc., 124 Ga. App. 25, 183 S.E.2d 92 (1971); Muth v. Leineke, 9 Cal. App.3d 433, 88 Cal. Rptr. 1 (1970). See, "Principal and Agent—Undisclosed Principal—Right of Set-Off Against Agent—Constructive Notice," *Australian Law Journal,* 6:105-106, July 1932. Partial disclosure does not prevent the third party from electing to hold the agent liable on the contract. However, it does cut off claims and setoffs from other transactions which the third party has against the agent and which the third party might otherwise set up against the principal if the agency were undisclosed. For an excellent analysis of this subject, see "Partially Disclosed Agency And Its Significance," *Kentucky Law Journal,* 39:208-214, January 1951.
12. Maxfield v. Carpenter, 32 N.Y.S. 381 (1895); Jensen v. Pitman, 236 Oreg. 59, 386 P.2d 803 (1963).
13. Darling-Singer Lumber Co. v. Commonwealth, 290 Mass. 488, 195 N.E. 723 (1935).
14. See, Floyd R. Mechem, "Notice To, Or Knowledge Of, An Agent", *Michigan Law Review,* 7:113 (1908).
15. Knowledge by an agent, even if unknown to his principal, is held to be constructive knowledge by his principal; see, "Agency-Knowledge of Agent-Transactions Occurring After Termination of Agency Relationship", *University of Pennsylvania Law Review,* 79:974-976, May 1931.
16. See, Restatement, Second, Agency, Sect. 189 Comment b, and Sect. 304 (1958).
17. Akwell Corp, v. Eiger, 141 F. Supp. 19 (S.D.N.Y. 1956).
18. Uniform Commercial Code, Sec. 3-401.
19. Under the Uniform Commercial Code, Sect. 3-403 (2) (b), the agent, to avoid personal liability for his signature on such an instrument, must state his representative capacity *and* name the person represented. See, Floyd R. Mechem, "The Execution Of Sealed Instruments By An Agent", *Michigan Law Review,* 6:552 (1908).
20. Under the Uniform Commercial Code, Sect. 3-401, no person is liable on an instrument unless his own signature appears thereon. An agent, authorized or not, is personally liable if he signs only his own name. He is also solely liable on the instrument if he signs his principal's name without also signing his own name as agent.
21. Uniform Commercial Code, Sect. 1-201 (20) defines a holder as "a person who is in possession of a document of title or an instrument or an investment security drawn, issued or indorsed to him or to his order or to bearer or in blank".
22. 37 Hun. 144, aff'd in 108 N.Y. 637 (1888). See, also, Montague Mailing Machinery Co. v. All-Package Grocery Stores Co., 182 App. Div. 500, 169 N.Y.S. 920 (1918).
23. Senor v. Bangor Mills, 211 F. 2d 685 (3d Cir. 1954); Restatement, Second, Agency, Sect. 208 (1958).
24. Poretta v. Superior Dowel Co., 153 Me. 308, 137 A. 2d 361 (1957). Professor Seavey notes the anomalous nature of the undisclosed principal doctrine and the unsettled nature of the cases where an agent has purchased goods for a principal on his own credit and where the principal pays the agent before the agent has paid the third party and said agent absconds without making payment. "Undisclosed Principal; Unsettled Problems," *Howard Law Journal,* 1:79-84, January 1955. See, also, note, "The Liability Of An Undisclosed Principal After Settlement With The Agent," *Mississippi Law Journal,* 18:436-448, May 1947. The English rule is that the undisclosed principal will have to pay twice unless his payment to his agent was induced by the words or conduct of the third party. The American courts remain divided but most jurisdictions hold that payment in good faith to the agent by the principal will preclude recovery by the third party against the principal. The Restatement has adopted the English rule, however.

Case 11
Cooper v. Epstein
308 A.2d 783 (D.C.1973)

Introduction

As a general rule, an undisclosed principal has the right to enforce an authorized contract made by his agent in his own name with a third party unless one of the legally recognized exceptions apply. The question arises whether an "non-assignment" clause in the agent-third party contract automatically bars the undisclosed principal from enforcing the contract or is merely evidence that the parties intended to exclude an undisclosed principal. The following case answers the question.

Fickling, Associate Judge

Appellant Warren R. Cooper, who claims to be an undisclosed principal, challenges the correctness of an award of summary judgment for appellees Benjamin and Molly Epstein defendants below. He contends that there were genuine issues of material fact which could not be resolved without a trial on the merits. We agree and reverse.

On August 20, 1969, appellees and one Jimmie Buford, the alleged agent of appellant Cooper, executed a document entitled "Lease and Purchase and Sale Agreement." This agreement was essentially a contract to sell certain real estate within the District of Columbia. Initially, however, the property was to be leased to Buford for a period of up to 36 months for a fixed monthly rental, plus real estate taxes and insurance. Buford was also obligated to pay all utility charges and to provide appellees with a $1,000 deposit. It was agreed that upon the cancellation of an identified encumbrance, the lease would automatically terminate and the sale provisions of the contract would come into play. By the sale terms of the agreement, the purchase price was to be $18,000—$3,000 in cash, the balance being secured by a first deed of trust on the property. The $1,000 deposit and the rental payments were to be credited toward the cash down payment. The agreement also contained the following non-assignment clause:

4. That he (Buford) will not transfer nor assign this agreement, nor let nor sublet the whole or any part of said premises without written consent of Landlord first had and obtained such consent shall not be unreasonably withheld.

The monthly payments on the lease were tendered in accordance with the contract terms from September 1969 until February 1970. The March 1970 payment, however, was two weeks late in arriving, and the check which constituted that payment was eventually returned to appellees marked "insufficient funds." The April 1970 payment was also late, and, on April 6, 1970, appellees notified Buford by registered mail that they intended to cancel the contract for nonpayment. (Money orders which were subsequently tendered for the March and April payments were rejected by appellees.)

On May 1, 1970, the encumbrance set out . . . was removed. Subsequently, Buford was advised by District-Realty Title Insurance Company that the property had been sold to the District of Columbia Redevelopment Land Agency and that settlement had taken place on June 1, 1970. This information was confirmed by appellees, who also informed appellant's counsel that the consideration for the sale had been $27,000 (less a $950 contingent deduction).

Appellant filed a complaint for an accounting and breach of contract. He alleged that Buford was his agent and was acting in that capacity when he signed the agreement.

After discovery, which consisted primarily of the deposing of appellant, the following was revealed.

Appellant, fearing that his credit standing might be suspect, arranged orally to have his employee, Buford, negotiate the purchase of the subject property. No documents were signed nor any receipt given for the $1,000 which appellant purportedly gave Buford for the initial deposit. Appellant can produce no record that he ever conveyed the $1,000 to Buford. Appellant has no records to show that he ever paid any of the rental payments or, in fact, was the principal to the contract. Appellant's knowledge of the terms of the contract was confused and quite limited. These facts and certain other collateral matters, when accepted as true, paint a picture of appellant as a man of enormous trust and that he was at best an undisclosed principal.

Later, when appellees' motion for summary judgment came on for a hearing, the judge, focusing on the nonassignment clause stated that, "to contract against assignment, to contract against subleasing, it seems to me, is to manifest an intent which also excludes the undisclosed principal." He therefore ruled that the agreement as a matter of law excluded suit by an undisclosed principal.

Appellant conceding—as he must—that the clause is some evidence of manifestation of an intent to exclude suit by an undisclosed principal, argues that the presence of the clause is not conclusive on the issue as a matter of law. We agree.

It is well settled that, absent some special exception, an undisclosed principal may sue and be sued on a contract made by his agent. . . . Even the fact that the agent denies that there is a principal, or represents himself to be the principal, is not sufficient to preclude suit by the undisclosed principal. However, where the express terms of the contract provide that it (the contract) is to be effective only between the agent and the third party, the undisclosed principal may not enforce the contract. See Restatement (Second) of Agency § 303 (1958). The undisclosed principal simply cannot sue where to do so would violate a term of the written contract. . . . Where the contract terms do not expressly exclude enforcement by or against an undisclosed principal, such liability may nevertheless be precluded if that was the intention of the parties. The resolution of the issue of whether the parties intended to exclude such liability is usually the duty of the fact finder.

We are of the opinion that when the motions judge ruled that Clause 4 . . . precluded suit by an undisclosed principal as a matter of law, he erred. Comment c to Section 303 of the Restatement of Agency (Second) states:

Non-assignment clause. A clause in the contract against assignment does not of itself prevent the principal from bringing suit upon the contract. The existence of such a clause, however, may be considered as evidence that the parties intended to exclude an undisclosed principal . . . (Emphasis added.)

We adopt this statement of the law and, therefore, remand this cause for trial on the merits. Additionally, on this record, mired as it is with factual and equitable considerations, we refuse to rule on other points pressed by appellees without such a trial.

Therefore, we reverse the decision of the motions judge and remand this cause for trial.

Discussion questions

1. What provision should a third party include in his contract to effectively exclude an undisclosed principal? Draft a simple provision.
2. Is a "non-assignment" clause, without more evidence, legally sufficient to bar enforcement of the agent-third party contract by the undisclosed principal? Why?

Case 12

Howell v. First of Boston International Corporation

34N.E.2d633
(Mass.1941)

Introduction

As a general rule an undisclosed principal can sue and be sued on a contract made by his agent in his own name with a third party, subject to certain exceptions. The following case illustrates one of the exceptions.

Lummus, Justice

Late in 1929 the defendant, then known as First National Corporation, was a registered broker in securities within the meaning of St.1921, c.499, G.L. (Ter. Ed.) c. 110A, the sale of securities act, popularly known as a blue sky law, which has since been superseded by revision contained in St.1932, c.290 and amendments. The present case depends upon the original law with its few amendments up to and including the year 1929.

Late in 1929 the Chase National Bank of the City of New York and the Chase Securities Corporation were selling their shares to the general public in blocks consisting of one share of each corporation. The State Street Trust Company, at the request of the plaintiff, undertook gratuitously in accordance with its custom to buy for her nine such blocks of stock. As it had done in similar cases for many years, it placed an order with the duly registered stock brokerage firm of Bright, Sears and Company to buy for it nine such blocks, represented by a receipt of Bankers Trust Company, the depositary of such blocks. Bright, Sears and Company knew of no purchaser except the State Street Trust Company, and relied upon its credit in making the purchase.

Bright, Sears and Company bought the receipt representing nine such blocks for $1,950 from the defendant, which relied upon the credit of Bright, Sears and Company and did not know whether that firm was buying as principal or agent. The defendant delivered the securities to Bright, Sears and Company in the form of "street certificates" negotiable by delivery, and received payment from that firm. That firm sent the State Street Trust Company a memorandum of the purchase made for the latter, in which the purchase price and the commission were stated. After the State Street Trust Company had received that memorandum it advised Bright, Sears and Company for the first time that it was buying for the plaintiff, and did so apparently for the purpose of having the shares registered in her name.

In September, 1935, the plaintiff learned for the first time that the securities that she had bought in 1929 had not been qualified for sale in Massachusetts. . . . On October 8, 1935, she tendered the securities to the defendant, together with all dividends received by her, and demanded a return of the purchase price. The tender was refused. She then brought this action of contract on October 10, 1935, for the purchase price with interest. The controversy was submitted to the trial judge in a district court upon a case stated. He found for the plaintiff, but his finding was vacated by the Appellate Division, which ordered judgment for the defendant. The plaintiff appealed to this court. . . .

The sale of securities act was intended to protect the general public, not security brokers. The latter were considered able to look out for themselves. Accordingly, Section 3 (n) of the act . . . provided that the provisions of the act should not apply to "The sale of securities directly or through a representative to a registered broker." All the defendant knew was that it was selling securities to Bright, Sears and Company, a registered broker. That sale was the defendant's entire transaction and only act.

The plaintiff invokes the familiar rules of law as to undisclosed principals. . . . It is one thing to pass over and disregard an apparent contracting party who is really an agent, in order to attach to his undisclosed principal the benefit of and liability upon a contract made by the agent, where no substantial right of the other contracting party will be impaired by so doing. . . . Where an undisclosed principal who had bought securities sold in violation of the sale of securities act was permitted to recover the price, the sale was equally invalid whether made to the agent or the undisclosed principal.

It is quite a different thing, where a defendant has made a sale to an apparent purchaser that was lawful on the facts known to the defendant, to pass over and disregard that apparent purchaser, to treat as the purchaser an undisclosed and unknown principal to whom the defendant could not lawfully make the sale, and thereby to convert the sale into a criminal offense. . . . We think that so doing is precluded by the rule that one may pass over the agent and consider the undisclosed principal as the contracting party only where the rights of the other contracting party are not thereby impaired.

Order of Appellate Division affirmed.

Discussion questions

1. Did the undisclosed principal have any recourse in this case since the court held that she could not rescind the contract? Why?
2. List four instances when an undisclosed principal cannot enforce a contract made by his agent in his own name with a third party.

Case 13

White Tower Management Corporation v. Taglino

19 N.E.2d 2700 (Mass.1939)

Introduction

When an undisclosed principal authorizes his agent to contract in his own name with a third party for the benefit of the undisclosed principal, the question arises as to what effect the agent's fraud and misrepresentation will have on the right of the undisclosed principal to enforce the contract against the third party. The following case illustrates the general rule of law applicable in such cases.

Cox, Justice

The plaintiff in this bill in equity seeks specific performance of a written agreement entered into by the defendants and one Taylor, admittedly acting as agent for the plaintiff, for the sale of a lot of land to Taylor by the male defendant. The agreement was assigned by Taylor to the plaintiff. The defendants, who are husband and wife, refused to carry out the agreement on the ground that they were induced to enter into it by false and fraudulent representations made by Taylor. The evidence, most of which was heard orally, is reported under G.L. (Ter.Ed.) c. 214, § 24, Rule 76 of the Superior Court (1932) the judge made findings of fact and, upon his order a final decree was entered denying specific performance of the agreement "and other relief contained in the Bill of Complaint and directing the male defendant to pay to the plaintiff $25 "deposited with him by the plaintiff." The plaintiff's appeal from this decree brings the case to this court. The judge found that there was inequitable conduct on the part of the agent of the plaintiff in negotiations leading to the execution of the agreement "in that he knew that the defendants would not enter into such an agreement if the purchaser were to be the White Tower Management Corporation, a corporation engaged in the restaurant business, and therefore concealed from the defendants the fact that he was agent for such corporation, and by misrepresentation led the defendants to believe that one or two individuals were to purchase the premises for the erection of a dwelling house thereon."

The plaintiff contends that a portion at least of the judge's findings is not supported by the evidence. It is for this court to examine the evidence and decide the case according to its own judgment as to the facts as well as the law, giving due weight to the findings of the trial judge. But his finding as to facts, either expressly made or necessarily implied from his disposition of the case, will not be reversed unless plainly wrong. . . .

The evidence as reported tends to show no mere concealment of the name of the purchaser. From the testimony of Taylor himself, as well as from that of the defendants, it appears that while Taylor did not affirmatively state that the plaintiff was not his principal, nevertheless he did represent that two individual buyers living in the Back Bay were the purchasers. Taylor admitted that the defendants asked him whom he represented. He was not bound to answer, but if he did, he was bound to tell the truth. . . . The affirmative statement that two people or a family consisting of two was the purchaser was, in the circumstances, a representation that the plaintiff was not the prospective purchaser. Taylor's answer could have been found to be a half truth, which in effect was a lie. . . .

It could have been found from the evidence that, if the defendants had known that the plaintiff was, in fact, the prospective purchaser, they would not have entered into the agreement. The plaintiff admittedly was engaged in the restaurant business, and there was evidence that the defendants would not sell to anyone who had a business or to "restaurant people," and so stated to Taylor. The representation by Taylor was material. . . . The plaintiff does not contend that it is not bound by Taylor's misrepresentation. It ought not to be permitted to take the benefit of false and fraudulent misrepresentations made by its agent. . . .

The finding by the judge of inequitable conduct on the part of Taylor, with the result of which the plaintiff is charged, brings the case within the rule stated in Shikes v. Gabelnick, 273 Mass.201, 173 N.E. 495, 87 A.L.R. 1339.

Although the judge found that the plaintiff was not entitled to specific performance, nevertheless he stated in his findings of fact that there was not sufficient fraud to warrant the rescinding of the contract. He also stated that the plaintiff's counsel had said in open court that it was not interested in the question of damages. The record discloses this to be the fact, and that counsel further stated that he was interested in the case at bar only in the question of specific performance, and that "We don't care about damages." The final decree includes an order that the male defendant pay the sum of $25 deposited with him by the plaintiff, and adjudges and decrees that "the prayers . . . for specific performance of the agreement and other relief contained in the Bill of Complaint be and are hereby denied." . . .

The plaintiff now contends that it never intended to waive a right for damages for breach of the agreement, and that that right ought not to be denied. If we attempt to reconcile the several findings of the judge, there is some difficulty in determining the reason for the order that the male defendant return the $25 deposit, unless the judge found, as we think he did, that the defendants relied upon Taylor's misrepresentation. We think it is clear that he did not intend the order by way of an assessment of damages. At the close of the evidence he stated to counsel that he did not think the plaintiff was entitled to damages, and after a statement of the plaintiff's counsel which was interrupted, the judge remarked that he had not decided the case "but it comes down to that." One prayer of the plaintiff's bill was for damages. The decree expressly denies the plaintiff's prayers for specific performance and "other relief."

On appeal in equity when the evidence is reported, such a decree should be entered as justice requires. . . . We think that the evidence warrants findings (as in fact the judge appears to have found) that the fraudulent misrepresentations by Taylor as to a material matter were relied on by the defendants, and that not only is there no ground for specific performance, but that rescission would be warranted, and that the order for the return of the deposit is to be considered as restoring the plaintiff to its original position. . . .

It follows that the words in the final decree, "and other relief," should be struck out; that it should be inserted in the decree that the plaintiff is not entitled to damages. In all other respects the decree is affirmed.

Ordered accordingly.

Discussion questions

1. Could the plaintiff have avoided the result of this case by asking Taylor to buy the property in his own name for his own benefit and then selling the property to the plaintiff thereafter at an agreed price which would compensate Taylor for his services? Why?
2. If Taylor agreed with the plaintiff to do so, would Taylor be committing fraud if he told the sellers that he was buying the property for himself without revealing that he had a contract to sell the property to the plaintiffs shortly thereafter?
3. If the agent, Taylor, committed fraud against the seller, could his undisclosed principal recover any money damages from him after the sellers rescinded the contract with the agent?

Case 14

Shields v. Coyne

127 N.W. 63 (Iowa 1910)

Introduction

An undisclosed principal who sues to enforce a contract made by his agent in his own name with a third party has the burden of proving that the agent acted for him at the time of contracting. The following case illustrates this rule as well as discusses one important exception to the general rule when an undisclosed principal cannot enforce a contract made on his behalf by his agent in his own name.

McClain, J.

The evidence tends to show an oral agreement between the defendant and Patrick Shields, the husband of plaintiff, by which, on certain contingencies not here material to mention, the defendant agreed to loan to said Patrick Shields $9,600 at 5½ per cent, interest for five years to enable the latter to purchase a piece of land, and that subsequently when the conditions had been complied with the defendant refused to advance the money in accordance with the agreement, rendering it necessary for this plaintiff, who alleges that the agreement was made for her and in her behalf, to borrow the money elsewhere at 6 per cent. Plaintiff seeks to recover, by way of damages for breach of contract, the difference in the interest which she was compelled to pay. It is not claimed that plaintiff's husband purported in the negotiations to be acting for his wife or for any person other than himself, or that defendant knew or had any reason to suppose that plaintiff's husband was making the contract as the agent of another. Indeed, we are unable to discover in the brief record presented to us any evidence of an arrangement or understanding between plaintiff and her husband that her husband was to act in her behalf in procuring the loan from defendant. This is a very material matter, for without some such arrangement or understanding between plaintiff and her husband, the contract would not be binding on the plaintiff, and therefore, as between her and defendant, there would be no mutuality. It does appear that the plaintiff, during the time these negotiations between her husband and defendant were pending, was carrying on a farm in her own name, and that all the marketing, buying, and selling was done by him for her. But we think that this evidence falls far short of constituting any proof that even as between plaintiff and her husband, it was understood that the proposed loan was being procured by plaintiff's husband for her, as undisclosed principal.

Under this state of facts it is very clear that plaintiff cannot maintain an action for the breach of this contract: First, because plaintiff's allegation that she entered into such contract through her husband as her agent, which allegation is covered by defendant's general denial, was not proven; and second, because, if proven, the contract would not be binding as between her and the defendant who had no knowledge that her husband was acting as her agent in the matter. One who sues as undisclosed principal on a contract purporting to have been made by his agent in the agent's own name has the burden of proving the fact of agency, and that in the making of a contract the alleged agent was acting for him. . . .

While the first of these reasons appears to us to be conclusive of the case, the argument of counsel relates to the second proposition, and we shall briefly express our views as to appellant's contentions. It is true that if one, as agent and acting for another, make a contract in his own name for the benefit of his undisclosed principal, the principal may be sued for breach of such contract, and on the other hand may recover damages for breach thereof by the other party. But this general rule is subject to well recognized exceptions, one of which is that if the party contracting with the agent having no knowledge of the agency may reasonably be supposed to have entered into such contract in consideration of some element of personal trust and confidence, and the contract remains wholly executory, the undisclosed principal cannot enforce the contract in his own name and right. This exception is based on the very good reason that a contracting party is not bound to accept performance of personal services from or extend confidence or credit to another person than the one with whom he supposed he was entering into the contract relation. . . .

The facts of this case bring it fully within the exception to the rule that the undisclosed principal may sue for breach of contract made by his agent. There is no evidence that Patrick Shields agreed to secure the payment of the money to be loaned by a mortgage of the land which as he represented he proposed to purchase, and even if it appeared that the loan was to be thus secured, there is no evidence that the defendant relied entirely upon such security, and not to any extent upon the personal responsibility of Patrick Shields. It is clear that he was under no obligation therefore to make the loan to plaintiff, and if he were under no such obligation, he is not liable for damages to plaintiff for refusing to make it. If the contract was by Patrick Shields as agent for plaintiff, it could only be carried out by the loan of the money to plaintiff, and plaintiff cannot recover damages if the contract was only for the loan of money to her husband.

The cases relied upon for appellant are not in point. In Winchester v. Howard, 97 Mass. 303, 93 Am. Dec. 93, it is said that an agent may sell the property of his principal without disclosing the fact of his agency, or that the property is not his own, and the principal may maintain an action in his own name to recover the price. But the court follows this general proposition with the statement that, on the other hand, every man has a right to elect what parties he will deal with, and to take into account in such dealing the character, credit, and substance of the person with whom he contracts. And in Kelly v. Thuey, 143 Mo. 422, 45 S.W. 300, the court, commenting upon the case of the same title above cited, simply holds that an agent may enter into a contract for the purchase of land for an undisclosed principal, and the principal may maintain suit in his own name and enforce the contract; but it is not indicated that any credit was extended or was to be extended to the agent as supposed principal in the transaction.

The reasons assigned by the defendant for refusing to carry out the contract with plaintiff's husband were wholly immaterial. If he incurred no obligation to this plaintiff, then his reasons for not carrying out his contract with her husband, even though not sufficient to justify him as against the husband, would not give rise to any right of action in favor of the plaintiff.

The judgment was correct, and it is affirmed.

Discussion questions

1. What should an undisclosed principal do before he has his agent contract on his behalf with a third party in order to meet the burden of proof that the agent acted for him at the time of contracting?
2. The court held that an agreement by a third party to lend money to another on an unsecured basis falls within the exception to the general rule that the undisclosed principal cannot enforce the contract made by an agent in his own name where the third party entered into such contract "in consideration of some element of personal trust and confidence". Would this exception apply if the undisclosed principal was extremely rich and the agent relatively poor in view of the court's statement that the exception applied because "every man has a right to elect what parties he will deal with, and to take into account on such dealing the character, credit, and substance of the person with whom he contracts."
3. Give two examples where the "character, credit, and substance" test would be applied by courts to bar an undisclosed principal from enforcing a contract made on his behalf by an agent in his own name with a third party.

Case 15

Kelly A.B. Co. v. Barber A.P. Co.

211 N.Y. 68 (1914)

Introduction

It is a fundamental rule of agency law that an undisclosed principal may enforce a contract made by his agent in the agent's name with a third party if the agent acted in accordance with the actual authority conferred upon him. However, there are several exceptions to this general rule, one of which is that an undisclosed principal cannot enforce such a contract if he knows that the third party would not contract with him. This leading case illustrates how the court evaluates whether or not the undisclosed principal "knows" such a fact.

Cardozo, J.

The plaintiff sues to recover damages for breach of an implied warranty. The contract was made between the defendant and one Booth. The plaintiff says that Booth was in truth its agent, and it sues as undisclosed principal. The question is whether it has the right to do so.

The general rule is not disputed. A contract not under seal, made in the name of an agent as ostensible principal, may be sued on by the real principal at the latter's election. . . . The defendant says that we should establish an exception to that rule, where the identity of the principal has been concealed because of the belief that, if it were disclosed, the contract would not be made. We are asked to say that the reality of the defendant's consent is thereby destroyed, and the contract vitiated for mistake.

The plaintiff and the defendant were competitors in business. The plaintiff's president suspected that the defendant might refuse to name him a price. The suspicion was not based upon any previous refusal, for there had been none; it had no other origin than their relation as competitors. Because of this doubt the plaintiff availed itself of the services of Booth, who, though interested to the defendant's knowledge in the plaintiff's business, was also engaged in a like business for another corporation. Booth asked the defendant for a price and received a quotation, and the asphalt blocks required for the plaintiff's pavement were ordered in his name. The order was accepted by the defendant, the blocks were delivered, and payment was made by Booth with money furnished by the plaintiff. The paving blocks were unmerchantable, and the defendant, retaining the price, contests its liability for damages on the ground that if it had known that the plaintiff was the principal, it would have refused to make the sale.

We are satisfied that upon the facts before us the defense cannot prevail. A contract involves a meeting of the minds of the contracting parties. If "one of the supposed parties is wanting," there is an absence of "one of the formal constituents of a legal transaction." . . . In such a situation there is no contract. A number of cases are reported where A had ordered merchandise of B, and C has surreptitiously filled the order. The question has been much discussed whether C, having thrust himself without consent into the position of a creditor, is entitled to recover the value of his wares. . . . That question is not before us, and we express no opinion concerning it. We state it merely to accentuate the distinction between the cases which involve it and the case at hand. Neither of the supposed parties was wanting in this case. The apparent meeting of the minds between determinate contracting parties was not unreal or illusory. The defendant was contracting with the precise person with whom it intended to contract. It was contracting with Booth. It gained whatever benefit it may have contemplated from his character and substance. . . . An agent who contracts in his own name for an undisclosed principal does not cease to be a party because of his agency. . . . Indeed, such an agent, having made himself personally liable, may enforce the contract though the principal has renounced it. . . . As between himself and the other party, he is liable as principal to the same extent as if he had not been acting for another. It is impossible in such circumstances to hold that the contract collapses for want of parties to sustain it. The contractual tie cannot exist where there are not persons to be bound, but here persons were bound, and those the very persons intended. If Booth had given the order in his own right and for his own benefit, but with the expectation of later assigning it to the plaintiff, that undisclosed expectation would not have nullified the contract. His undisclosed intention to act for a principal who was unknown to the defendant was equally ineffective to destroy the contract in its inception.

If, therefore, the contract did not fail for want of parties to sustain it, the unsuspected existence of an undisclosed principal can supply no ground for the avoidance of a contract unless fraud is proved. We must distinguish between mistake such as we have been discussing, which renders the contract void ab initio, because the contractual tie has never been completely formed, and fraud, which renders it voidable at the election of the defrauded party. . . . In the language of Holmes, J., in the case cited: "Fraud only becomes important, as such, when a sale or contract is complete in its formal elements, and therefore valid unless repudiated, but the right is claimed to rescind it. If one who is in reality an agent denies his agency when questioned, and falsely asserts that his principal has no interest in the transaction, the contract, it may be, becomes voidable, not because there is a want of parties, but because it has been fraudulently procured. That was substantially the situation in Winchester v. Howard (97 Mass. 303). When such a case arises, we shall have to consider whether a misrepresentation of that kind is always so material as to justify rescission after the contract has been executed. . . . But no such situation is disclosed in the case at hand. Booth made no misrepresentation to the defendant. He was not asked anything, nor did he say anything, about the plaintiff's interest in the transaction. Indeed, neither he nor the plaintiff's officers knew whether the defendant would refuse to deal with the plaintiff directly. They suspected hostility, but none had been expressed. The validity of the contract turns thus, according to the defendant, not on any overt act of either the plaintiff or its agent, but on the presence or absence of a mental state. We are asked to hold that a contract complete in form, becomes a nullity in fact because of a secret belief in the mind of the undisclosed principal that the disclosure of his name would be prejudicial to the completion of the bargain. We cannot go so far. . . . It is unnecessary, therefore, to consider whether, even if fraud were shown, the defendant, after the contract was executed, could be permitted to rescind without restoring the difference between the price received for the defective blocks and their reasonable value. It is also unnecessary to analyze the evidence for the purpose of showing that the defendant, after notice of the plaintiff's interest in the transaction, continued to make delivery, and thereby waived the objection that the contract was invalid. . . .

Other rulings complained of by the defendant have been considered, but no error has been found in them.

The judgment should be affirmed, with costs.

Discussion questions

1. How could the seller have avoided the holding of this case? Why?
2. List three other cases where an undisclosed principal cannot enforce an authorized contract his agent made in his own name with a third party.

Name: ______________________

PROBLEMS

Date: ______________________

Section Number: ______________________

1. An agent for an undisclosed principal

______ a. Has less express authority than would be the case if he were acting as an agent for a disclosed principal.

______ b. Has liability on a contract he made with a third party, if the third party elects to hold him liable thereon.

______ c. Must derive whatever authority he may have from a written power of attorney.

______ d. Must disclose his principal's identity prior to performance.

2. P wished to acquire a site for a warehouse. Knowing that if it negotiated directly for the purchase of the property the price would be substantially increased, it employed A to secure lots without disclosing that he was acting for P. A's authority was evidenced by a writing signed by the proper officers of P. A entered into a contract in his own name to purchase T's lot, giving T a negotiable note for $1,000 signed by A as first payment. P wrote A acknowledging the purchase. P also disclosed its identity as A's principal to T. In respect to the rights and liabilities of the parties, which of the following is a correct statement?

______ a. T is not bound on the contract since A's failure to disclose he was A's agent was fraudulent.

______ b. P, A, and T are potentially liable on the contract.

______ c. Unless T formally ratifies the substitution of P for A, he is not liable.

______ d. A has no liability since he was acting for and on behalf of an existing principal.

3. Wishing to acquire a site for its factory without provoking a rise in price, P engaged A to purchase land without disclosing P's name. A did so and signed a contract in its own name with T to purchase T's land. Under these circumstances

______ a. The transaction is fraudulent.

______ b. A is not personally liable on the contract.

______ c. P must formally ratify the contract if it is to hold T liable.

______ d. T may obtain recourse against either P or A if the contract is not performed.

4. P hires A as his agent to acquire T's land at a price not to exceed $50,000, the land is badly needed to provide additional parking space for P's shopping center. In order to prevent T from asking for an exorbitant price, P told A not to disclose his principal. A subsequently purchased the land for $45,000. Under these circumstances

______ a. A and P committed fraud when they did not disclose the fact that A was P's agent.

______ b. Absent an agreement regarding the compensation to be paid A, he is entitled to the difference between the $50,000 limitation and the $45,000 he paid for the land; i.e., $5,000 based upon quasi contract.

______ c. T may rescind the contract upon his learning the truth as long as the conveyance has not been accomplished.

______ d. T may sue either P or A on the contract in the event of default by P.

5. If an agent makes a contract for his undisclosed principal

______ a. As between the principal and his agent, the agent has no implied authority.

______ b. The principal has committed a fraud upon any and all third parties with whom the agent deals.

______ c. The agent is personally liable on the contract if the third party sues him.

______ d. The contract between the undisclosed principal and his agent must be in writing, witnessed, and duly notarized to be valid.

6. P engaged A as her agent. It was mutually agreed that A would not disclose that he was acting as P's agent. Instead he was to deal with prospective customers as if he were a principal acting on his own behalf. This he did and made several contracts for P. Assuming P, A or the customer seeks to avoid liability on one of the contracts involved, which of the following statements is correct?

_____ a. A has no liability once he disclosed that P was the real principal.

_____ b. P must ratify the contracts of A in order to be held liable.

_____ c. The third party may choose to hold either A or P liable.

_____ d. The third party can avoid liability because he believed he was dealing with A as a principal.

7. P engaged A as her agent. It was mutually agreed that A would not disclose that he was acting as P's agent. Instead he was to deal with prospective customers as if he were a principal acting on his own behalf. This he did and made several contracts for P. Assuming P, A, or the customer seeks to avoid liability on one of the contracts involved, which of the following statements is correct?

_____ a. The third party may choose to hold either A or P liable.

_____ b. The third party can avoid liability because he believed he was dealing with A as a principal.

_____ c. P must ratify the contracts of A in order to be held liable.

_____ d. A has no liability once he disclosed that P was the real principal.

8. P, a wealthy art collector, orally engaged A to obtain a rare and beautiful painting from T. T did not know that P had engaged A to obtain the painting for P because as P told A "that would cause the price to skyrocket." Regarding the liability of the parties if a contract is made or purported to be made, which of the following is correct?

_____ a. Since the appointment of A was oral, no agency exists, and any contract made by A on P's behalf is invalid.

_____ b. Because P specifically told A not to reveal for whom he (A) was buying the painting, A can not be personally liable on the contract made on P's behalf.

_____ c. If A makes a contract with T which A breaches, T may, after learning of the agreement between P and A, elect to recover from either P or A.

_____ d. If A makes a contract to purchase the painting, without revealing he is P's agent, T has entered into a contract which is voidable at his election.

9. Alston represents Pepper, an undisclosed principal. Pepper instructs Alston to buy goods in his own name on credit from Tonner. Alston does so and when Tonner discovers the facts, he refuses to deliver the goods to Alston or Pepper.

   a. In an action by Alston against Tonner for breach of contract, judgment for whom? Why?

____

____

____

____

   b. In an action by Pepper against Tonner for breach of contract, judgment for whom? Why?

____

____

____

____

10. Atwater represents Parker, an undisclosed principal. Atwater negotiates to purchase a tract of 100 acres from Chin. Chin informs Atwater that he will not deal with him if he is representing Parker. Atwater replies that he is dealing in his own behalf. They enter into the contract and the deed is subsequently delivered to Atwater. One day later Chin discovers the true facts and promptly seeks to rescind the sale.

    a. In Chin's action against Atwater to rescind the sale, judgment for whom? Why?

    b. Assume that when Chin stated to Atwater that he, Chin, would not deal with Atwater if he was representing Parker, Atwater made no statement. What rights, if any, would Chin have? Why?

11. Winslow, an artist, appoints Dalton, another artist to enter into a contract to paint a portrait of Booth. Winslow instructs Dalton not to disclose to Booth that Dalton is acting for Winslow. Dalton contracts in his own name with Booth for the painting of the portrait for $5,000. When Booth discovers that Dalton acted for Winslow he refuses to allow Winslow to paint the portrait.

    a. In an action by Winslow against Booth for breach of contract, judgment for whom? Why?

    b. Would your answer to a. be different if Winslow was universally recognized in the art world as being a much better painter than Dalton? Why?

    c. Has Dalton committed fraud against Booth? Why?

12. Pratt authorizes Avid to buy $2,500 of goods for him from Timmons on credit. Pratt instructs Avid not to disclose that he is buying the goods for Pratt. Avid makes the purchase on credit in his own name. Two days before payment is due, Pratt gives Avid his $2,500 check and tells Avid to deposit the check and to issue his own check to Timmons. Instead, Avid absconds with the money. Three days later Timmons discovers that Pratt was the undisclosed principal and sues him for the $2,500 purchase price.

    a. Judgment for whom? Why?

    b. Under what circumstances would Timmons not be able to recover from Pratt?

13. Andrews owes Thornton $2,000. Parton authorizes Andrews to sell certain antique furniture owned by Parton to Thornton for $10,000. Parton instructs Andrews not to disclose that he is contracting on behalf of Parton but rather to contract in his own name. Andrews does as he is instructed. When Thornton discovers that Parton is the principal in the sale, he offers to pay only $8,000 of the $10,000 purchase price because he wants to set-off the $2,000 claim he has against Andrews. Parton refuses and sues Thornton for $10,000.

    a. How much may Parton recover from Thornton? Why?

    b. If Parton recovers only $8,000 from Thornton, what rights, if any, does he have against Andrews? Why?

14. Pilsen authorizes Alsop to buy on credit a painting from Towbin for $5,000 and instructs Alsop not to reveal that he is acting on behalf of Pilsen. Alsop buys the painting from Towbin in his own name for $5,000 and decides to keep the painting for himself.

    a. Pilsen learns of the transaction and seeks to ratify it. May he do so? Why?

    b. What rights, if any, does Pilsen have against Alsop? Why?

15. Astor, conducting a business under her own name issued and delivered her promissory note to the order of Taggert for the purchase of $10,000 worth of goods. Later, Taggert discovered that Astor was in fact conducting the business as an agent for an undisclosed principal, Perry. The note was not paid at maturity.

    a. In an action by Taggert against Astor on the note, judgment for whom? Why?

    b. In an action by Taggert against Perry on the note, judgment for whom? Why?

    c. In an action by Taggert against Perry on the underlying contract for the purchase of the goods, judgment for whom? Why?

16. Higgins Electronics, Inc. wanted to purchase some valuable used electronic equipment from Ladd, a competitor. The company hired Lemmon to make the purchase in his name and instructed him not to disclose that he was acting for the Company. Lemmon signed a contract in his own name to purchase the equipment from Ladd for $75,000 with delivery and payment to be made 30 days later. Before the payment date the company learned of a major technological breakthrough in electronic equipment and decided to buy new equipment which incorporated the discovery. Lemmon was instructed immediately to neither pay nor accept delivery of the used equipment. When Ladd learned subsequently that the company was Lemmon's principal, he sued the company for breach of contract. The company defended contending that it was not liable to Ladd because (1) Ladd intended to contract with Lemmon only and (2) recovery was barred because Ladd discovered the identity of the company after the contract was executed.

    Discuss the validity of each defense raised by Higgins Electronics, Inc.

____

____

____

____

____

17. When an agent acts for an undisclosed principal, the principal will **not** be liable to third parties if the

_____ a. Principal ratifies a contract entered into by the agent.

_____ b. Agent acts within an implied grant of authority.

_____ c. Agent acts outside the grant of actual authority.

_____ d. Principal seeks to conceal the agency relationship.

18. Easy Corp. is a real estate developer and regularly engages real estate brokers to act on its behalf in acquiring parcels of land. The brokers are authorized to enter into such contracts, but are instructed to do so in their own names without disclosing Easy's identity or relationship to the transaction. If a broker enters into a contract with a seller on Easy's behalf,

_____ a. The broker will have the same actual authority as if Easy's identity has been disclosed.

_____ b. Easy will be bound by the contract because of the broker's apparent authority.

_____ c. Easy will **not** be liable for any negligent acts committed by the broker while acting on easy's behalf.

_____ d. The broker will **not** be personally bound by the contract because the broker has express authority to act.

19. An agent will usually be liable under a contract made with a third party when the agent is acting on behalf of a (an)

		Disclosed principal	*Undisclosed principal*
_____	a.	Yes	Yes
_____	b.	Yes	No
_____	c.	No	Yes
_____	d.	No	No

20. Cox engaged Datz as her agent. It was mutually agreed that Datz would not disclose that he was acting as Cox's agent. Instead he was to deal with prospective customers as if he were a principal acting on his own behalf. This he did and made several contracts for Cox. Assuming Cox, Datz or the customer seeks to avoid liability on one of the contracts involved, which of the following statements is correct?

_____ a. Cox must ratify the Datz contracts in order to be held liable.

_____ b. Datz has **no** liability once he discloses that Cox was the real principal.

_____ c. The third party can avoid liability because he believed he was dealing with Datz as a principal.

_____ d. The third party may choose to hold either Datz or Cox liable.

21. Which of the following rights will a third party be entitled to after validly contracting with an agent representing an undisclosed principal?

_____ a. Disclosure of the principal by the agent.

_____ b. Ratification of the contract by the principal.

_____ c. Performance of the contract by the agent.

_____ d. Election to void the contract after disclosure of the principal.

22. Able, as agent for Baker, an undisclosed principal, contracted with Safe to purchase an antique car. In payment, Able issued his personal check to Safe. Able could not cover the check but expected Baker to give him cash to deposit before the check was presented for payment. Baker did not do so and the check was dishonored. Baker's identity became known to Safe. Safe may **not** recover from

_____ a. Baker individually on the contract.

_____ b. Able individually on the contract.

_____ c. Baker individually on the check.

_____ d. Able individually on the check.

23. When a valid contract is entered into by an agent on the principal's behalf, in a nondisclosed principal situation, which of the following statements concerning the principal's liability is correct?

		The principal may be held liable once disclosed	*The principal must ratify the contract to be held liable*
_____	a.	Yes	Yes
_____	b.	Yes	No
_____	c.	No	Yes
_____	d.	No	No

Items 24 and 25 are based on the following information:

Frey entered into a contract with Cara Corp. to purchase televisions on behalf of Lux, Inc. Lux authorized Frey to enter into the contract in Frey's name without disclosing that Frey was acting on behalf of Lux.

24. If Lux repudiates the contract, Cara may

_____ a. Obtain specific performance, compelling Lux to perform on the contract.

_____ b. Hold Frey liable on the contract whether or not Cara discovers that Lux is the principal.

_____ c. Hold Frey liable on the contract but only if Cara fails to discover that Lux was the principal.

_____ d. Not hold Lux liable because proof that Lux was the principal will be barred by the parol evidence rule.

25. If Cara repudiates the contract, which of the following statements concerning liability on the contract is **not** correct?

_____ a. Frey may hold Cara liable and obtain money damages.

_____ b. Frey may hold Cara liable and obtain specific performance.

_____ c. Lux may hold Cara liable upon disclosing the agency relationship with Frey.

_____ d. Cara will be free from liability to Lux if Frey fraudulently stated that he was acting on his own behalf.

26. When an agent acts for an undisclosed principal, the principal will **not** be liable to third parties if the

_____ a. Principal ratifies a contract entered into by the agent.

_____ b. Agent acts within an implied grant of authority.

_____ c. Agent acts outside the grant of actual authority.

_____ d. Principal seeks to conceal the agency relationship.

27. Parc contracted with Furn Brothers Corp. to buy hotel furniture and fixtures on behalf of Global Motor House, a motel chain. Global instructed Parc to use Parc's own name and not to disclose to Furn that Parc was acting on Global's behalf. Who is liable to Furn on this contract?

		Parc	*Global*
_____	a.	Yes	No
_____	b.	No	Yes
_____	c.	Yes	Yes
_____	d.	No	No

CHAPTER 7

THE PRINCIPAL-AGENT RELATIONSHIP: RIGHTS, DUTIES, AND LIABILITIES

63. Introduction.

When a principal and agent enter into a written contract, usually prepared by the principal's attorney, they will be more explicit in setting forth the rights, duties, and liabilities each has than when they contract orally. However, in either case, it is virtually impossible to articulate precisely each right and duty under every conceivable circumstance. Therefore, courts will apply rules of agency law and contract law applicable to the agency relationship which have been judicially established over several hundred years to define the rights, duties, and liabilities that each has to the other when the oral or written principal-agent contract is silent or ambiguous.[1] In the sections that follow, we will examine these well-settled rules which govern the principal-agent relationship.

64. Duties of agent: introduction.

The principal-agent relationship is legally recognized as a fiduciary relationship in which the agent owes his principal certain fiduciary duties imposed not by the terms of their contract but rather by operation of law. As a consequence of this fiduciary relationship, the agent owes his principal the fiduciary duty of undivided loyalty and the duty to act in good faith at all times. This fiduciary relationship is imposed by law upon the agent because the very nature of the agency relationship involves the principal entrusting his fortune, reputation, and legal rights and responsibilities to his agent whose actions, for better or worse, vitally affect the economic well-being and reputation of the principal. Since the principal entrusts so much to his agent, the law of agency requires that the agent perform his responsibilities not according to the morals of the ordinary marketplace, where parties deal with each other at arm's length, but according to the higher standards imposed by law upon those in a position of trust who handle the business affairs of others, such as those in the position of trustee, partner, or corporate director. It is in the context of the agent's fiduciary relationship with his principal that each of the agent's duties hereafter discussed is imposed by operation of law where the contract between principal and agent is silent or ambiguous.

The broad concept of fiduciary relationship imposes upon the agent numerous duties including the duty to: exercise reasonable care and skill in the performance of his duties, act in good faith at all times, account fully to his principal for all his actions on behalf of his principal, keep his principal fully informed as to all matters relevant to the principal's interest, obey all lawful instructions given to him by his principal, no matter how arbitrary or capricious, and act properly at all times to further the principal's legal interests. Although the principal and agent may expressly agree to modify or exclude completely one or more of the agent's fiduciary duties, courts are reluctant to permit the substantial erosion of the agent's fiduciary duty. In the event the agent breaches his fiduciary duty, the principal may bring an action against him based upon breach of contract or tort or both.

65. Agent's duty to obey principal's instructions.

An agent has the duty to obey all of his principal's lawful instructions no matter how arbitrary or capricious any of those instructions seem to the agent or anyone else. Thus, where the principal instructs his agent not to drink alcoholic beverages during the work-day, the agent must obey or he will be liable to his principal for any loss resulting from his failure to obey. Even where the principal suffers no loss as a result of the agent's disobeying his lawful instructions, the principal may consider the same a breach of their contract and a legal basis for justifiably terminating the principal-agent contract. By contrast, if the principal's instructions are illegal, immoral, unethical, or opposed to public policy, as where the principal instructs his agent to bribe another to obtain business for his principal, the agent has no duty to obey.[2] Indeed, if the agent obeys such unlawful instructions, it is well-settled that the agent is personally liable for any crime or tort he commits. In such a case the agent cannot immunize himself from criminal or civil liability on the ground that he was simply following his principal's orders.

To determine the extent to which an agent must obey his principal's lawful instructions, the law makes a distinction between instructions which do not require the agent to use any discretion to perform and those which do. Thus, where the principal instructs his agent to perform a duty that involves no discretion, such as to sell only for cash, the agent must strictly obey or he will be liable to his principal for any damages resulting from the agent's failure to obey. However, where the principal's instructions require the agent to use discretion in performing his duties, such as to buy or sell at the best price possible, the agent has more latitude and discretion in performing his duties. In such a case, if the agent acted in good faith and with reasonable care and skill and did not abuse his discretion, he is not liable for any damages suffered by his principal even if the agent did not in fact buy or sell for the best price possible.

These rules are subject to exceptions in the case of an emergency and an agency coupled with an interest. In an emergency when the agent is unable to communicate with his principal to obtain special instructions, he may depart from his principal's prior instructions which he believes in good faith will cause loss to his principal. In such an event he may pursue a different course of conduct provided he acts in good faith and exercises sound discretion in order to protect the principal's interests, even if previously prohibited from doing so.

In the case of an agency coupled with an interest, where the agent has possession of the principal's property or a non-possessory security interest therein to secure a debt, the agent may properly refuse to obey his principal's instructions which imperil the agent's rights with respect to the principal's property.

The agent's duty to obey applies equally whether he is a compensated or noncompensated agent.[3] Moreover, he must obey any lawful instructions that his principal gives him even where the principal agreed not to give such instructions according to their original contract. In such an event, the agent may treat such instructions as a breach of their contract and may hold his principal liable for any loss the agent incurs as a result of obeying his principal's different instructions.[4]

66. Agent's duty to exercise reasonable care and skill.

The agency relationship requires only that the agent exercise the degree of care, diligence, and skill that the nature of the authority and the circumstances of the case dictate.[5] Thus, an agent properly performs his duty if he acts with reasonable care, diligence, and skill as an ordinary reasonable person would act under the same circumstances.[6] Applying this fundamental rule, an agent does not insure or guarantee that his performance of his duties will earn a profit or not cause a loss to his principal, unless he expressly agrees otherwise with his principal. Rather, the agent is liable to his principal for any loss only where he fails to exercise reasonable care, diligence and skill. An agent who fails to do so is negligent in the performance of his duties and is liable to his principal for any proximate (reasonably foreseeable) loss that results. Thus, an agent employed to sell on credit to qualified buyers who sells without investigating the credit of the buyer is liable to his principal for any resulting loss because of his negligence arising from his failure to exercise reasonable care and skill in performing his duties. The principal has the burden of proving that the agent was negligent in performing his duties and the issue of negligence is usually a question of fact to be decided by the jury.

67. Agent's duty of undivided loyalty and good faith.

The fiduciary relationship between agent and principal requires that the agent have undivided loyalty to his principal and that he act in good faith at all times. This duty is relentless and supreme.[7] Accordingly, an agent breaches his fiduciary duty of undivided loyalty and good faith when, without his principal's consent, (a) he acquires any interest directly or indirectly in the subject matter of the agency, or (b) buys the principal's property given to him to sell or sells his own property to the principal when engaged by his principal to buy property, or (c) where he also represents the third party to the contract. It is obvious that the agent in the circumstances mentioned is acting with divided loyalty and in bad faith. His attempt to serve two masters is a breach of his fiduciary duty of undivided loyalty and good faith.

In any case where the agent breaches his fiduciary duty by engaging in self-dealing, the principal may disaffirm the contract made by the agent upon discovery of the breach or within a reasonable time thereafter. The principal's absolute right to disaffirm applies even where he suffers no loss and there is no fraud as where the agent buys the principal's property for sale at the price offered without the principal's consent. And where the agent makes any profit as a result of his self-dealing, he must also disgorge the profit and turn it over to his principal, as where he secretly buys the principal's property that he has been authorized to sell for him and sells it thereafter at a profit.[8]

The absolute duty of undivided loyalty also requires the agent to report to his principal promptly all acquired information related to his principal's interests.[9] Where the agent fails to do so, he has breached his fiduciary duty of undivided loyalty and is liable to his principal for any loss proximately caused. And even where no loss occurs, the agent's breach will still justify termination of the agency relationship regardless of the specified duration of their agreement.

Furthermore, the duty of undivided loyalty is so pervasive that an agent may not use confidential trade secrets or customer lists to which he had access while an agent after the termination of the agency.[10] However, the former agent may properly use the skill and experience he acquired in any new employment because he is not required to "wipe clean the slate of his memory."

In every case where the agent breaches his fiduciary duty of undivided loyalty and good faith, the agent is not entitled to compensation, reimbursement, indemnification, or to an agent's lien. Moreover, he is liable for any loss caused by his breach and may be dismissed without liability regardless of the specified duration of the agency agreement.

68. Agent's duty to account to his principal.

An agent has the fiduciary duty to account to his principal for all the principal's funds which comes into his possession as a result of the agency relationship. The particular form of accounting which the agent must render depends upon community customs and standards for that type of business. Unless otherwise provided in their contract, the agent must render an accounting within a reasonable time after receipt or disbursement of funds and must render a final accounting upon termination of the agency. Moreover, he must keep his principal's funds in an account separate from his own funds at all times. Applying this rule, where the agent commingles his principal's funds with his own funds in one savings or checking account, the agent will be absolutely liable as an insurer for any resulting loss if the bank fails, even though the agent acted in good faith when commingling such funds and was not negligent in selecting the bank that subsequently failed.

Although it is well-settled that an agent does not guarantee that the performance of his duties will earn a profit, the rule is equally well-settled that the agent must account to his principal for all profits made and must turn them over to his principal promptly.[11] He simply cannot keep some of the profit without his principal's consent because he made a particularly good deal for his principal. Moreover, the agent has a duty to turn over promptly to his principal any property that he received from anyone in connection with the performance of his duties as agent,[12] including secret bribes, kickbacks, gifts, or commissions.[13] However, in the case of routine small gratuities given to agents, as at holiday season, the agent may properly keep the same if the effect, according to common knowledge, custom and practice, is not to influence or corrupt the agent, unless the principal and agent agree otherwise. Most principals expressly or impliedly allow their agent-employees to keep small gifts. Some corporations and partnerships have adopted a formal written policy binding upon their agent-employees which define the kinds, values, and amounts of gifts which their agent-employees may accept and keep from third parties who do business with the corporation or partnership and require their employees to submit written detailed reports of gifts received by them and members of their immediate families from such third parties.

To aid the principal in his claim against his agent to recover profits or other property belonging to the principal, the courts will impose a constructive trust upon any funds or property in the agent's possession which belong to the principal.[14] This constructive trust imposes upon the agent the absolute duty to hold such funds or property as a trustee in trust for his principal and to turn them over promptly together with a full accounting.[15] Moreover, the principal may obtain an injunction to restrain the agent from disposing of the funds or property belonging to the principal.

69. Agent's duty not to delegate his authority to another.

The fiduciary nature of the agency relationship, based in part upon the principal's trust and confidence in his selected agent, imposes upon the agent the duty to perform personally the duties entrusted to him when such duties involves the exercise of discretion, personal judgment or particular skill. In such a case, the agent may not properly delegate his duty to perform to another without the principal's consent. Thus, where the agent wrongfully delegates his duty to perform, even to one who is equally or even more competent than himself, he will be in breach of his fiduciary duty; the agency relationship may be properly terminated by the principal regardless of the specified duration of their agency agreement, and the agent will be liable for any loss resulting from his wrongful delegation.

The principal's consent to such delegation, when given, may be express[16] or implied.[17] In some cases, based upon the custom of the trade or the prior course of dealing between principal and agent, the principal understands that the agent will act through another agent.[18] In such a case, the other agent is called a subagent and he becomes the agent of the principal, and all of the rights, duties, and liabilities of the principal-agent relationship are applicable to that relationship,[19] including the duty to compensate his subagent. By contrast, where the agent's duties do not require discretion or personal judgment or particular skills, or where an emergency occurs, the agent may properly delegate his duty to perform to a subagent without permission unless prohibited by their contract.[20] Moreover, if the agent selected his subagent with reasonable care, he will not be liable to his principal for any loss caused by the subsequent negligence of the subagent in the performance of his duties.[21] In such a case the principal's sole recourse will be against the subagent who is liable to the principal for any loss caused by his negligence in the performance of his duties as subagent.

If the agent has wrongfully delegated his duty to perform to a subagent without the principal's consent, where required, the principal will not be liable for the subagent's contracts made on his behalf or for any torts he commits while performing in the capacity of a subagent. In such a case, the third party can hold the subagent personally liable based upon the subagent's breach of his implied warranty of authority because every agent impliedly warrants to the third party he contracts with in his principal's name that he had actual authority to contract for his principal. In that event, the subagent can hold the agent who appointed him as a subagent for any loss that the subagent incurs to the third party with whom he contracted for the benefit of the principal based upon the agent's breach of his implied warranty of authority. This is so because the agent who appointed him as a subagent for the principal impliedly warranted to him that he had authority to contract for his principal when he appointed him as a subagent for his principal. Thus, every agent who appoints a subagent without express or implied authority does so at his peril.[22]

70. Agent's duty to comply with law.

It is a fundamental rule of law that an agent must comply with the law no matter what the principal-agent contract otherwise provides. Thus, where the principal proposes that his agent do an act which is illegal at the time it is proposed or which becomes illegal at the time it is to be performed, the agent may not do it and he will not be liable to his principal for his failure to perform the requested illegal act.[23] This rule applies whether or not the principal or agent knew the proposed act was illegal. However, if one party knows the proposed act is illegal and the other does not, the party with such knowledge will be liable to the party without such knowledge where loss is sustained by the ignorant party as a result of the performance of an illegal act. Moreover, where the agent commits an illegal act at the principal's direction, both principal and agent will be liable. In the event both principal and agent are aware that the consummated act of the agent is illegal, neither party may enforce the contract against the other because of the judicial application of the "clean hands doctrine" which results in the court leaving the parties as it finds them since neither party has "clean hands".

The agent's duty to comply with the law not only applies to the avoidance of illegal acts but also to licensing requirements imposed by statute. Thus, where a person is required by law to be licensed by the state in order to practice his profession or occupation, such as law or real estate, he will be denied the right to receive compensation from his principal where he acts as agent for another without such required license even though he has fully performed and the effect of this rule is to give a windfall to his principal. This rule is rationalized upon desirable social policy of state regulation of certain professions and occupations.

71. Agent's duty to notify principal of material matters.

It is a fundamental rule of agency law that every agent has an implied duty to notify his principal promptly of all matters that come to the agent's attention during his agency which may materially affect his principal's interest. Moreover, even where the agent does not so inform his principal, whether due to benign neglect or willful omission, the principal is bound by such notice given to his agent. If the agent breaches this imperative duty, he will be liable for any resulting loss to his principal as well as be subject to dismissal regardless of the specified duration of the agency. However, this general rule does not apply where the notice given to the agent is adverse to the agent's personal interest. In that case, notice to the agent would not constitute notice to the principal.[24]

72. Principal's duties: introduction.

The principal is not a fiduciary as is his agent. However, under the law of agency, the principal has certain implied duties to his agent such as the duty to compensate his agent reasonably, to reimburse him for reasonable expenses incurred in the performance of his duties, to indemnify him for any loss he incurs in the proper performance of his duties and to afford his agent every reasonable opportunity to perform his duties. While these duties may be express according to the terms of the principal-agent contract (oral or written), they will be implied in every other case where the contract is silent or ambiguous unless the parties have expressly excluded or modified these duties. Each of these major implied duties will be discussed separately in the four sections that follow.

73. Principal's duty to compensate his agent.

The principal's duty to compensate his agent is usually expressly agreed in their oral or written contract. However, where their agreement is silent or ambiguous, it is a fundamental rule of agency law that the principal has an implied duty to pay his agent reasonable compensation. What constitutes reasonable compensation will depend upon the nature of the services rendered, the custom of the trade or business, and any prior course of dealing between the parties.[25] Unless the agreement provides otherwise, the agent must complete his performance before he becomes entitled to reasonable compensation.[26] Furthermore, where the agent receives a draw against future commissions to be earned, his draw is legally presumed to be his salary unless the parties expressly agree that it is a loan.

If the principal wrongfully terminates the agency contract, he is liable to his agent for damages for breach of contract in addition to reasonable compensation for services rendered up to the date of termination. By contrast, if the agent wrongfully terminates his employment or breaches any of his fiduciary duties prior to completing his performance, he forfeits his right to receive any compensation where he was not to be paid until he fully performed.[27] However, if he was entitled to payment as he performed his duties, he is entitled to payment of compensation previously earned subject to the principal's claim for damages for breach of contract.

To aid the agent in enforcing and collecting his claim for reasonable compensation, as well as for reimbursement of reasonable expenses and indemnification against losses as discussed in the next two sections, the law provides that the agent has a lien against the principal's property that is in his possession. This extremely valuable remedy, called an agent's lien, gives the agent priority over other creditors of the principal and entitles the agent to satisfy his lawful claims out of the principal's property in his possession. However, if the agent turns over possession of the principal's property to the principal, the agent's lien terminates and the agent then becomes a general unsecured creditor of his principal.

74. Principal's duty to indemnify his agent.

The principal-agent contract may expressly provide the terms and conditions under which the principal will indemnify the agent for losses incurred by the agent in the performance of his duties. However, where their contract is silent or ambiguous, it is well-settled that the principal has the implied duty to indemnify his agent for any losses that the agent may incur in the course of his performance provided the loss was not incurred as a result of the agent's negligence, misconduct, or illegal act.[28]

Applying this rule, an agent is not entitled to obtain indemnification from his principal for losses sustained by the agent due to the agent's negligent operation of his automobile or to parking tickets issued to the agent for illegal parking even though the agent's loss was incurred while he was performing his duties for his principal.[29] However, the agent is entitled to obtain indemnification for losses sustained when he performs an act in good faith at the principal's direction when said act is not manifestly illegal or known to be wrong, as where the agent is held liable for wrongful repossession which he does pursuant to his principal's instructions.

Where the agent is entitled to indemnification, he may resort to the remedy of his agent's lien with respect to the principal's property in his possession as discussed in the preceding section.

Where the agent has paid for goods that he bought for his principal and has shipped them to his principal, he has the right to stop the goods in transit and to repossess them where the principal becomes insolvent.[30] And where the agent has not yet shipped the goods, he may hold the goods in his possession, pursuant to his agent's lien, to satisfy his claim for indemnification or reimbursement for the purchase price he advanced.

75. Principal's duty to reimburse his agent.

Although it is customary for the principal-agent contract to expressly provide the terms and conditions under which the principal shall reimburse his agent for advances, expenses, and disbursements, the law of agency imposes upon the principal the implied duty to reimburse his agent for all reasonable advances, expenses, and disbursements incurred by the agent in the performance of his duties. The agent has the burden of proof as to their reasonableness and that they were reasonably related to the duties he was performing.

Where the agent is entitled to reimbursement, he may resort to the remedy of his agent's lien with respect to the principal's property in his possession as discussed in the preceding section.

76. Principal's duty to perform.

A principal has the implied duty to do everything reasonably necessary to enable the agent to perform his duties.[31] In the event the principal breaches his duty, as where he does not provide his agent with (a) required funds to purchase goods from a third party, or (b) a required automobile to enable the agent to cover his assigned territory, or (c) a list of prospective customers for the agent to call upon, the agent may properly terminate the agency agreement and hold the principal liable for any damages suffered by the agent.

Current References

"Expensive day at the office: can corporations indemnify their agents who suffer personal liability for regulatory offenses?" (Canada) by Peter Bowal, 45 *University of Toronto Law Journal,* 247-278, Summer 1995.

"Principal's duty to indemnify agent," by Clarence E. Hagglund and Britton D. Weimer, 40 *Federation of Insurance and Corporate Counsel Quarterly* 274-280, Spring 1990.

Notes

1. For an analysis of rights and duties of principal and agent flowing from the principal-agent relationship, see "The Relationship Of Principal And Agent," *Modern Law Review,* 17:24-40, January 1954. The strict fiduciary standards which must be followed by an agent are examined in Alvin E. Evans, "Fiduciary Obligations of Agents," *Western Reserve Law Review,* 2:5-26, June 1950.
2. Ford v. Wisconsin Real Estate Examining Bd., 48 Wis.2d 91, 179 N.W.2d 786 (1970); Hunter v. Payne, 113 Misc. 385, 184 N.Y.S. 433 (1920).
3. Stanton v. Weber, 218 Oreg. 282, 341 P.2d 1078 (1959); Wilson v. Southern Pac. Land Co., 61 Cal. App. 545, 215 P. 396 (1923); Murray v. Gamble, 127 Ga. App. 855, 195 S.E.2d 461 (1973); Barile v. Wright, 256 N.Y. 1, 175 N.E. 351 (1931).
4. Theis v. DuPont, Glore Forgan Inc., 212 Kan. 301, 510 P.2d 1212 (1973); People v. Mead, 36 N.Y. 224 (1867); Day v. American Machinists Press, 86 App. Div. 613, 83 N.Y.S. 263 (1903).
5. Bucholtz v. Sirotkin Travel Ltd., 74 Misc.2d 180, 343 N.Y.S.2d 438 (1973); Heinemann v. Heard, 50 N.Y. 27 (1872); Krafft v. Citizens Bank of Dyersburg, 139 App. Div. 610, 124 N.Y.S. 214 (1910).

6. State Auto. & Cas. Underwriters v. Salisbury, 27 Utah2d 229, 494 P.2d 529 (1972); McCauley v. Georgia Railroad Bank, 245 N.Y. 245, 157 N.E. 125 (1927); Barney v. Bond and Mort. Guaranty Co., 118 Misc. 241, 193 N.Y.S. 19 (1922).
7. Bennett v. Shamilzadeh, 121 N.Y.S.2d 805 (1953); Laub v. Genway Corp., 60 F.R.D. 462 (S.D.N.Y. 1973); Franco v. Stein Steel & Supply Co., 227 Ga. 92, 179 S.E.2d 88 (1970); Finnerty v. Frenchman, 118 N.Y.S.2d 790 (1952); Elco Shoe Mfrs. Co. v. Sisk, 260 N.Y. 100, 183 N.E. 191 (1932). See, also, the case of Meinhard v. Salmon, 249 N.Y. 458, 164 N.E. 545 (1928) where the court found that an agency relationship existed between two coadventurers-partners requiring undivided loyalty. See comments on *Meinhard* in *Calif. Law Review* 29:367, *Harvard Law Review* 42:953, *Minn. Law Review* 13:711, *St. Johns Law Review* 3:287, and *Yale Law Journal* 38:782.
8. There have been numerous cases concerning agent self-dealing. See, Otsego Aviation Service v. Glens Falls Ins. Co., 277 App. Div. 612, 102 N.Y.S.2d 344 (1951); Donovan & Schuenke v. Sampsell, 226 F.2d 804 (9th Cir. 1955); Groh v. Shelton, 428 S.W.2d 911 (Mo. App. 1968); Schultz v. Manufacturers and Traders Trust Co., 128 F.2d 889 (2d Cir. 1942); Blakeley v. Bradley, 281 S.W.2d 835 (Mo. 1955); Phelan v. Middle States Oil Corp., 220 F.2d 593 (2d Cir. 1955), cert. denied 349 U.S. 929 (1955); In Re Krabbe's Estate, 1 Misc. 2d 810, 147 N.Y.S.2d 498 (1956); Boulevard Plaza Corp. v. Campbell, 254 Minn. 123, 94 N.W.2d 273 (1959); Frank Sheridan Jonas, Inc. v. Romanat, 94 N.Y.S.2d 727 (1950); Anderson Corp. v. Blanch, 340 Mass. 43, 162 N.E.2d 825 (1959); Singer v. A. Hollander & Son, Inc., 202 F.2d 55 (3rd Cir. 1953); Ritterpusch v. Lithographic Place Serv., Inc., 208 Md. 592, 119 A.2d 392 (1956); In Re Williams's Estate, 37 Misc. 2d 542, 235 N.Y.S.2d 815 (1962); In Re Willet's Estate, 173 Misc. 199, 17 N.Y.S. 2d 578 (1939).
9. Hawkeye Cas. Co. v. Frisbee, 316 Mich. 540, 25 N.W.2d 521 (1947); Moore v. Commonwealth State Real Estate Commission, 9 Pa. Commonwealth 506, 309 A.2d 77 (1973); Edmonstone v. Hartshorn, 19 N.Y. 9 (1859); Village of Burnsville v. Westwood Co., 290 Minn. 159, 189 N.W.2d 392 (1971); Klien v. 20th Century Fox International Corp., 201 Misc. 32, 108 N.Y.S.2d 767 (1951); O'Neal v. Employment Sec. Agency, 89 Idaho 313, 404 P.2d 600 (1965).
10. Gilmore Indus., Inc. v. Ridge Instrument Co., 288 Ala. 127, 258 So.2d 55 (1972); Franke v. Wiltschek, 115 F. Supp. 28 (S.D.N.Y. 1953), aff'd 209 F.2d 493 (2d Cir. 1953); Shook v. United States, 238 F.2d 952 (6th Cir. 1956), cert. denied 353 U.S. 924 (1957); Byrne and Bowman v. Barrett, 268 N.Y. 199 (1935); Fairchild Engine and Airplane Corp. v. Cox, 50 N.Y.S.2d 643 (1944); Diamond v. Oreamuno, 24 N.Y.2d 494, 301 N.Y.S.2d 78 (1969).
11. Williams v. Queen Fisheries, Inc., 2 Wash. App. 691, 469 P.2d 583 (1970); La Forge v. Cornell, 127 N.Y.S. 453 (1911); Wilson v. Wilson, 4 N.Y. 413 (1868); May v. Hettrick Bros. Co., 181 App. Div. 3, 167 N.Y.S. 966 (1917); New York Trust Co. v. American Realty Co., 244 N.Y. 209, 155 N.E. 102 (1926). See "Agency and Secret Profits," *Manitoba Law Journal*, 3:17-29, 1968.
12. Alexopoulos v. Dakouras, 48 Wis.2d 32, 179 N.W.2d 836 (1970); Stuber v. Taylor, 200 N.W.2d 276 (N.D. 1972); Jewett v. Commonwealth Bond Corp., 241 App. Div. 131, 271 N.Y.S. 522 (1934).
13. In Re Browning's Estate, 172 Misc. 647, 15 N.Y.S.2d 864 (1939).
14. United States v. Drisko, 303 F. Supp. 858 (E.D. Va. 1969); Hunter v. Shell Oil Co., 198 F.2d 485 (5th Cir. 1952).
15. Adkins v. Moody, 228 Ark. 175, 306 S.W.2d 333 (1957); Blackburn's Administratrix v. Union Bank & Trust Co., 269 Ky. 699, 108 S.W.2d 806 (1937); Polley v. Daniels, 289 App. Div. 181, 264 N.Y.S. 194 (1933); Sears, Roebuck & Co. v. Kelly, 1 Misc. 2d 624, 149 N.Y.S.2d 133 (1956).
16. Stauter v. Walnut Grove Prods., 188 N.W.2d 305 (Iowa 1971).
17. Cleaveland v. Gabriel, 149 Conn. 388, 180 A.2d 749 (1962).
18. For example, when an agent cannot legally perform himself or it is impractical for him to perform. See, Cleaveland v. Gabriel, 149 Conn. 388, 180 A.2d 749 (1962).
19. For example, when the principal deposits a check in his agent bank but the check is drawn at another bank in a distant location, it is understood by the principal that the agent bank will forward the check to a correspondent bank for collection. In this case, the correspondent bank becomes an agent of the principal rather than a subagent of the forwarding bank. Should the collection bank be negligent or otherwise cause loss to the principal, he may hold it directly liable and not the forwarding bank. The only way the forwarding bank can be held liable to the principal is if it was in breach of its duty to exercise due care in selecting the correspondent bank. UCC, sects. 4-201(1), 4-202(3), 4-204.
20. Knudsen v. Torrington Co. 254 F.2d 283 (2d Cir. 1958); Cowan v. Pearson, 354 P.2d 194 (Okla. 1959).
21. Cowart v. Jordan, 75 Ga. App. 855, 44 S.E.2d 804 (1947).
22. Great Atl. & Pac. Tea Co. v. Noppenberger, 171 Md. 378, 189 A. 434 (1937).
23. Ford v. Wisconsin Real Estate Examining Bd., 48 Wisc. 2d 91, 179 N.W.2d 786 (1970).
24. Restatement, Second, Agency, Sect. 389 (b) and Sect. 418 (1958) state that notice to the agent would not constitute notice to the principal because the agent is privileged to protect his own interests when these are adverse to those of his principal. However, Sections 271 and 275 note that the principal would still be bound by his "imputed knowledge" even where his agent had adverse interests unless the third party knew or should have known of such adverse interests.
25. McCollum v. Clothier, 121 Utah 311, 241 P. 2d 468 (1952); Flinsch v. Viele, Blackwell and Buch, 194 App. Div. 460, 185 N.Y.S. 520 (1920). However, there is a different result with a gratuitous agent. As long as no services were requested by the principal and the services do not discharge an obligation owed by the principal, the principal has no duty to compensate the other even though he may have benefited from such services. See, for example, Rogers v. Garrigues, 185 Md. 544, 45 A. 2d 277 (1946); Spencer v. General Electric Co., 243 F. 2d 934 (8th Cir. 1957); and Silver v. Missouri, K. & T. Railway Co., 125 Mo. App. 402, 102 S.W. 621 (1907). Restatement, Second, Agency, Sects. 441, 443-449 deal with the principal's duty to compensate his agent and Sects. 438-440 (1958) deal with his duty to indemnify his agent.
26. The agreement may also provide that the agent is not to be paid merely upon completion but upon completion to the

satisfaction of the principal. See, the Restatement of Contracts, sect. 265 (1932); Ard Dr. Pepper Bottling Co. v. Dr. Pepper Co., 202 F. 2d 372 (5th Cir. 1953). The contract may also expressly provide that services be completed within a specified time as a condition precedent to payment. See, Smith v. Gilbraltar Oil Co., 254 F. 2d 518 (10th Cir. 1958); Walker v. American Optical Corp., 509 P. 2d 439 (Ore. 1973).

27. Sundland v. Korfund Co., 260 App. Div. 80, 20 N.Y.S. 2d 819 (1940); La Forge v. Cornell, 127 N.Y.S. 453 (1911); Palmer v. Pirson, 4 Misc. 455, 24 N.Y.S. 333 (1893); Cahill v. Gilman, 84 Misc. 372, 146 N.Y.S. 224 (1914); Labinsks v. Holst, 84 N.Y.S. 991 (1903).
28. Bacon v. Fourth National Bank, 9 N.Y.S. 435 (1889); Howe v. Buffalo, New York and Erie R.R. Co., 37 N.Y. 297 (1867). In re Lessig's Estate, 165 Misc. 706, 1 N.Y.S. 2d 566 (1937).
29. Buckley v. City of New York, 170 Misc. 412, 10 N.Y.S. 2d 650 (1939); Vogel v. Graham, 167 N.Y.S. 886 (1917).
30. Restatement, Second, Agency, Sect. 466 (1958).
31. Sidella Export Import Corp. v. Rosen, 273 App. Div. 490, 78 N.Y.S. 2d 155 (1948).

Case 16

Freeport Ridge Estates, Ltd. v. Reckner

266 So.2d 129 (Fla. 1972)

Introduction

Agents frequently hire subagents to assist them in the performance of their duties. Where the agreement between principal and agent is silent or ambiguous as to whether the agent has authority to hire subagents, the question arises whether the agent has implied authority to do so and what are the rights, duties, and liabilities of agent, subagent, and principal. The following case illustrates the judicial analysis applied to resolve these important questions.

Per Curiam

In an action for services and goods sold and delivered appellant, co-defendant below, seeks review of an adverse final judgment in the amount of $39,650.

The record on appeal reflects that Canaveral International Corporation is a publicly owned holding corporation which conducts various businesses through wholly owned subsidiaries. One such wholly owned corporation is Freeport Ridge Estates, Ltd., an organization which owned, developed and subdivided a large tract of land on Grand Bahama Island for the purpose of selling lots to members of the public at a profit. Heritage Land Sales, Inc. is a corporation founded in 1964 for the express purpose of acting as a sales broker, promoter and agent for the sale of real estate in the Bahamas. Most of the stock in Heritage was owned by Bert Dubbin, the son of Canaveral's board chairman, Henry Dubbin, and nephew of Canaveral and Freeport's president, Daniel Dubbin. The familial relationships that existed between the Dubbins was the only link Heritage had with Canaveral and Freeport. Canaveral and Freeport did not own any of Heritage's stock nor did they place any person upon Heritage's board of directors.

In 1965 Heritage entered into an agreement with Freeport to act as Freeport's broker or agent for the sale of Bahamian lots. Heritage was to get a commission on each lot sold and on two subsequent occasions the commission Heritage was to receive increased. This increase was due in part to Heritage's mounting financial problems and as these problems increased, the operational relationship between these two corporations became closer. Heritage moved from its main offices into the Canaveral Building and over a two and one-half year period Freeport advanced to Heritage between $600,000 and $700,000. These advances allowed Heritage to operate and provide working capital that was used for, among other things, payrolls and advertising. In the beginning of 1967, Daniel Dubbin, president of Freeport, had his secretary become a signatory on all checks written by Heritage to make certain that the funds were being properly disbursed. Eventually the relationship of Heritage and Canaveral and Freeport was terminated and the uncollected sums owed by Heritage were written off as bad debts.

Richard G. Reckner, appellee, was retained to fly prospective buyers from the United States to Grand Bahama Island to view lots that were for sale. When Reckner was first hired he met with Bert Dubbin and Daniel Dubbin to discuss the proposed operation and an oral contract was entered. Reckner was to be in charge of the flights, hire the pilots and maintain the airplanes used for the flights. The plane service commenced in September, 1966 and for his services Reckner was to bill Heritage although he did not know the exact relationship between Freeport and Heritage. Evidence of Freeport's subsequent control over Reckner include: Reckner's schedules were set by Freeport executives, any problems he had were to be taken to a Freeport vice president, he acted as a private pilot for Daniel Dubbin in an aircraft owned by one of Canaveral's subsidiaries, and the bills submitted to Heritage were subject to approval by Freeport.

During the deterioration of Heritage's financial position, Reckner had difficulty receiving payment for bills submitted to Heritage and as the amount increased, Reckner sought payment from Freeport but was told he could only collect from Heritage. The flights were discontinued after June, 1967, after which date all payments to Reckner ceased with an outstanding bill of $39,650 and a plan was arranged to help satisfy the debt owed to Reckner. Reckner agreed to purchase certain lots for which Heritage would earn its standard commission from Freeport. When the commission was received by Heritage it would be paid to Reckner, then he would endorse the check over to Freeport as the down payment for the lots. The balance of the sale price for the lots was reflected by a purchase money mortgage. Reckner planned to sell the lots at a profit.

On June 30, 1967 the plan was put into effect and Reckner received a check from Heritage for $25,600 which he then endorsed over to Freeport. Reckner, however, was unable to sell any of the lots and defaulted on his mortgage payments to Freeport. This lawsuit was brought against Freeport and Canaveral to recover the total amount owed to Reckner, $39,650. At trial the jury returned a verdict in favor of Reckner for $39,650 and this appeal was taken by Freeport and Canaveral.

Relying upon the record on appeal, the relationship between Freeport and Reckner was one of principal and sub-agent. An overview of the facts clearly establishes that Heritage, by reason of Freeport's complete control of financial affairs and policy decisions, was the agent of Freeport and that Reckner was to function as a sub-agent. In his capacity as a sub-agent appointed pursuant to the implied authority of the principal, Reckner in the absence of an express agreement to the contrary which does not exist in the instant case, can look directly to the principal for his compensation.

The power of an agent to delegate authority to a sub-agent is proper if the delegation merely involves a ministerial act such as the showing of land. Reckner's duty to fly prospective purchases to Grand Bahama Island will qualify as the requisite ministerial act.

The $25,600 received by Reckner from Heritage used in part payment of his purchase of the Bahamian lots should reduce the jury's verdict of $39,650 to $14,050. The plan initiated by the parties and this sum of money was voluntarily accepted by Reckner and he cannot now be heard to the contrary.

For the reasons stated, the judgment is affirmed in part and modified in part as set out herein, and the cause is remanded to the Circuit Court for further proceedings not inconsistent herewith.

Discussion questions

1. How could the principal have avoided the result in this case? Why?
2. Under what circumstances may an agent appoint a subagent? Why?

Case 17

Tarnowski v. Resop

51 N.W.2d 801 (Minn. 1952)

Introduction

The agent owes his principal the fiduciary duty of undivided loyalty and the duty to act in good faith at all times. When an agent breaches this significant duty, not only may his principal disaffirm the agent's contract made in the principal's name with a third party who bribes his agent, but he may also seek damages from his agent. The following case illustrates how a court assesses damages against the agent and what limitations exist in determining damages.

Knutson, Justice

Plaintiff desired to make a business investment. He engaged defendant as his agent to investigate and negotiate for the purchase of a route of coin-operated music machines. On June 2, 1947, relying upon the advice of defendant and the investigation he had made, plaintiff purchased such a business from Phillip Loechler and Lyle Mayer of Rochester, Minnesota, who will be referred to hereinafter as sellers. The business was located at LaCrosse, Wisconsin, and throughout the surrounding territory. Plaintiff alleges that defendant represented to him that he had made a thorough investigation of the route; that it had 75 locations in operation; that one or more machines were at each location; that the equipment at each location was not more than six months old; and that the gross income from all locations amounted to more than $3,000 per month. As a matter of fact, defendant had made only a superficial investigation and had investigated only five of the locations. Other than that, he had adopted false representations of the sellers as to the other locations and had passed them on to plaintiff as his own. Plaintiff was to pay $30,620 for the business. He paid $11,000 down. About six weeks after the purchase, plaintiff discovered that the representations made to him by defendant were false, in that there were not more than 47 locations; that at some of the locations there were no machines and at others there were machines more than six months old, some of them being seven years old; and that the gross income was far less than $3,000 per month. Upon discovering the falsity of defendant's representations and those of the sellers, plaintiff rescinded the sale. He offered to return what he had received, and he demanded the return of his money. The sellers refused to comply, and he brought suit against them in the district court of Olmsted county. The action was tried, resulting in a verdict of $10,000 for plaintiff. Thereafter, the sellers paid plaintiff $9,500, after which the action was dismissed with prejudice pursuant to a stipulation of the parties.

In this action, brought in Hennepin county, plaintiff alleges that defendant, while acting as agent for him, collected a secret commission from the sellers for consummating the sale, which plaintiff seeks to recover under his first cause of action. In his second cause of action, he seeks to recover damages for (1) losses suffered in operating the route prior to rescission; (2) loss of time devoted to operation; (3) expenses in connection therewith; (4) nontaxable expenses in connection with prosecution of the suit against the sellers; and (5) attorneys' fees in connection with the suit. The case was tried to a jury, and plaintiff recovered a verdict of $5,200. This appeal is from the judgment entered pursuant thereto.

Defendant contends that after recovery of a verdict by plaintiff in his action for rescission against the sellers he cannot maintain this action against defendant. Principally, defendant argues that recovery in the action against the sellers is a bar to this action for the following reasons: (1) That plaintiff has elected one of alternative remedies and cannot thereafter pursue another; (2) that successful pursuit of one remedy constitutes a bar to another remedy for the same wrong, even though the outcome of the first action did not make plaintiff whole in point of actual loss; (3) that the satisfied verdict in the rescission case is a bar; and (4) that defendant and the sellers were joint tort-feasors, and the discharge of one discharged them all.

1. With respect to plaintiff's first cause of action, the principle that all profits made by an agent in the course of an agency belonging to the principal, whether they are the fruits of performance or the violation of an agent's duty, is firmly established and universally recognized. . . . It matters not that the principal has suffered no damage or even that the transaction has been profitable to him. . . .

The rule and the basis therefore are well stated in Lum v. McEwen, 56 Minn. 278, 282, 57 N.W. 662, where, speaking through Mr. Justice Mitchell, we said: "Actual injury is not the principle the law proceeds on, in holding such transactions void. Fidelity in the agent is what is aimed at, and, as a means of securing it, the law will not permit him to place himself in a position in which he may be tempted by his own private interests to disregard those of his principal. . . . It is not material that no actual injury to the company (principal) resulted, or that the policy recommended may have been for its best interest. Courts will not inquire into these matters. It is enough to know that the agent in fact placed himself in such relations that he might be tempted by his own interests to disregard those of his principal. The transaction was nothing more or less than the acceptance by the agent of a bribe to perform his duties in the manner desired by the person who gave the bribe. Such a contract is void. This doctrine rests on such plain principles of law, as well as common business honesty, that the citation of authorities is unnecessary."

The right to recover profits made by the agent in the course of the agency is not affected by the fact that the principal, upon discovering a fraud, has rescinded the contract and recovered that with which he parted. Restatement, Agency, § 407 (2). Comment e on Subsection (2) reads: "If an agent has violated a duty of loyalty to the principal so that the principal is entitled to profits which the agent has thereby made, the fact that the principal has brought an action against a third person and has been made whole by such action does not prevent the principal from recovering from the agent the profits which the agent has made. Thus, if the other contracting party has given a bribe to the agent to make a contract with him on behalf of the principal, the principal can rescind the transaction, recovering from the other party anything received by him, or he can maintain an action for damages against him; in either event the principal may recover from the agent the amount of the bribe."

2. Plaintiff's second cause of action is brought to recover damages for (1) losses suffered in the operation of the business prior to rescission; (2) loss of time devoted to operation; (3) expenses in connection with rescission of the sale and investigation

therewith; (4) nontaxable expenses in connection with the prosecution of the suit against the sellers; and (5) attorneys' fees in connection with the suit.

The case comes to us on a bill of exceptions. No part of the testimony of the witnesses is included, so we must assume that the evidence establishes the items of damage claimed by plaintiff. Our inquiry is limited to a consideration of the question whether a principal may recover of an agent who has breached his trust the items of damage mentioned after a successful prosecution of an action for rescission against the third parties with whom the agent dealt for his principal.

The general rule is stated in Restatement, Agency, § 407 (1), as follows: "If an agent has received a benefit as a result of violating his duty of loyalty, the principal is entitled to recover from him what he has so received, its value, or its proceeds, and also the amount of damage thereby caused, except that if the violation consists of the wrongful disposal of the principal's property, the principal cannot recover its value and also what the agent received in exchange therefore."

In Comment a on Subsection (1) we find the following: " . . . In either event, whether or not the principal elects to get back the thing improperly dealt with or to recover from the agent its value or the amount of benefit which the agent has improperly received, he is, in addition, entitled to be indemnified by the agent for any loss which has been caused to his interest by the improper transaction. Thus, if the purchasing agent for a restaurant purchases with the principal's money defective food, receiving a bonus therefore, and the use of the food in the restaurant damages the business, the principal can recover from the agent the amount of money improperly expended by him, the bonus which the agent received, and the amount which will compensate for the injury to the business."

The general rule with respect to damages for a tortious act is that "The wrong-doer is answerable for all the injurious consequences of his tortious act, which according to the usual course of events and the general experience were likely to ensue, and which, therefore, when the act was committed, he may reasonably be supposed to have foreseen and anticipated." . . . The general rule is given in Restatement, Torts, § 910, as follows: "A person injured by the tort of another is entitled to recover damages from him for all harm, past, present, and prospective, legally caused by the tort."

Bergquist v. Kreidler, 158 Minn. 127, 196 N.W. 964, involved an action to recover attorneys' fees expended by plaintiffs in an action seeking to enforce and protect their right to the possession of real estate. Defendant, acting as the owner's agent, had falsely represented to plaintiffs that they could have possession on August 1, 1920. It developed after plaintiffs had purchased the premises that a tenant had a lease running to August 1, 1922, on a rental much lower than the actual value of the premises. Defendant (the agent) conceded that plaintiffs were entitled to recover the loss in rent, but contended that attorneys' fees and disbursements expended by plaintiffs in testing the validity of the tenant's lease were not recoverable. In affirming plaintiffs' right to recover we said, " . . . the litigation in which plaintiffs became involved was the direct, legitimate, and a to be expected result of appellant's misrepresentation. The loss sustained by plaintiffs in conducting that litigation 'is plainly traceable' to appellant's wrong and he should make compensation accordingly."

So far as the right to recover attorneys' fees is concerned, the same may be said in this case. Plaintiff sought to return what had been received and demanded a return of his own down payment. The sellers refused. He thereupon sued to accomplish this purpose, as he had a right to do, and was successful. His attorneys' fees and expenses of suit were directly traceable to the harm caused by defendant's wrongful act. As such, they are recoverable.

The Bergquist case is distinguished in the later case of Stickney v. Goward, 161 Minn. 457, 201 N.W. 630, 39 A.L.R. 1216, where he held that attorneys' fees might not be recovered in a separate suit against the same parties that were involved in a prior suit. That situation does not prevail here. In this case, defendant was not a party to the suit against the sellers. As in the Bergquist case, the attorneys' fees and expenses of litigation against the sellers became necessary because of defendant's tortious conduct. The general rule applicable here is stated in 15 Am.Jur., Damages, § 144, as follows: "It is generally held that where the wrongful act of the defendant has involved the plaintiff in litigation with others or placed him in such relation with others as makes it necessary to incur expense to protect his interest, such costs and expenses, including attorneys' fees, should be treated as the legal consequences of the original wrongful act and may be recovered as damages."

The same is true of the other elements of damage involved. . . .

3. Defendant contends that plaintiff had an election of remedies and, having elected to proceed against the sellers to recover what he had paid, is now barred from proceeding against defendant. It is true that upon discovery of the fraud plaintiff had an election of remedies against the sellers. It is not true, however, that, having elected to sue for recovering of that with which he had parted, he is barred from proceeding against his agent to recover damages for his tortious conduct. While some of the allegations in plaintiff's complaint against the sellers are similar to or identical with those in his complaint in this case, insofar as the fraud is concerned, the right of recovery here against the agent goes much further than the action against the sellers. Many of the elements of damage against the agent are not available to plaintiff against the sellers. For instance, he has no right to recover attorneys' fees and expenses of the litigation against the sellers. He has that right against the agent. Plaintiff may recover profits made by the agent, irrespective of his recovery against the sellers. Losses directly flowing from the agent's tortious conduct are not recoverable against the sellers in an action for rescission, but they may be recovered against the agent, whose breach of faith has caused such losses.

4. Nor is the settlement and dismissal of the action against the sellers a bar to an action against the agent, for the same reasons as stated above. The sellers and agent are not joint tort-feasors in the sense that their wrongful conduct necessarily grows out of the same wrong. Their individual torts may have been based on the same fraud, but their liabilities to plaintiff do not have the same limitations. In simple terms, the causes of action are not the same.

Defendant relies principally upon Martin v. Setter, 184 Minn. 457, 239 N.W. 219, 80 A.L.R. 471. In that case, plaintiffs and defendant contracted to exchange land. One Rieger acted as agent for defendant in the transaction. In a suit to recover for a default, defendant interposed a counterclaim for damages alleged to have resulted from fraudulent representations as to the value of the land which defendant received in the trade. It developed that defendant had instituted an action against his agent, Rieger, to recover damages for the identical misrepresentations plaintiffs were charged with, and that defendant had made a settlement with Rieger and had dismissed his action against Rieger with prejudice. We held that Rieger and plaintiffs were joint tort-feasors; that the action asserted against Rieger and the one against plaintiffs were one and the same; consequently, that a release of Rieger released plaintiffs.

The case is readily distinguishable from the instant case. The Martin case was not one for rescission. There, defendant's counterclaim sought to recover his damages, he retaining what he had received. He had previously settled an action brought against his agent to recover the same damages. In the case now before us, the two actions, though based on the same fraud, are not the same, as we have pointed out above. The Martin case is not authority for the proposition for which defendant now contends. Settlement of the action for rescission against the sellers is not a bar to an action against the agent to recover those elements of damages not involved in the action for rescission brought against the sellers.

Affirmed.

Discussion questions

1. Are there any circumstances where an agent can keep something of value that he received from a third party in connection with the contract made by the agent on his principal's behalf with the third party? Why?
2. Is there any way the principal could have avoided liability for his agent's fraud in this case? Why?

Case 18

Berenson v. Nirenstein et al

93 N.E.2d 610
(Mass. 1950)

Introduction

In the event an agent breaches his fiduciary duty to his principal, the wrongful profits reaped by the agent may be reached by the principal. The following case illustrates the judicial response and judicial remedy available to the aggrieved principal.

Qua, Chief Justice

Material allegations of the amended bill may be summarized as follows: The plaintiff lives in Newton and does business in Boston. The defendant Nirenstein lives and does business in Springfield. In January, 1949, Nirenstein called on the plaintiff in Boston, stated that all the shares of Bowles Lunch, Inc., which had its principal business in Springfield, could be purchased, and offered "to act as agent and broker for the plaintiff in seeking to buy" these shares. The plaintiff expressed interest. Nirenstein handed to the plaintiff detailed audits of Bowles Lunch, Inc., and "represented that he was peculiarly in a position to negotiate a purchase of these shares of stock on behalf of the plaintiff because of his knowledge of the situation and his acquaintance with the parties" in Springfield. The plaintiff then "retained the defendant (Nirenstein) as his broker and agent to effect a purchase of the shares of stock at an agreed commission of Five Dollars ($5.00) per share, to be paid by the plaintiff to the defendant (Nirenstein) at the time when such purchase was consummated, and the defendant (Nirenstein) agreed to act as such broker and agent on behalf of the plaintiff and to use his best efforts to purchase said shares of stock for him." After further conferences and some negotiations by Nirenstein, the plaintiff authorized that defendant to make a firm offer of $70 a share for four thousand seven hundred four shares held by certain trustees. Thereafter Nirenstein, while still representing to the plaintiff that he was acting in the plaintiff's behalf, entered into a written agreement with the trustees for the purchase of the shares himself at $70 a share.

There are further allegations to the effect that the defendant Bowles, with knowledge of the defendant Nirenstein's fiduciary obligations to the plaintiff, induced Nirenstein to break them, to the profit of Bowles, who has acquired some of the assets of the corporation; and that after the bringing of this suit, and after the plaintiff in reliance upon an oral agreement for the settlement of the entire case had permitted a restraining order to be dissolved, the defendant Nirenstein repudiated the settlement, completed his purchase of the stock and started to liquidate the corporation. The prayers are for injunctive relief, that Nirenstein be held as trustee of the purchase agreement and the stock, that Nirenstein and Bowles be required to account for profits or damages, and that the stock be reached and applied in satisfaction of what is found due.

The trial judge sustained demurrers to the bill and stated, not without considerable justification, that he did so in reliance upon Salter v. Beal, 321 Mass. 105, 71 N.E.2d 872, and the cases there cited.

In Salter v. Beal the defendant had been employed by the plaintiff to appraise certain machinery which the plaintiff contemplated buying, and had bought the machinery for himself. This court held that no fiduciary obligation was shown. We do not intend to cast doubt upon the correctness of that decision on the facts. But we reached our conclusion in that case largely, though not wholly, because of a line of cases which appeared to be "authority for the proposition that a mere engagement to buy in behalf of another without more is not deemed in this Commonwealth to create a fiduciary relation." . . . For convenience, we repeat the citations of these cases in the footnote. On the other hand, it is established by a long line of decisions here and elsewhere that the relation of principal and broker is a fiduciary one involving trust and confidence. And a fiduciary is ordinarily chargeable as constructive trustee for the benefit of one rightfully entitled to property acquired by the fiduciary in breach of trust. Restatement: Restitution, § § 190, 194.

So far as we are aware this is the first time when possible conflict between these two lines of cases has been squarely brought to the attention of this court by the issues and the argument in any case, and it has become necessary to consider them in relation to each other. The fiduciary obligation toward his principal of one who is acting in the full sense as a broker in the sale or purchase of property rests upon fundamental principles of business morality and honor which are of the highest public interest, and which it is the bounden duty of courts to preserve unimpaired. We do not believe that in deciding the cases listed in the first footnote the court had in mind a case where the full relation of principal and broker existed. That the court at one time thought a constructive trust might arise in such a case seems apparent from the reasoning of Chief Justice Knowlton in Clark v. Delano, 205 Mass.224,91 N.E.299,29 L.R.A., N.S.,595. It may be significant that in all of the cases in the first list, so far as appears, the relation between the parties was substantially different from that ordinarily obtaining between principal and broker, and in none of them is the principal and broker relation mentioned. Even if this is not a wholly satisfactory distinction, we are nevertheless impelled to the conclusion that at least where, by the conduct of the parties, the full relation of principal and broker has come into existence, including the carrying on of a negotiation between seller and buyer, there has come into existence with it a confidential and fiduciary relation which gives rise to a constructive trust in favor of the principal in property which the broker has acquired for himself in violation of his duty to his principal. We by no means suggest that all of the cases in the first list were wrongly decided, but we do hold that in so far as broad expressions in some of them might be thought at variance with what has just been stated such expressions must be deemed to be qualified by what is here said. That other courts have struggled with similar problems and have reached differing conclusions appears from many cases collected in 42 A.L.R. 28, and 135 A.L.R.236.

We think that the amended bill in this case sufficiently alleges the existence of a full and complete relation of principal and broker between the plaintiff and the defendant Nirenstein, out of which arose all the fiduciary obligations incident to such a relation, and that the bill sufficiently shows a breach of such obligations by the defendant Nirenstein at the instigation and to the profit of the defendant Bowles. The bill can therefore stand on the theory of a constructive trust in the shares of stock and their proceeds. . . .

The interlocutory decrees sustaining the demurrers of the defendants Nirenstein and Bowles are reversed, and decrees are to be entered overruling the demurrers. The final decree dismissing the bill is reversed, with costs to the plaintiff.

So ordered.

Discussion questions

1. According to this decision would a fiduciary relationship arise if the prospective buyer of the stock merely asked the broker to *evaluate* the stock being offered for sale rather than to purchase it as an agent for the buyer? Why?
2. If there is no fiduciary relationship under the facts stated in the preceding question, how could the prospective buyer protect himself from the possibility that the broker might appropriate the opportunity to buy the stock? Why?

Case 19

Colonell v. Goodman

78 F. Supp.845
(D.C.E.D.Penn. 1948)

Introduction

Included within the agent's fiduciary duty of undivided loyalty and good faith is the duty not to do anything which competes with his principal's interests. The following case illustrates this rule of law and the operative effect it has when the agent tries to recover the fruits of his own wrong from third parties.

Kirkpatrick, District Judge

The plaintiff brought this action upon a contract by which, as he alleges, he was promised, for services in connection with the sale of the business of Parkway Oil Company, one of the defendants, a commission of five per cent upon the sale price.

The case was tried to the Court with a jury. The verdict was for the plaintiff and against all the defendants except David Pleet. The other defendants have filed a motion for judgment under Federal Rules of Civil Procedure; Rule 50(b), 28 U.S.C.A. following section 723c, and also an alternative motion for a new trial.

The following is the substance of the plaintiff's case:

From 1937 until 1945 he was in the employ of American Oil Company as sales manager in charge of sales for Pennsylvania and six other states.

In 1939 and 1940 Parkway Oil Company, which operated a number of service stations in Philadelphia, was under contract with American to buy all its oil and gasoline from the latter. It was not, however, an exclusive distributor.

The plaintiff, beginning in the early part of 1939, in pursuance of his duties as sales manager for American, had numerous contacts and interviews with Goodman, the president of Parkway, in the course of which he made a number of suggestions for the improvement of its business and gave advice and assistance. During 1939 and the early part of 1940, the possibility of the plaintiff's leaving American and becoming interested in Parkway, either as a part owner or as an employee, was discussed. There never was any definite agreement but the plaintiff had some reason to think that the talk would lead to one.

In February or March, 1940, the plaintiff told Goodman that if he was to become financially interested in Parkway he would want it to have an exclusive distributorship and suggested that the Texas Company, a competitor of American, was the logical concern to negotiate with, adding that he was acquainted with a number of the Texas Company officials. Goodman agreed and authorized him to see the Texas Company with a view to obtaining an exclusive distributorship from it.

The plaintiff went to New York where he interviewed one of the Texas vice-presidents and learned from him that Texas would not give an exclusive distributorship. However, in view of what was said at the interview, he came to the conclusion that Texas might be interested in purchasing Parkway and, on his return to Philadelphia, so advised Goodman. He, however, pointed out to Goodman that if Texas should buy Parkway there would be no possibility of his obtaining an interest in or employment with Parkway, whereupon Goodman promised him that if a sale to Texas should be consummated he would receive a commission of five per cent. At the same time Goodman told the plaintiff that he, Goodman, would handle all future negotiations with the Texas Company.

Thereafter from time to time over a period of more than a year, Goodman told the plaintiff that he was in contact with Texas and, although the plaintiff did not himself have any further direct dealings with Texas, he assisted Goodman in preparing data of various kinds to submit to Texas, showing the value of the Parkway properties and its financial position, and also advised Goodman as to the proper method of approach and what steps to take in the conduct of the negotiations.

At the end of 1941, the war caused a suspension of all further efforts to sell until the latter part of 1944, at which time Goodman told the plaintiff that Texas was again interested. Goodman reiterated his promise to pay the five per cent commission and the plaintiff resumed his activities in connection with the negotiations which consisted, as before, of advice and assistance to Goodman without any direct dealing on the plaintiff's part with Texas.

In June, 1945, the plaintiff learned through a third party that Parkway had been sold to Texas and went to see Goodman who confirmed the news and also told the plaintiff that he would not get any commission.

The foregoing facts, which represent the evidence in its most favorable light to the plaintiff, present the case of an important official of a corporation, entrusted particularly with the promotion and maintenance of sales, who, without his employer's knowledge, sets about detaching one of his employer's largest customers and endeavoring to give its business to one of his employer's competitors, his purpose being to improve the business position of the customer with which he hopes (though without any definite assurance) to associate himself. When it appears that the competitor may be interested in purchasing the customer's business outright, he informs the customer of that fact, makes a contract with the customer to receive a commission on the sale and thereafter continues to advise and consult with the customer in the negotiations until the sale is consummated.

As to the nature of the cause of action; the plaintiff, in his complaint and consistently throughout the trial, maintained that the action was by an agent to recover a commission, under an express contract by which it was agreed that if a sale of the property was effected the commission would be paid in consideration of the agent's having brought the purchaser to his principal, the understanding being that the plaintiff's right to his commission would accrue when the sale was made, without regard to how or by whom the result was finally accomplished. In view of the large amount of the commission claimed and the comparatively small amount of work done by the plaintiff, as well as of the fact that the work had been done when the promise was made, the Court in the course of the trial, in conference with counsel, suggested that the plaintiff might be basing his action not on a claim for commission as such but on a promise of compensation in return for his failure to receive an interest in Parkway. This theory was expressly repudiated by plaintiff's counsel and the case was argued by counsel and submitted to the jury on the sole theory that the plaintiff was claiming an agent's commission on a sale.

The plaintiff, as a managing official or executive of a corporation, owed it a fiduciary as well as a contractual duty. "An agent is a fiduciary with respect to matters within the scope of his agency.", Restatement, Agency, Sec. 13.

> . . . any bargain that tends to induce a violation of a fiduciary's duty as such, is illegal except when effectively consented to by the beneficiary or principal . . . Restatement, Contracts, Sec. 570. Broad considerations of public policy condemn such contracts.

It can hardly be asserted, nor could a jury find, that a promise by a third party to compensate a sales manager of a corporation for his services in taking a large customer away from his employer is not one that tends to induce a violation of his duty. A bargain which, it seems to me, was less clearly against the employer's interest and not so great a deviation from the employee's duty as that in the present case put the plaintiff out of court in Pollock v. MacElree, D.C.56 F.Supp. 961, 963, Judge Kalodner observing "Obviously the Court should not assist the plaintiff to profit in this unconscionable transaction." Reiner v. North American Newspaper Alliance, 259 N.Y. 250, 181 N.E.561, 564, 83 A.L.R. 23, was a bargain which committed the plaintiff to a breach of his contract with a third person, but the opinion of Judge Crane contains a statement of public policy transcending the precise situation before the Court. He said, "Fraud, deceit, breach of trust, are general terms covering divers situations and circumstances, and seldom yield to definition or limitation; in other words, the facts differ in every case, but the principle remains the same."

It is true that, as stated in Sec. 393(e), Restatement, Agency, that an employee who expects to terminate his employment may, before the close of his employment, make certain arrangements to establish himself in a new business, even with a view toward competing with his employer. "He may not, however, before the termination of his employment, solicit customers for such rival business, nor may he do other similar acts in direct competition with the employer's business.", Restatement, Agency, Sec. 393(e). I do not believe that the plaintiff in the present case, even during the time when he had some prospect of becoming associated with Parkway, was justified in working, without his employer's knowledge, to switch Parkway's business from his employer to a competitor. However, that question is really not in the case because when he concluded, after his first interview with the Texas people, that they would not give Parkway a distributorship and made up his mind to advise Parkway of a possible sale and to do what he could to promote the sale, he ceased to be an employee planning to terminate his employment and became an employee working for compensation against his employer's interests.

There was some rather equivocal testimony on the part of the plaintiff to the effect that American was not greatly interested in retaining Parkway as a customer. In view of the facts that no witness was called to substantiate this testimony, that American renewed its contract with Parkway, after the plaintiff made his contract with Goodman, for a further period of three years during which period American could have cancelled on six months' notice but did not, and the further fact that the plaintiff did not advise American of what he was doing (and in fact made some effort to conceal it by directing Texas to write him at his home address), no finding could have been made that his violation of duty was "effectively consented to by the beneficiary or principal of the fiduciary." Restatement, Contracts, Sec. 570. Beyond all this, however, it is to be remembered that the rule is a prophylactic one. "Actual injury is not the principle the law proceeds on, in holding such transactions void." Lum v. McEwen . . . '"the rule is not intended to be remedial of actual wrong, but preventive of the possibility of it.'" . . .

Out of what appeared to the Court an abundance of caution, the defendants at the close of the plaintiff's case offered an amendment to the answer, specifically raising the defense of illegality. The Court allowed the amendment but the defense could have been made just as well without it. "Thus, although illegality is an affirmative defense, if the illegality appears on the face of the contract, or from the opening statement of plaintiff's counsel, or from plaintiff's proof, the defendant could take advantage of it by proper motion, and if necessary the court will raise the objection itself."

Summing up, "The law leaves the plaintiff to be judged by his own standards; his complaint that the defendant treated him as he treated others falls upon deaf ears; the law is silent; it has nothing to say." Reiner v. North American Newspaper Alliance, supra.

Judgment may be entered for the defendants. . . .

Discussion questions

1. Would the court's decision be the same if the employee's agreement to assist the customer in the sale of its business to a competitor of the employee's principal involved a very small customer who the principal intended to terminate its business relationship with in the near future? Why?
2. Does the agent's fiduciary relationship survive termination of his employment and bar him from disclosing confidential information to a new employer he acquired during his former agency relationship in the absence of any express agreement when the new employer is in direct competition with the former employer? Why?

Case 20

Thompson v. Hoagland

242 A.2d 642
(N.J.1968)

Introduction

As Judge Cardozo has written, the agent's fiduciary duty of undivided loyalty to his principal and his duty to act in good faith at all times is "relentless and supreme". Within the parameters of this broad principle of law is the requirement that the agent make full disclosure to his principal of any circumstances that might reasonably be expected to influence the complete loyalty of the agent to the interests of his principal. The following case illustrates the application of this rule and the effect of the agent's breach upon his right to obtain compensation.

Conford, S.J.A.D.

Plaintiff, a real estate broker, appeals from the dismission by the Law Division at the end of plaintiff's case, in an action tried to the court without a jury, of his complaint for commissions earned in procuring a purchaser for defendants' real estate. Defendants had refused to enter into a contract of sale with the proposed purchaser. The action of the trial court was based upon the alleged failure of plaintiff to inform defendants that the purchaser was an individual with whom plaintiff had a number of joint investments in real estate.

There must be a reversal for the reason that there was some testimony on plaintiff's case which, if believed, would have permitted the court to find that plaintiff made substantial revelation to defendants of his relationship with the purchaser. It is true that under R.R. 4:42-2(b), the trial court was authorized, if it chose to do so, to decide the motion for involuntary dismissal at the end of plaintiff's case on its merits. But its remarks on granting the motion indicate that it was not purporting to find the facts against the plaintiff on the merits, but rather dealing with the motion as though the case were being tried before a jury. The court stated it was viewing the record "in its most favorable terms" to the plaintiff and not weighing the credibility or probative value of plaintiff's proofs but accepting them "all as true." On this approach, as will be demonstrated hereinafter, the plaintiff's proofs required a denial of the motion. Since the case must be retried, however, we will deal with another ground of reversal argued by plaintiff as well as with alternative grounds of affirmance advanced by defendants.

The following facts were developed on plaintiff's case. On June 11, 1963 plaintiff entered into a written, exclusive right-to-sell agreement with defendants for their 76-acre tract of land in Franklin Township for a period of 365 days. Sale was authorized at a price of $65,000, with terms specified. Commission was to be 10% of the sale price. In the agreement plaintiff undertook to advertise, offer and show the property for sale. Advertising was to be for a sale price of $70,000. Plaintiff advertised and showed the property to prospects, but without early success. Six to eight weeks later defendants sought an alteration of the agreement to fix the sale price at $80,000, but plaintiff refused. He did agree, however, to change the asking price to $80,000.

On April 22, 1964, one Dr. Abrams offered plaintiff $60,000, which was refused by defendants. On June 8, 1964 he offered $65,000. Again defendants refused. On or about June 8, 1964 plaintiff tendered defendants for execution Dr. Abrams' signed contract to purchase the property for $65,000, with terms as specified in the sales agreement. Dr. Abrams also deposited a $6,500 earnest-money check with plaintiff. Defendants rejected the contract. There was proof from which it could have been found that defendants at that time were resolved not to sell the property to anyone for $65,000, being satisfied that it was worth more.

As of the time of Dr. Abrams' offers, he and plaintiff jointly held three or four tracts of land which they had purchased for speculative purposes, and they were both stockholders, along with a number of other investors, in an active real estate investment corporation of which they were officers and directors. Plaintiff testified that when he was negotiating the brokerage agreement with defendants he informed them of his purchase with Dr. Abrams of a nearby tract, as the price was relevant to the question of the price to be fixed for the subject property. He gave equivocal testimony as to whether he told defendants about his other land investments with Dr. Abrams at the time the latter submitted his offers, but on cross-examination by the court he testified:

> The Court: So, then, you say you did tell the Hoaglands that Dr. Abrams was interested in the property and that you and he had some prior business relationships or partnership arrangements in properties you had bought in the past?
> The Witness (plaintiff): Right.
> The Court: And that he had offered $60,000?
> The Witness: That's correct.

We conclude that this testimony created at least a fact issue as to plaintiff's revelation to defendants of his association with Dr. Abrams, calling for controversion by the defense, and that it was therefore error to dismiss, at least in the absence of any purposed decision of the factual merits pursuant to R.R. 4:42-2(b). See supra.

Plaintiff argues that it is immaterial in any event whether he ever informed defendants of his association with Dr. Abrams since the proof is clear that circumstance was not material to their refusal to sell—they having decided to sell to no one at the figure listed in the agreement. We do not agree. If the failure to apprise defendants of the relationship bore upon a circumstance which could have generated a fair suspicion as to whether plaintiff had exercised his very best efforts as defendants' agent to obtain the best price possible for the property, this constituted an absolute defense to any action for a commission, whether or not defendants were in fact prejudiced by the nondisclosure. For reasons to be indicated, we are satisfied that plaintiff's relationship to Dr. Abrams was of a character requiring full apprisal of defendants thereof and their consent, express or implied, to the submission of an offer by him, in consequence of the fiduciary status of plaintiff toward defendants inherent in the broker-principal relationship.

Only recently the Supreme Court restated the fundamental relationship between broker and principal as follows:

> The broker was and is looked upon as a fiduciary and is required to exercise fidelity, good faith and primary devotion to the interests of his principal. . . . He cannot permit his interests to interfere with those of his principal. As the Court of Errors and Appeals said in Young v. Hughes, 32 N.J.#1.372, pp.384-385 (E. & A. 1880), the rule which applies to trustees has been equally applied to the relation between the real estate broker and his principal. He must show perfect good faith and openness of dealing. The rule was not intended to be remedial of actual wrong done alone, but also to be preventive of the possibility of it. (Emphasis ours). . . .

It is a corollary of the principle discussed above that failure of the broker to inform the principal that the purchaser he produces is an alter ego of the broker or a relative or partner renders the transaction voidable as between broker and principal at the option of the principal. . . . The rule is prophylactic in purpose, and, by the better view, not qualified by the actual bona fides of the broker in the matter or the absence of harm to the principal. . . . In this context the principal is entitled to be informed of "any circumstance that might reasonably be expected to influence the complete loyalty of the agent to the interest of his principal." . . .

We are satisfied that the close and continuing business relationship between plaintiff and Dr. Abrams, amounting in substance, although not with legal technicality, to a partnership in land speculation, was such as to foster a temptation on the part of plaintiff to favor the interests of his associate at the expense of undivided loyalty to defendants in submitting a purchase offer by the former. This brought the case within the spirit of the rule cited above making an undisclosed partner of the broker an impermissible source of an offer or purchase to be submitted to a principal-seller in purported satisfaction of the brokerage undertaking.

In view of the foregoing, if plaintiff failed to make the necessary disclosure it would be inconsequential that defendants refused to accept the offer because they did not desire to sell at the stipulated price to any one at all.

Defendants' alternative ground for sustaining the judgment in their favor—that they had revoked the brokerage agreement by their letter requesting a change in the selling price from $65,000 to $80,000—is not borne out by the evidence. Plaintiff's testimony was that defendants requested the modification but he refused to accede thereto. Moreover, it is doubtful whether in the case of an "exclusive right" agreement for a fixed period the principal can defeat the broker's right to earn a commission during that period by revoking the authorization. . . .

Judgment reversed; the cause is remanded for a new trial.

Discussion questions

1. The court reversed the lower court's dismissal of plaintiff's action for commissions earned at the end of plaintiff's case because "there was some testimony on plaintiff's case which, if believed, would have permitted the court to find that plaintiff made substantial revelation to defendants of his relationship with the purchaser." Must the "revelation" be in writing? Why?
2. The court held that even if the agent's failure to disclose his association with the prospective purchase to his principal was not the reason that induced his principal to breach his agreement to sell, his principal still had an absolute defense when sued for commissions. Would the agent be also barred from recovering his reasonable expenses for advertising the property for sale? Why?

Case 21

Herzog v. Capital Co.

California Supreme Court
27 Cal.2d 349, 164 P.2d 8 (1945)

Introduction

It is a fundamental rule of agency law that information acquired by the agent during the performance of his duties is imputed to his principal. The application of this rule is illustrated in the following case.

Gibson, C. J.

In June, 1938, defendants, acting through their local agent, Yakel, sold plaintiff a house in San Diego for $9,500, representing that it was in "sound condition" and "perfectly intact." The house began to leak badly during a heavy rain in January, 1940, and a subsequent inspection disclosed that the leakage was due to the use of defective materials and improper bracing. This action for damages for alleged fraud in the sale of the house resulted in a judgment in favor of plaintiff in the sum of $3,500. . . .

The complaint alleged that when plaintiff inspected the house, it had been freshly painted thereby concealing from him, or anyone else making a reasonable inspection of the premises, the defective condition which caused the leaks, and that since there were no heavy rains until January, 1940, he did not sooner discover that the house leaked. . . .

It is claimed, however, that the trial court erred in holding defendants liable because the agreement of sale expressly provided that there were no promises, representations, verbal understandings or agreements except those contained therein.

A defrauded purchaser is not precluded by a provision of this kind from rescinding and pursuing the innocent seller far enough to secure a return of the consideration paid (citing cases). Such a provision, however, will relieve an honest seller from liability for damages arising from the fraudulent representations of his negotiating agent (citing cases). This rule, of course, applies only to recovery of damages based upon the misrepresentations of the agent, and it does not exempt the principal from liability for his own conduct.

Although plaintiff was notified by the contract provision that Yakel had no authority to make representations or enter into verbal understandings in connection with the sale of the property, it is clear that Yakel knew of the defective condition of the house and that he was acting within the scope of his authority when he caused it to be refinished and newly painted, thereby effectually concealing the structural defects. The knowledge of an agent, which he is under a duty to disclose to his principal, is to be imputed to the principal (Rest., Agency, § 275), and, accordingly, defendants are charged with Yakel's knowledge. Under these circumstances they had a duty to reveal the hidden and material facts concealed by their agent and of which they had knowledge, and their failure to disclose them constituted fraud (citing cases). With respect to this positive duty of disclosure plaintiff could rely on Yakel's actual as well as ostensible authority, for the provision in the contract related only to the exclusion of liability for representations and verbal understandings. A principal under a positive duty to make a disclosure cannot escape liability for failure to do so by relying on a contract provision to the effect that there are no other representations except those contained in the written agreement. . . .

The judgment is affirmed.

Discussion questions

1. How could the principal have avoided this result? Why?
2. What rights, if any, does the principal have against his agent? Why?

Case 22
Jansen v. Williams
Nebraska Supreme Court
36 Neb. 869, 55 N.W. 279 (1893)

Introduction

One of the most important duties the agent owes his principal is the fiduciary duty of undivided loyalty and the duty to act in good faith at all times. The following case illustrates the application of this rule and the remedy given to the injured principal when the agent breaches his fiduciary duty.

Ryan, C.

This action was brought by the defendant in error to recover the sum of $100, retained as commission from the proceeds of the sale of real property, effected by the plaintiffs in error. . . .

It was fairly deducible from the testimony that Williams employed Jansen and Murphy to sell the real property in question; that he afterwards had negotiations with said Hartley for an exchange of said property for property owned by Mr. Hartley, of the fair value of $3,300; that Hartley, pending these negotiations, went to Messrs. Jansen and Murphy, and, learning from them that the property could be purchased from them for $3,000, he dropped the negotiations with Williams; that for some reason the title to the property was taken from Williams and wife to A.W. Jansen, one of the plaintiffs in error, whose identity with his agent of that name Williams testifies he was unaware of when said deed was executed; that Williams inquired of Murphy who was the purchaser, and was informed by Murphy that the purchaser did not wish his name known in the matter and therefore did not disclose it; that Jansen, in answer to the same inquiry of Williams, met it with the same refusal, at the same time saying that it made no difference, as the party was good. It was testified by Jansen and Murphy on the trial in the district court that the reason the title was taken in Jansen's name was, that Hartley was not able just then to advance the money to make the cash payment, and therefore this money was advanced by plaintiffs in error to insure the present consummation of the trade, rather than to wait ten or twelve days until Hartley would have money which would then be due him. . . .

At the request of the defendant in error the court instructed the jury as follows:

> An agent ought as far as possible to represent his principal, and to the best of his ability he should endeavor to successfully accomplish the object of his agency. It is also his duty to keep his principal fully and promptly informed of all the material facts or circumstances which come to his knowledge, and since he is expected to represent his principal, he cannot have a personal interest adverse to the interest of his principal, and if he deals with the subject-matter of the agency, the profits will, as a general rule, belong to the principal and not to the agent. In all things he is required to act in entire good faith towards his principal. There are duties which the law imposes upon an agent without any express stipulations on the subject, and one of these duties of an agent is to keep his principal informed of his acts, and to inform him within a reasonable time of sales made, and to give him a timely notice of all facts and circumstances which may render it necessary for him to take measures for his security. An agent cannot act for his principal and for himself in the same transaction by being both buyer and seller of property, and has no right to act as the agent for others for the purchase of property without the knowledge or consent of such owner, nor to take any advantage of the confidence which his position inspires to obtain the title in himself. If you find that the defendants were the agents of the plaintiff for the sale of the property mentioned in the petition, and that in making the sale they purposely kept from the plaintiff any of the material facts touching said sale for the purpose of subserving their own interest, and intended to and did keep the plaintiff in the dark as to such facts until after the said sale was consummated and deed executed by said plaintiff, then I instruct you that they are not entitled to a commission for selling the same. . . .

It is unnecessary to quote further illustrations of the correctness of the instructions given the jury at the request of the defendants in error. The same principles announced in these instructions pervade all the textworks and the decisions of the courts which have to deal with the relations of principal and agent. In none of them is recognized the right of the suppression of important facts of which the principal had a right to be informed as a part of the "secrets of the real estate business," as was claimed by plaintiff in error Murphy in his testimony. The evidence fully sustains the verdict which was rendered by the jury. Indeed, a verdict different would probably of necessity have been set aside, as has been shown by abundant citation of text-writers and authorities. The instructions clearly gave the law to the jury as applicable to the evidence, and the judgment of the district court must therefore be

Affirmed.

Discussion questions

1. Under what circumstances could the agent buy property that his principal authorizes him to sell for the principal? Why?
2. If the agent sells his principal's property as authorized and the third party afterwards gives the agent a gratuity, which was not agreed to in advance, would the agent be entitled to keep the gratuity or must he turn it over to his principal? Why?
3. Must the agent report every "innocent gratuity" he received to his principal which arises out of the agent's performance of his duties? Why?
4. If an agent makes a direct offer to buy his principal's property, after the principal rejected an earlier offer from someone the agent found, does the agent's fiduciary duty terminate when he submits his own offer in his own name? Why?
5. Would your answer to the prior question be the same if the agent resold the property to another at a large profit 30 days later? Why?

Case 23

Glenn v. Rice

174 Cal.269, 162P. 1020 (1917)

Introduction

It is a fundamental rule of agency law that a principal may not serve two masters at the same time unless both masters consent. In the following case the agent was not allowed to collect his commission even from the principal who knew of the double agency even though this resulted in a windfall for the principal. The court explained its reasoning as follows:

> The authorities, with practical unanimity, declare that if an agent is engaged by both parties to effect a sale of property from one to the other, or an exchange between them, not as a mere middleman to bring them together, but actively in inducing each to make the trade, he cannot recover compensation from either party, unless both parties knew of the double agency at the time of the transaction. The reason for the rule is that he thereby puts himself in a position where his duty to one conflicts with his duty to the other, where his own interests tempt him to be unfaithful to both principals, a position which is against sound public policy and good morals. His contract for compensation being thus tainted, the law will not permit him to enforce it against either party. It is no answer to this objection to say that he did, in the particular case, act fairly and honorably to both. The infirmity of his contract does not arise from his actual conduct in the given case, but from the policy of the law, which will not allow a man to gain anything from a relation so conducive to bad faith and double dealing. And the fact that the party whom he sues was aware of the double agency and of the payment, or agreement to pay, compensation by the other party, and consented thereto, does not entitle him to recover. He must show knowledge by both parties. One party might willingly consent, believing that the advantage would accrue to him, to the detriment of the other. The law will not tolerate such an arrangement, except with the knowledge and consent of both, and will enter into no inquiry to determine whether or not the particular negotiation was fairly conducted by the agent. It leaves him as it finds him, affording him no relief. (citing cases.)

Discussion questions

1. If the agent obtained buyer and seller's consent to the agent's dual representation, could he keep two commissions? Why?
2. Must an agent disclose the exact amount of commission he is receiving from each party to the other party he is also representing? Why?

Case 24

Columbus Bar Association v. Grelle

Supreme Court of Ohio,
14 Ohio St.2d 209, 237 N.E.2d 298 (1968)

Introduction

Attorneys are agents for their clients and therefore owe the same fiduciary duty that other agents owe to their principal. The following case illustrates the application of this rule to attorneys as well as the application of the Canons of Professional Ethics which attorneys are subject to.

Per Curiam

The respondent, Walter W. Grelle, Jr., was admitted to the practice of law in August 1938, and, with the exception of the four years that he served in the United States Navy during World War II, he has been engaged in practice in Columbus, Ohio, ever since. During his years of practice the respondent has been active in the bar associations and various fraternal, civic, and veterans' organizations. The complaint forming the basis of this disciplinary action is the only complaint that has ever been filed against the respondent.

The facts that led to the filing of this complaint by the Columbus Bar Association are as follows:

On April 23, 1963, the respondent filed a personal injury action on behalf of Lloyd I. Perine in the Franklin County Court of Common Pleas. On July 19, 1963, the respondent and his secretary witnessed the signing of a separation agreement between Lloyd I. Perine and his wife, Dorothy J. Perine. This agreement had been prepared by the respondent, but the terms had been previously agreed upon by the Perines, with little or no advice from the respondent. The part of this separation agreement that is relevant to this action provided that Mrs. Perine was to receive one-third of the net proceeds of Mr. Perine's personal injury case.

Mrs. Perine subsequently requested the respondent to obtain a divorce for her. It is clear that Mr. Perine knew of this request and acquiesced in it, and that Mrs. Perine knew that the respondent was representing her husband in the personal injury action. The testimony of Mrs. Perine and the respondent conflicted as to whether the respondent accepted the divorce case or declined it on the basis of conflict of interest. In any case, a divorce petition was filed in the Domestic Relations Division of the Franklin

County Court of Common Pleas on behalf of Mrs. Perine in September of 1983. This petition was prepared by the respondent. It was signed, and the acknowledgment for it was taken by Richard J. Giovanetti, an attorney who rented office space in the same suite as respondent. The petition itself was in simple form, and it did not plead the facts constituting the alleged grounds of divorce.

At the hearing on the divorce petition on November 27, 1963, which was uncontested, the respondent appeared for Mrs. Perine, the reason given for his appearance being that attorney Giovanetti was out of town. A decree was granted which incorporated the terms of the separation agreement.

After the divorce, the former Mrs. Perine remarried and became Mrs. Pinto. She later obtained another attorney to enforce the child support order of $10 per week against Mr. Perine.

In February 1965, the personal injury action of Mr. Perine was settled by the respondent for $19,000, and respondent paid the net proceeds directly to Mr. Perine. On May 11, 1965, Mrs. Pinto called the respondent and asked about the personal injury case. Respondent then told her that the case had been settled, but refused to disclose the amount of the settlement without permission of Mr. Perine. On May 18, 1964, Mrs. Pinto filed a motion to reduce to a money judgment that part of the separation agreement which had formalized the agreement that she was to share in the net proceeds of the settlement. Respondent, representing Mr. Perine, successfully resisted this motion. The propriety of the order dismissing this action is not before us.

Subsequently, Mrs. Pinto brought these facts to the attention of the Columbus Bar Association which filed the complaint in this case. On these facts, the Board of Commissioners on Grievances and Discipline concluded that the respondent had violated his oath of office and Canons 6 and 37 of the Canons of Professional Ethics. The recommendation of the commissioners was that the respondent be suspended for an indefinite period from practice of law.

The matter is before us on the findings of the board and the respondent's objections thereto, and for disciplinary action if we conclude that the facts properly found require such action.

One of the major objections of respondent pertains to the conclusion of the board that his conduct violated Canon 6 of the Canons of Professional Ethics. Canon 6 reads as follows:

> Adverse Influences and Conflicting Interests.
>
> It is the duty of a lawyer at the time of retainer to disclose to the client all the circumstances of his relations to the parties, and any interest in or connection with the controversy, which might influence the client in the selection of counsel.
>
> It is unprofessional to represent conflicting interests, except by express consent of all concerned given after a full disclosure of the facts. Within the meaning of this canon, a lawyer represents conflicting interests when, in behalf of one client, it is his duty to contend for that which duty to another client requires him to oppose.
>
> The obligation to represent the client with undivided fidelity and not to divulge his secrets or confidences forbids also the subsequent acceptance of retainers or employment from others in matters adversely affecting any interest of the client with respect to which confidence has been reposed.

Respondent notes that there was no finding that he did not disclose to each of the Perines his representation of the other, and he argues that the evidence shows that there was, in fact, full disclosure of this mutual representation. We agree with respondent on this point. Dorothy Pinto testified at the hearing that when she went to the respond-ent's office it was with full knowledge and approval of her husband, Lloyd Perine. She also testified that she had previously agreed with Lloyd Perine that he would pay for any divorce received.

There was no misrepresentation by the respondent as to his position with respect to either of the parties. It appears that with respect to the separation agreement and the divorce appearance he was not primarily protecting anyone or advising anyone, but was rather carrying out the mutual wishes of the parties. Conflicting interest arose out of the separation agreement, but not until over a year after the divorce was final. Any representation of the wife by the respondent had long since ceased.

The agreement between the parties which had reference to a division of the net proceeds of the contemplated settlement of Mr. Perine's claim for damages contained no promise by the respondent to protect the rights assigned to Mrs. Perine at the time of distribution. There is no claim that there was any representation that attorney Grelle would represent her or protect her interest in that fund upon distribution. It is understandable, however, that Mrs. Perine might have concluded that this was to be one of Mr. Grelle's functions. The fact that such misunderstandings are likely to occur under such circumstances must lead to the conclusion that only in the clearest cases should counsel hazard to represent interests which are or may become adverse, even after disclosing dual representation.

In retrospect, this was not such a case. Too many experienced lawyers have accepted such employment in separation or divorce matters under such circumstances, only to ultimately abandon the interest of one or the other of their clients. In such instances of dual representation, a party disappointed in the financial results, as was Mrs. Pinto, may validly argue after the fact that the dual representation brought about the omission from the agreement of specific language protecting her upon distribution of the anticipated settlement fund.

At all events, when Mrs. Pinto filed her motion to reduce to judgment that part of the agreement drawn by respondent which gave her a one-third interest in the proceeds of the personal injury settlement, Mr. Grelle should have withdrawn from the matter. His failure promptly to disclose to Mrs. Perine the fact that a settlement had occurred and that distribution to Perine had been made, and his ardent advocacy of the husband's adverse interest to the agreement violated the second paragraph of Canon No. 6, and was unprofessional conduct which justifies a reprimand.

We find, however, in view of all the facts of this case, including his full disclosure to the parties of his position and their consent to that position, that Mr. Grelle did not violate his oath of office. In view of the previously unblemished record of the respondent the reprimand which we here impose is judged to be suitable disciplinary action.

Judgment accordingly.

Discussion questions

1. What should the attorney have done to avoid the holding of this case? Why?
2. Could the attorney have properly made full disclosure if Mr. Perine objected thereto? Why?
3. Would the attorney have been liable to Mr. Perine if he made full disclosure without Mr. Perine's consent? Why?

Case 25

Soam v. Trane Company

202A.D.2d162 (1994)

This case illustrates the significant legal consequences when an agent breaches his duty of undivided loyalty.

Plaintiff, a New York corporation formed in 1975 to represent American companies in connection with the potential sale of goods and services to the Soviet Union, commenced the underlying action against, *inter alia*, defendant Trane Company ("Trane"), a nationally known manufacturer of heating, ventilating and air-conditioning equipment, seeking to recover commissions plaintiff is alleged to have earned pursuant to a letter agreement from the sale of air-conditioning equipment to be utilized in the Moscow World Trade Center ("the Moscow Center"), located in the Soviet Union.

The trial court, in dismissing the amended complaint for, *inter alia*, breach of contract as against defendant Trane, properly determined that the plaintiff had breached its duty of loyalty to Trane as its agent and had forfeited its commission by representing Trane's competitor, Chrysler Corporation, and promoting Chrysler, rather than Trane air-conditioning equipment to the mechanical contractor for the Moscow Center project, for use in that project.

On a nonjury trial, the decision of the fact-finding court should not be disturbed on appeal unless the court's conclusions could not have been reached under any fair interpretation of the evidence. Applying the foregoing standard of review, we find that the trial court's conclusion that plaintiff forfeited its commission should not be disturbed on appeal since that determination is supported by the impartial testimony of Monroe Kolber, an employee of the mechanical contractor, that in late August of 1976 the plaintiff had promoted Chrysler equipment, rather than that of Trane, for use at the Moscow World Trade Center; a contemporaneous document confirming that Kolber had reported the plaintiff's disloyal efforts on behalf of Chrysler; and the plaintiff's admission that it had, in fact, received a commission from the sale of Chrysler air-conditioning equipment while the plaintiff was purporting to represent Trane.

An agent is held to the utmost good faith in his dealings with his principal, and forfeits any right to compensation for his services if he acts adversely to his employer "in any part of the transaction," or promotes and sells any product made by the principal's competitor.

Plaintiff's contention that forfeiture is an "unconscionable penalty" is negated by New York's strict application of the forfeiture doctrine which mandates the forfeiture of all compensation, whether commissions or salary, where, as here, one who owes a duty of fidelity to a principal is faithless in the performance of his services.

We have reviewed the plaintiff's remaining claims and fine them to be without merit.

Discussion questions

1. Could the plaintiff have avoided this result by entering into a non-exclusive agency agreement with Trane which provided that the plaintiff would also represent competitors of Trane?
2. Could the plaintiff have avoided this result by contracting with Trane that plaintiff would sell competitor products only AFTER customers refused to purchase Trane products from the plaintiff?

Case 26

Island Associated Coop., Inc. v. Hartman and Fram Corporation

118A.D.2d830 (1986)

Introduction

This case examines the legal issue of when an employer is liable for theft of property when the employee steals property of a customer of the employer while the employee is making a delivery to the customer on behalf of the employer. Note the different legal theories under which an employer may be held liable for an employee's torts.

An employee of the defendant Fram Corporation (hereinafter Fram), the defendant Edward Hartmann, was caught removing inventory from the warehouse of the plaintiff, one of Fram's customers. The plaintiff's first cause of action against Fram is based on the doctrine of respondeat superior. Special Term correctly concluded that Hartmann did not act within the scope of his employment. Hartmann's actions were in no way *"incidental to the furtherance of the employer's interest"*. While torts committed by an employee who inartfully tries to carry out his employer's assignment may be found to be within the scope of employment, torts committed for personal motives unrelated to the furtherance of the employer's business are not, especially if the tortious acts are serious in nature.

The plaintiff presented no evidence to support its second cause of action that the defendant Fram had any knowledge of Hartmann's actions, or its third cause of action that Fram in any way acted negligently in the selection or supervision of its employees. Mere speculation or surmise is not enough.

Discussion questions

1. Would the employer be liable for the employee's theft if it learned that its employee stole the property shortly thereafter and did not do anything?
2. Would the employer be liable for the employee's theft if the employer hired the employee without checking his background and the employee had a criminal record involving similar acts while previously employed by another employer?
3. Give an example of negligent supervision by the employer which would trigger employer liability.

Case 27

TPL Associates v. Helmsley-Spear, Inc.

146A.D.2d468 (1989)

Introduction

Every agent is a fiduciary and owes his principal the duty of undivided loyalty. Moreover, the agent has an absolute duty not to act adversely to his principal. The agent must make prompt, full and complete disclosure of any interest the agent has whenever there is a conflict of interest between the agent and principal. He must disclose the conflict of interest in the words of Judge Cardozo "without ambiguity or reservation, in all its stark significance." The following case illustrates the legal consequences when the agent breaches his fundamental duties.

Supreme Court erred in granting summary judgment because a triable issue of fact existed as to whether defendants-respondents had met their fiduciary obligation of disclosing their conflict of interest "without ambiguity or reservation, in all its stark significance" (*Wendt v Fischer,* 243 NY 439, 443 [1926, Cardozo, J.]). Respondents undertook to act as broker for plaintiff-appellant, a general partnership, which owned commercial property located at 610-620 West 132nd Street in Manhattan. Appellant's asking price for the property was "$3,000,000 all cash". In June 1984, respondent informed appellant's general partners, Theodore Sofia, Jr. and Paul Greenberg, that there was a prospective purchaser willing to pay $2.7 million for the property. The partners were told that Lal Sani would take title, together with members of his family, through an entity to be formed for that purpose. Respondent Earle S. Altman, a senior vice-president of Helmsley-Spear, Inc., successfully negotiated an agreement between the parties, and it was also agreed that appellant would pay a brokerage commission of $96,000.

Shortly before the contract of sale was to be signed on June 18, 1984, Jerome Gellman, appellant's attorney, learned that Altman might have an interest in the purchasing entity to be formed by Sani. When confronted with this, Altman claimed that he and other Helmsley-Spear brokers had agreed to acquire "nominal" interests in the purchasing entity in order to assure Sani that they would be aggressive in seeking tenants for the property after the sale. According to appellant, Altman assured Gellman that the Helmsley-Spear brokers would acquire no more than a 1 or 2% interest each and that their aggregate interest would not exceed 10% of the purchasing entity. Appellant also claims Altman was told that if, in fact, Helmsley-Spear brokers were the purchasers of the property, appellant would not pay any brokerage commission at all. Altman assured Gellman that this was not the case and he agreed to a $10,000 reduction in the brokerage commission. A paragraph was inserted into the contract of sale, acknowledging that certain members of Helmsley-Spear "may be principals" of the purchasing entity in addition to acting as brokers for the sale. Appellant then executed both the contract of sale and the brokerage agreement.

In February 1985, a limited partnership was formed to acquire title to the property. At the closing on February 11, the limited partnership certificate was provided to Gellman as proof that the persons signing on behalf of the partnership were authorized to do so. The certificate named Sani and Altman as general partners and Alan Helman, who, unbeknownst to Gellmann, was a Helmsley-Spear broker, was listed as the sole limited partner with a 22.5% interest in the partnership profits.

The first $43,000 installment of the brokerage commission was paid by appellant at the closing. Thereafter, Greenberg and Sofia, who knew that Helman was a Helmsley-Spear broker, reviewed the closing documents including the limited partnership certificate. Their suspicions were aroused when they saw that Helman had made a capital contribution of only $100 to the partnership. Upon checking the records of the New York County Clerk's office, they found that an amended certificate had been executed on the date of the closing and filed several weeks later. The amended certificate indicated that 6 of the 10 general partners were Helmsley-Spear brokers and the two limited partners were both corporate entities. Altman and Sani were the managing general partners and Helman, who had withdrawn as the original limited partner, was a general partner. The amended certificate also revealed that Altman, and his Helmsley-Spear colleagues (identified in the amended certificate as the "Altman Partners") had contributed more capital and acquired a greater ownership interest in the partnership than the "Sani Partners".

Appellant refused to pay the second installment of the brokerage commission. Instead, it commenced this action to recover that portion of the commission already paid and the $300,000 reduction in the original listing, alleging breach of fiduciary duty, fraudulent representation and unjust enrichment. Supreme Court granted respondents motion to dismiss the complaint on the ground that respondents interest in the transaction had been disclosed to appellant and that this was evidenced by the provision inserted in the contract of sale. Further, the court noted that neither the contract of sale nor the brokerage agreement warranted that respondents interest would not exceed 10%. The court held that parol evidence to the contrary was not admissible as the brokerage agreement was an integrated writing. The court also relied on the fact that, at the closing, appellant's counsel was shown the limited partnership certificate indicating that one of the Helmsley-Spear brokers interest exceeded 10%.

Supreme Court erred in treating the relationship between the parties as one at arm's length, rather than as a fiduciary relationship between principal and agent. An agent is charged with a duty of loyalty and may not have interests in the subject transaction which are adverse to those of his principal. Where a conflict of interest exists, nothing less than full and complete disclosure is required of the agent. The question is not whether respondents represented that their interest in the purchasing entity would not exceed 10%, but whether appellant was "fully informed of every fact material to [its] interests" and whether it freely consented in the presence of such knowledge. Disclosure which is "indefinite and equivocal does not set the agent free to bargain for his own account or for the account of a corporation which acts through him alone" (*Wendt v Fischer*, 243 NY, supra, at 443) or even for a partnership in which he has a substantial interest. The failure to make independent inquiries which would reveal the agent's adverse interest is immaterial, inasmuch as the principal is entitled to rely on the agent's representations and his complete, undivided loyalty.

A breach by the agent of this duty of loyalty is a fraud for which the agent is answerable in damages, and any compensation paid to him may be forfeit. The record in this case raises a substantial issue as to whether respondents have met their duty, as fiduciaries, of complete and unequivocal disclosure. Summary judgment was therefore improper.

Discussion Questions

1. What should the broker have done which would have enabled it to keep the agreed real estate commission and also be a part of the group that purchased the property from the seller?
2. Would the result be the same if the wives or the broker-individuals were the members of the limited partnership?

Name: ______________________________

PROBLEMS

Date: ______________________________

Section Number: ______________________________

1. On March 15, A received an oral offer to work as an account executive for P. A orally accepted the offer on April 1, and agreed to begin work on May 1. The duration of the contract was one year from May 1, and provided a $20,000 salary plus a bonus based on commission earned. Under these circumstances, which of the following is true?

______ a. A has an agency coupled with an interest.

______ b. The contract in question is not subject to the statute of frauds.

______ c. A would be permitted to delegate his performance to another equally competent person.

______ d. Although A's contract is silent on the point, A has an implied right to reimbursement for the reasonable and necessary expenses incurred on behalf of P.

2. What fiduciary duty, if any, exists in an agency relationship?

______ a. The principal owes a fiduciary duty to his agent.

______ b. The agent owes a fiduciary duty to third parties he deals with for and on behalf of his principal.

______ c. The agent owes a fiduciary duty to his principal.

______ d. There is no fiduciary duty in an agency relationship.

3. P hired A as an assistant vice president of sales at $2,000 a month. The employment had no fixed duration. In light of their relationship to each other, which of the following is correct?

______ a. A has a legal duty to reveal any interest adverse to that of P in matters concerning his employment.

______ b. If A voluntarily terminates his employment with P after working for P for several years, he can not work for a competitor for a reasonable period after termination.

______ c. P can dismiss A only for cause.

______ d. The employment contract between the parties must be in writing.

4. P engaged A for six months as his exclusive agent to sell specific antiques.

______ a. The creation of such an agency must be in writing.

______ b. If the principal sells the antiques through another agent, he will be liable to A for damages.

______ c. The principal does not have the legal power to terminate the agency since it is an agency coupled with an interest.

______ d. A has impliedly guaranteed that he will sell the antiques within the six-month period.

5. A has been engaged as a general sales agent for P. P owes A several duties which are implied as a matter of law. Which of the following duties is owed by P to A?

______ a. Not to compete.

______ b. To reimburse A for all expenditures as long as they are remotely related to A's employment and not specifically prohibited.

______ c. Not to dismiss A without cause for one year from the making of the contract if the duration of the contract is indefinite.

______ d. To indemnify A for liability for acts done in good faith upon P's orders.

6. A has been engaged as sales agent for P. Under which of the following circumstances may A delegate his duties to another?

______ a. Where an emergency arises and the delegation is necessary to meet the emergency.

______ b. Where it is convenient for A to do so.

______ c. Only with the express consent of P.

______ d. If P sells its business to another.

7. Colton had a claim against Poppins for goods sold to him in the amount of $100,000. The claim was disputed because some of the merchandise was claimed to be defective. Poppins retained an agent, Anton, to represent him to negotiate a settlement with Colton. Anton settled the claim for $86,000 which Poppins paid. Poppin paid Anton $1,000 for his services. Poppins then discovered that Colton paid Anton a gratuity of $2,000 to obtain the $86,000 settlement from Poppins.

   a. In an action by Poppins against Anton to recover the $2,000 gratuity and $1,000 fee, judgment for whom? Why?

   b. In an action by Poppins against Colton to recover $2,000, judgment for whom? Why?

8. Paulson sent a ship he owned to International Boat Brokers, doing business in Hong Kong and Yokohama, to be sold for not less than $1,000,000 cash. International, believing that Oriental Boat Sales had wider contacts in Japan, hired Oriental to make the sale without obtaining Paulson's consent. Oriental was unable to find a buyer for an all-cash sale but found a customer, Kinezawa, who would pay $1,200,000, payable $800,000 in cash and $400,000 in three months. Oriental reported to International that they could not sell the ship for all-cash but that they would buy it themselves for $1,000,000 cash. The sale was made to Oriental. Oriental promptly resold it to Kinezawa, eventually receiving $1,200,000.

   a. In an action by Paulson against Oriental, judgment for whom? Why?

   b. In an action by Paulson against International based upon Oriental's actions, judgment for whom? Why?

9. Adams was a salesman employed by Prince to travel a certain territory and to solicit orders from hardware dealers. Adams received a $1,000 order from Tippet, a hardware dealer. Adams sent the order to Prince who shipped the merchandise to Tippet. At the end of the month Adams collected the $1,000 but failed to remit to Prince. Prince had not given Adams any express authority to collect.

   a. In an action by Prince against Tippet to recover $1,000, judgment for whom? Why?

   b. Assume Adams had been given express authority to collect for Prince. If Adams had deposited the funds he collected in his own personal checking account in good faith and his bank had failed, could Prince hold Adams liable for the funds collected? Why?

   c. Assume that Adams promised to have the order shipped promptly to Tippet and that, in gratitude and without ulterior motive or prior agreement, Tippet gave Adams a clock-radio as a gift. Assume further that there was no custom or agreement between Prince and Adams permitting Adams to accept a gift in such circumstances. Prince learned of the gift and demanded the clockradio. Must Adams give it to Prince? Why?

   d. Would your answer to c. be different if the gift was cash? Why?

10. Purdy instructed his agent, Avery, to purchase certain bonds at a certain price on a certain date. Avery, in the course of performance, learned from sources he believed in good faith to be reliable that the price of the bonds was expected to be lower in the week following the date he was instructed to buy. Avery waited the extra week, but the price increased by $5,000 above the price on the date Avery should have bought them.

    a. Is Avery personally liable for the extra cost of $5,000? Why?

    b. If the price decreased and Avery saved Purdy $5,000 by waiting one extra week, would Avery be entitled to an extra commission? Why?

11. Pawling directs his stockbroker, Akins, to purchase, as his agent, 1,000 shares in Nikal Corporation at $50 a share. Akins, having such shares on hand and being unable to obtain them elsewhere, conveys 1,000 shares to Pawling without disclosing these facts. Three days after receiving the stock, Pawling discovers the foregoing facts.

    a. In an action by Pawling against Akins to rescind the sale, judgment for whom? Why?

    b. Would your answer to a. be different if Pawling waited one month to see what happened to the market value and decided to rescind when the market price fell ten percent below what he had paid for it? Why?

12. Arrow was the agent of Limestone Products Corp. Arrow sought the assistance of Barton in order to sell rocks for use on state highway projects because Barton knew many state officials. Arrow introduced Barton to Philips, the president of Limestone Products Corp. and it was agreed that Barton was to use his influence with state officials on behalf of the company. Philips orally agreed to pay Arrow twice the usual commission for sales made by Arrow to the state with the understanding that Arrow would turn over 50% of his commissions to Barton. Barton, through his contacts, had the specifications for road building changed so that only Limestone's products could be used. As a result, large purchases were made by the state. Arrow received the commissions from the company but refused to give Barton his share.

    a. In an action by Barton against Arrow to recover his share, judgment for whom? Why?

    b. In an action by Barton against Limestone Products Corp. to recover commissions, judgment for whom? Why?

13. Bishop, a California orange grower, ships two carloads of oranges to his factor, Lemel, in New York City. Twenty one hours before they are due to arrive, the factor learns that the wholesale price of oranges in New York City is depressed and will continue to be depressed during the next few days because of the glut of oranges on the market. Lemel checks the market price in Philadelphia and learns that the wholesale price is 30% higher there, or $10,000 more for the two carloads, and the same price is expected tomorrow and that there is only a nominal extra cost for rerouting the oranges to Philadelphia. Lemel tries unsuccessfully to communicate this information to Bishop but cannot reach Bishop. Lemel then reroutes the oranges to Philadelphia, where they are destroyed by a flood. The agreement between Bishop and Lemel provided that Lemel could not reroute any shipment without Bishop's prior consent.

    a. Did the factor have the authority to reroute the oranges? Why?

    b. Is Lemel liable for the loss? Why?

c. If Lemel did not reroute the oranges but sold them in New York City for $10,000 less than they could have been sold for in Philadelphia, would Lemel be liable to Bishop for $10,000 less the extra freight cost assuming there was no flood and Lemel could not reach Bishop to obtain authorization to reroute the oranges to Philadelphia? Why?

14. Howard insured his house against loss by fire with Everystate Insurance Company. Howard's house was partially destroyed by fire. The company sent its agent, Davis, to adjust the loss. Davis delegated his authority to Williams, a well-known, highly regarded insurance adjuster, without the company's consent. Williams agreed on behalf of the company to settle Howard's claim for $10,000. When the company learned the facts, it promptly repudiated the settlement by advising Howard that Williams had no authority to act for the company.

a. In an action by Howard against the company to recover $10,000, judgment for whom? Why?

b. In an action by Howard against Davis and Williams to recover $10,000, judgment for whom? Why?

c. If Howard recovers a judgment against Williams for $10,000, does Williams have any recourse against Davis? Why?

15. Aarons was a well-known food broker. He entered into a written contract with All American Food Products Corp. to be its exclusive sales agent for five years in a tri-state area on a commission basis. The contract was silent about assignment. After Aarons performed for three years, he organized a corporation which took over all of his business. Aarons assigned his contract with All American to the new corporation. Aarons was the sole stockholder. All American then refused to permit the new corporation to act as its agent. Moreover, All American informed Aarons that it regarded Aarons' assignment of its contract as a breach and terminated its agency agreement with Aarons.

    a. In an action by the new corporation against All American for breach of contract, judgment for whom? Why?

    b. In an action by Aarons against All American, judgment for whom? Why?

    c. Would your answer to a. be different if Aarons held only 50% of the stock of the new corporation and the other 50% was held by two other persons who contributed substantial sums to the new corporations but who had no experience in the food business? Why?

16. Duval was the agent for Sunshine Pools, Inc. He sold pools, related equipment, and accessories for Sunshine. Holmes, president of Tilden Sporting Equipment, Inc., approached Duval and offered him an excellent deal on a commission basis if he would secretly sell their brand of diving boards and platforms instead of the Sunshine products. Duval agreed. The arrangement which was worked out between them was to have Duval continue to act as a general sales agent for Sunshine and concurrently act as the agent for an "undisclosed" principal in respect to Tilden diving boards. He could then sell both lines to new pool customers and go back to prior customers to solicit sales of the Tilden boards. Duval was not to mention his relationship with Tilden to the prospective customers, and of course, no mention of these facts would be made to Sunshine. Duval was told to use his discretion insofar as effectively misleading the prospective customers about whose diving board they were purchasing.

    Things went smoothly for the first several months until Tilden began to manufacture and ship defective diving boards. Subsequently, Tilden became insolvent, and Holmes absconded with advance payments made by purchasers including those who had purchased from Duval.

    a. What are the rights of the various customers against Duval?

    b. What are the rights of the various customers against Tilden and/or Holmes?

    c. What rights does Sunshine have against Duval?

    d. What rights does Sunshine have against Tilden and/or Holmes?

17. John Barry, a world famous golfer, represents Golf Cart Company, Inc. as a sales agent to promote sales of the Company's product, a golf cart. The company sells a new type of golf cart which it has named the "Barry Golf Cart" and it has commenced an extensive marketing campaign. As a part of this campaign, the company sends letters advertising the carts to presidents of golf clubs. In its letter the company represents that the new cart "can be driven a full 18 holes of golf under any conditions" and that "the cart will not require any major repairs for two years". Also in the letter, which is signed by John Barry as vice president in charge of sales promotion, there is a statement by John Barry that he "personally tested the cart and was delighted with its performance."

    Jones, a president of a golf club, bought a golf cart after reading the letter and corresponding with the company to determine the model which best suited his needs. He now finds that the cart is totally unsatisfactory since it continuously breaks down when it is driven on the golf course. He has informed Barry that he intends to bring a suit for damages against both the company and Barry in his individual capacity. However, he further states that if he could be sure that Golf Cart Company, Inc. is solvent he would not sue Barry individually but would sue only the company. To determine the company's financial status, he asks Barry to secretly allow him access to the company's financial records. Barry suspects that Jones may have other motives for wishing to secretly view the company's records.

    a. What should Barry do with regard to arranging for Jones to secretly examine the company's financial records to avoid a suit against himself individually? Explain.

____

____

____

____

____

    b. In the event that Barry is sued individually by Jones, what defense (s) is (are) available to him? Explain.

____

____

____

____

____

18. Ogden Corp. hired Thorp as a sales representative for nine months at a salary of $3,000 per month plus 4% of sales. Which of the following statements is correct?

______ a. Thorp is obligated to act solely in Ogden's interest in matters concerning Ogden's business.

______ b. The agreement between Ogden and Thorp formed an agency coupled with an interest.

______ c. Ogden does **not** have the power to dismiss Thorp during the nine-month period without cause.

______ d. The agreement between Ogden and Thorp is **not** enforceable unless it is in writing and signed by Thorp.

19. Ritz hired West for six months as an assistant sales manager at $4,000 a month plus 3% of sales. Which of the following is correct?

______ a. The employment agreement must be in writing and signed by the party to be charged.

______ b. The agreement between Ritz and West formed an agency coupled with an interest.

______ c. West must disclose any interests he has which are adverse to Ritz in matters concerning Ritz's business.

______ d. West can be dismissed by Ritz during the six months only for cause.

CHAPTER 8

LIABILITY OF PRINCIPAL AND AGENT FOR TORTS AND CRIMES COMMITTED BY AN AGENT

77. Introduction.

We have seen in an earlier chapter that a principal, whether disclosed, partially disclosed, or undisclosed, will be liable on a contract made by his agent on behalf of the principal with a third party if the agent acted within the scope of his actual authority, express or implied. Moreover, a disclosed principal will also be liable on a contract made on his behalf by his agent with a third party where the agent had apparent authority even though the agent had no actual authority. However, a principal will not be liable on any contract where the agent did not have actual or apparent authority to contract unless the principal ratifies such unauthorized contract.

The question arises as to when and to what extent the principal and agent are liable to third parties when the agent commits a tort (civil wrong) or crime and what are the rights, duties, and liabilities of the principal, agent, and third party in such a case to each other. Each will be discussed separately in the sections that follow.

During the first half of the 20th century, the Federal government and every state enacted legislation to abolish the centuries old common law doctrine of sovereign immunity. This historic doctrine barred lawsuits and tort claims against the United States and states as well as against any political subdivision of the state, such as county, city, town, village or any other municipality whenever government employees, such as police officers, firemen, sanitation employees, or doctors employed by hospitals owned by municipalities, committed torts while acting within the scope of their employment.

The impetus for the legislation abolishing the doctrine of sovereign immunity and permitting tort claims against municipalities was the advent of the automobile which many municipalities acquired for use by their uniformed employees (e.g., police officers) in the performance of their duties. An increasing number of automobile accidents involving negligent municipal employees causing serious injuries and economic losses to members of the public, many of which were widely reported in the daily newspapers, led newspaper publishers, lawyers and others to successfully lobby for the repeal of the doctrine of sovereign immunity at the Federal and state level.

The statutes abolishing the doctrine of sovereign immunity typically permit the injured person or his estate (if he dies) to sue the municipal employer for torts committed by municipal employees while acting within the scope of their employment. However, these statutes typically require that the injured person **first** serve a written and sworn notice of claim upon the municipal employer within a specified time after the tort occurred (within 90 days in New York, and in the event of the victim's death, within 90 days after the judicial appointment of a representative of the decedent's estate). The injured plaintiff must then typically wait a minimum period of time (30 days in New York) after serving the notice of claim to allow the municipal employer time to investigate and possibly negotiate a settlement without the added legal expense of defending a lawsuit. If the injured plaintiff wants to commence an action against the municipal employer, he or she must do so in accordance with the applicable statute of limitations (in

New York, one year and 90 days after the tort occurred except where the plaintiff has died, the statute of limitations is two years from the date of death).

Since the advent of state and Federal legislation permitting claims against municipalities to recover money damages for torts committed by municipal employees, more than 50 billion dollars has been paid to several million plaintiffs by the Federal government and municipalities in all 50 states. Some municipalities have liability insurance to cover some or all of their tort liability but many large municipalities, like the Federal government, state governments and major cities such as New York City, are self-insurers that pay tort claimants out of the public treasury because they believe they can control settlements and verdicts more effectively than liability insurance companies and avoid liability insurance premium expenses. The amount paid each year has been steadily increasing.

Thus, during the ten year period from 1986-1995, New York City paid a steadily increasing amount each year to tort claimants and for the entire ten year period paid approximately $2 billion out of its public treasury (i.e., the taxpayers pocketbook). Between 1991 and 1995 alone, New York City paid tort claimants between $225 million and $275 million each year. By comparison, in 1977, New York City paid tort claimants only $24 million.

Similarly, the number of tort claims filed against New York city each year has markedly increased from approximately 22,000 claims in 1986 to approximately 30,000 claims in 1995 (an average of 80 tort claims each day).

The vast bulk of both settlements and verdicts against New York City are paid in personal injury cases (in contrast with property damage claims). In 1995 personal injury settlements and verdicts amounted to $235.8 million or 91% of the total which was paid as follows:

1. Medical Malpractice	$71.3 million
2. Sidewalk Accidents	$45.5 million
3. Motor Vehicle Accidents	$33.1 million
4. Police-Related Accidents	$21.9 million
5. School Accidents	$14.4 million
6. All other accidents	$49.6 million

The following cases illustrate when a tort committed by a municipal employee is within or outside the scope of his or her employment.

78. Liability of agent for his own torts and crimes.

It is a fundamental rule of agency law that an agent is personally liable for every tort or crime he commits while employed by his principal, whether his principal was disclosed, partially disclosed, or undisclosed at the time he committed the tort or crime.[1] The agent is liable even though he committed the tort or crime in the furtherance of the principal's business or upon the express instructions of his principal or solely for the benefit of his principal. Thus, the agent cannot immunize himself from liability to the injured third party or to his principal for any loss that either suffers as a result of his torts or crimes unless a statute exempts the agent from liability to the injured party. An example of such a statute was enacted by Congress in 1961 as an amendment to the Federal Tort Claims Act of 1946. It provides that an employee of the United States is immune from personal liability for any tort he causes while operating a motor vehicle in the course of his employment. This result is achieved by making the injured party's remedy against the United States "exclusive of any other civil action . . . against the employee or his estate. . . . " 28 U.S. Code 2679. This provision was adopted in order to save federal employees the expense of buying liability insurance because the United States does not carry automobile liability insurance since it elects to be a self-insurer with respect to any liability it incurs as a result of the negligence of its employees while operating a motor vehicle in the course of their employment.

The agent who commits a tort or crime while acting within the scope of his employment has breached his contract with his principal because he has failed to act in accordance with the implied duty imposed by law upon every agent: the duty to act lawfully and with reasonable care, diligence and skill. In such a case, the principal is legally justified in terminating the agency immediately even though the agent may have satisfied the injured third party for any loss sustained and even though the agency agreement has not yet expired. And where the agent's tort or crime causes loss to his principal, the agent is also liable to his principal for such loss.

The question arises whether an agent who satisfies his tort liability to the injured third party has any right to obtain reimbursement or indemnification from his principal because the agent committed the tort while attempting to further the principal's interests? Under general principles of agency law, the agent's right to reimbursement or indemnification is limited to those cases where the agent acted properly and lawfully.[2] Thus, the agent who commits a tort intentionally or negligently is not entitled to any reimbursement or indemnification from his principal no matter how great the agent's loss is. However, a narrow exception applies where the agent intentionally commits a tort at the principal's direction in good faith and without knowledge that he is committing a tort. In such a case, he is entitled to indemnification from his principal for any loss he sustains, whether or not the principal knew that the agent's act was a tort, as where the agent is held liable for wrongful repossession which he does pursuant to his principal's instructions.

79. Liability of principal for agent's torts and crimes.

In the evolution of agency law it was judicially established that every principal, whether disclosed, partially disclosed, or undisclosed, was liable for the torts committed by his agent while he was acting within the scope of his employment.[3] This absolute rule applies no matter how much care the principal exercised in selecting, training, and supervising his agent or in instructing him not to commit any torts during his employment. Thus, the principal simply cannot immunize himself from liability to the injured third party for any loss caused by his agent's torts while the agent was acting within the scope of his employment. This rule applies equally to the public sector where Federal, State and local governments, by waiver of their sovereign immunity, are liable for the torts committed by their employees within the scope of their employment. In a recent year over 30,000 torts claims were filed against the city of New York which in the same year paid out over $275,000,000 in satisfaction of tort claims against it.

This major principle of law is a classic example of judicial imposition of liability without fault. The principal's liability for his agent's torts committed within the scope of his employment is rooted in the legal doctrine of respondeat superior[4]—"let the principal respond," also known as the doctrine of vicarious liability. This extremely important doctrine is based on desirable social policy because the principal has "deeper pockets" than his agent and is more likely to be able to compensate the injured third party than the agent. Any different rule would result often in the injured party being unable to collect for his injury[5] and would serve to foster a socially undesirable policy of actually discouraging a principal from exercising care in selecting, training and supervising his agents who are his employees. Thus, the principal who sends his agent into the marketplace assumes the risk of liability arising from his agent's torts committed within the scope of his employment under the doctrine of respondeat superior. Obviously, the principal may and often does purchase liability insurance which will insure and indemnify him against loss to particular enumerated torts committed by his agent. The principal's premium expense will become a cost of doing business and be reflected in the price he charges for his goods or services so that in the final analysis all of society bears the loss caused by the agent's torts which cost insurance companies billions of dollars annually.

The litmus test of the principal's liability for his agent's torts is that the agent must commit the tort while acting within the scope of his employment. Thus, the first question that arises is what constitutes "employment"? The concept of "employment" is that the agent must be an employee of the principal and not an independent contractor. Whether the agent is an employee or an independent contractor depends upon the degree of control and supervision that the principal has over the agent's activities. An employee, by definition, is subject to substantial control and supervision as to the method, manner, time and place of how, where and when he performs his duties. By contrast, an independent contractor is engaged by his principal to obtain a particular objective or result, but the independent contractor retains substantial control over the details as to how, when and where he performs his duties. The legal distinction between employee and independent contractor is extremely significant because it is a fundamental principle of agency law that a principal is not liable for the torts of his agent where the agent is an independent contractor even though the tort was committed while the independent contractor was acting on behalf of his principal.[6]

However, one exception to this rule has been made where the principal employs an independent contractor to perform work for him when the work can be classified as "inherently dangerous." This exception to non-liability for the torts of an independent contractor is stated in the Restatement, Second, Agency, Section 416:

> One who employs an independent contractor to do work which the employer should recognize as likely to create

during its progress a peculiar risk of physical harm to others unless special precautions are taken, is subject to liability for physical harm caused to them by the failure of the contractor to exercise reasonable care to take such precautions, even though the employer has provided for such precautions in the contract or otherwise.

This exception is frequently used in cases where a principal employs an independent contractor to perform work on his premises which endangers those who pass by. A related exception applied where non-delegable duties are imposed by statute or by a franchise. For example, activity by licensed public utilities and common carriers is frequently held to be non-delegable if the act causing injury is directly related to the performance of the franchise rights.

The second question that arises is what constitutes "scope of employment"? Certainly, the agent is not acting within the scope of his employment where he commits a tort at a time and place and under circumstances where he is not acting on behalf of or in furtherance of his principal's interests as where he shoots at pedestrians for target practice while driving a company truck to make a delivery. In such a case, he is said to be committing a tort while off on an "independent frolic" of his own and his principal has no liability for his torts under the independent frolic rule. This is true even though the tort was committed by the agent during his scheduled working hours or while in company uniform or on his employer's premises. Accordingly, the term "scope of employment" does not refer to the agent's working hours but rather to whether the tort was committed by the agent in furtherance of the principal's interest.

The most difficult and vexatious cases to decide are those where the agent's tort is not clearly within or outside the scope of the agent's employment. In such a case, the courts and juries will examine how far the agent has deviated in time, place and circumstance from the scope of his employment. The greater the deviation, the more likely that courts and juries will hold that the principal is not liable for his agent's tort because the tort was committed outside the agent's scope of employment regardless of whether or not he intended to further his principal's interest. This problem is illustrated by the delivery route cases where the agent makes a detour from his prescribed delivery route solely for his own purposes. Where the detour is substantial and the tort is committed while detouring, the agent is outside the scope of his employment and the principal is not liable for his tort.[7] However, where the agent has completed his personal business after detouring and is on his way back to his prescribed delivery route, the courts have frequently held that he is once again acting within the scope of his employment when he is reasonably close to his authorized delivery route and any tort he commits while reasonably close to his authorized delivery route will impose liability on his principal. Thus, the agent need not return to the precise place from which he deviated in order to be within the scope of his employment.[8]

In the event the agent commits a tort while acting within the scope of his employment, the injured third party may hold the principal and agent jointly and severally liable.[9] Accordingly, the injured third party may at his option sue either the principal or the agent or both of them. However, where an injured third party releases the agent from liability for his tort, the principal will also be released from his liability.[10] In the event the injured third party sues both and recovers a judgment against both, he may satisfy his judgment against either one, in whole or in part, but cannot recover more than the amount of his judgment.

If the injured third party recovers some or all of his loss from the principal, the principal in turn may recover his loss from his agent unless he has authorized or ratified the agent's tort. As noted earlier, the agent who commits a tort while acting in the scope of his employment has breached his contract with his principal because he has failed to comply with his implied duty to exercise reasonable care, diligence and skill. Therefore, he must indemnify his principal for any loss the principal incurs, including his reasonable legal expenses. Moreover, the principal may discharge his agent for such breach of contract without liability even though the agency agreement has not expired.

All of the foregoing rules are also applicable where the employee is not an agent for his employer but rather is his servant, that is, an employee who is not acting in the capacity of an agent. Thus, the rights, duties, and liabilities of the employer and employee for the torts of his employee are the same whether the employee is designated an agent or a servant.

In the event the agent or servant commits a crime, the doctrine of respondeat superior does not apply. Rather, the principal is not criminally liable for his agent's or employee's crime unless he planned, directed, ordered it, or acquiesced in its commission. However, some statutes have imposed criminal responsibility vicariously upon principals for their agent's or employee's criminal acts, as where the agent or employee commits a criminal violation of the pure food laws or the laws regulating the sale of alcohol beverages to minors.[11]

Current References

"Agency—Vicarious Liability—Attorneys incur vicarious liability for the torts of associated counsel [Case Note] Duggins v. Guardianship of Washington, 632 So.2d 420 (Miss. 1993)," by Susan C. Spears, 64 Mississippi Law Journal 275-289, Fall 1994.

"Attending Physician not vicariously liable for covering physician's negligence," 38 Trial Lawyer's Guide, 210-214, Summer 1994.

"Criminal liability of a parent company for the conduct of its subsidiary: the spillover of the Exxon Valdez," by Robert Iraola, 31 Criminal Law Bulletin 3-18, Jan.-Feb. 1995.

"Discrimination by managers and supervisors: recognizing agent liability under Title VII," by Scott B. Goldberg, 143 University of Pennsylvania Law Review 571-594, Dec. 1994.

"Does Title VII contemplate personal liability for employee/agent defendants?" by Janice R. Franke, 12 Hofstra Labor Law Journal 39-63, Fall 1994.

"Employer Liability for sexual harassment: the morass of agency principles and respondeat superior," by Rachel E. Lutner, 1993 University Of Illinois Law Review 589-628, Summer 1993.

"Employer liability for acts of sexual harassment in the workplace: respondeat superior and beyond," by N. James Turner, 68 Florida Bar Journal 41 (5), Dec. 1994.

"Employment sexual harassment liability under agency principles: a second look at Meritor Savings Bank, FSB v. Vinson," by Michael J. Phillips, 44 Vanderbilt Law Review 1229-1272, Nov. 1991.

"Evidence was insufficient to establish corporation's complicity in driver's actions, precluding award of punitive damages," 38 Trial Lawyer's Guide 355-358, Fall 1994.

"Finding the road to strict liability for the intentional torts of employees [Case Note] Rodebush v. Oklahoma Nursing Homes, Ltd., 867 P.2d 1241 (Okla. 1993)," by Robert J. Winter, 30 Tulsa Law Journal 375-393, Winter 1994.

"Franchise vicarious liability in Florida: a survey and recent developments (part 1)," by David A. Beyer, 69 Florida Bar Journal 18 (7), Feb. 1995.

"The negligent hiring doctrine—a growing dilemma for employers," by Donald J. Petersen and Douglas Massengill, 15 Employee Relations Law Journal 419-432, Winter 1989.

"A lender's liability for agent misdeeds," by Kenneth M. Lodge, Ronald L. Sandack and Thomas J. Cunningham, 33 Santa Clara Law Review 811-858, Fall 1993.

"Scope of employment redefined: holding employers vicariously liable for sexual assaults committed by their employees," by Rochelle Rubin Weber, 76 Minnesota Law Review 1513-1541, June 1992.

"Title VII sexual harassment: recognizing an employer's non-delegable duty to prevent a hostile workplace," Justin S. Weddle, 95 Columbia Law Review 724-748, April 1995.

"Tort law—fiduciary theory imposes higher duty and direct liability on church for clergy sexual misconduct [Case Note] Tenantry v. Diocese of Colorado, 863 P.2d 310 (Colo. 1993)," by Jennifer L. Wallace, 28 Suffolk University Law Review 331-339, Spring 1994.

"Up against the wall: municipal liability for police brutality under respondeat superior," by J.M. Marcus, 18 Southern Illinois University Law Journal 655-672, Spring 1994.

"When the fiduciary's agent errs—who pays the bill—fiduciary, agent or beneficiary?" by Charles M. Bennett, 28 Real Property Probate and Trust Journal 429-534, Fall 1993.

"Workplace violence and the duty of care: the scope of an employer's obligation to protect against the violent employee," by Alfred G. Feliu, 20 Employee Relations Law Journal 381-406, Winter 1994.

Notes

1. The principle of law that an agent is liable for his own torts is analyzed in Floyd W. Mechem, "The Liability Of An Agent To Third Persons In Tort," *Yale Law Journal,* 20:239 (1911).
2. See, Restatement, Second, Agency, Sects. 438-440 (1958).
3. Oganaso v. Mellow, 356 Mo. 228, 201 S.W. 2d 365 (1947). Where an agent is not acting for his principal's interest or is outside the scope of his employment, his principal is not liable. See, Bioens v. Manhattan For Hire Car Corp., 159 S.E. 395 (Va. 1931); Uhrig v. Hanke Motor Car Co., 89 Ind. App. 429, 166 N.E. 611 (1929); Barnes v. Hampton, 149 Va. 740, 141 S.E. 856 (1928); Stone v. Commonwealth Coal Co., 259 Mass. 360, 156 N.E. 737 (1927); Floyd R. Mechem, *Agency,* vol. 2 (2d ed. 1914) sect. 1879. However, where the deviation is slight and usual the court may, as a matter of law, determine that the servant was acting within the scope of his employment. Wagnitz v. Scharetz, 89 Cal. App. 511, 265 Pac. 318 (1928); Jackson v. Bardelaben, 22 Ala. App. 615, 118 So. 504 (1928). See, also, "Agency-Liability Of Principal For Torts Committed Outside Agent's Scope Of Employment," *Virginia Law Review,* 18:95-96, November 1931.
4. Restatement, Second, Agency, Sects. 216, 219(1) (1958).
5. The policy basis of vicarious liability, which imposes tort liability on one who is not personally at fault, is also to encourage principals to hire the best personnel as agents as a means of avoiding accidents to third parties. This extra burden has been described as "the most valuable check in the conduct of social life." See, Harold Laski, "The Basis of Vicarious Liability," *Yale Law Journal,* 26:105 at 114 (1916).
6. See, Scammon v. Chicago, 25 Ill. 425 (1861); Floyd R. Mechem, *Agency,* vol. 2 (2d ed. 1914), sect. 1917; "Responsibility For The Torts Of An Independent Contractor," *Yale Law Journal,* 39:861-873, April 1930. The distinction between employee and independent contractor is based on their function rather than their designation. In M.F.A. Mutual Ins. Co. v. U.S., 314 F. Supp. 590 (W.D. Mo. 1970), the federal district court found that an insurance company's agreement with its new agents, who were defined as "independent contractors," was not determinative when these agents were specially supervised, received instructions in training and were fully compensated for expenses incurred for their work in selling and servicing insurance contracts. In fact, the court held, these agents occupied the legal sta-

tus of agents rather than independent contractors. See, also, Eitel v. Schmidlapp, 459 F.2d 609 (4th Cir. 1972); McCarty v. King County Medical Serv. Corp., 26 Wash.2d 660, 175 P.2d 653 (1946); Green v. Independent Oil Co., 414 Pa. 477, 201 A.2d 207 (1964); Moriarty v. W. T. Grant Co., 155 N.Y. S.2d 218 (1956), where the court held that a general contractor is not liable for the torts of his sub-contractor. See, also, chapter one, footnote 7.

7. Nelson v. Nelson, 282 Minn. 487, 166 N.W.2d 70 (1969); Kroiak v. Chicago Express, Inc., 10 N.J. Super. 60, 76 A.2d 266 (1950).
8. Marriott v. National Mut. Cas. Co., 195 F.2d 462 (10th Cir. 1952); Cook v. United States, 240 F. Supp. 353 (D. Ore. 1964).
9. Biel, Inc. v. Kirsch, 130 Ind. App. 46, 153 N.E.2d 140 (1958).
10. Stewart v. Craig, 208 Tenn. 312, 344 S.W.2d 761 (1961).
11. Certain regulatory statutes established an absolute duty upon the principal to exercise due care and penalize him for the criminal acts of his agents even though he had no specific intent to violate the statute. See, Rietze v. Williams, 458 S.W.2d 613 (Ky. 1970), and United States v. Hilton Hotels Corp., 467 F.2d 1000 (9th Cir. 1972), cert. denied 93 S. Ct. 938 (1973) where the court held that a landlord may be subjected to penalties for criminal negligence when he attempts to delegate to another his duties and responsibilities for maintenance of the premises. Statutes imposing vicarious *criminal* liability upon principals do so to protect the public. See, Floyd R. Mechem, "The Liability Of A Principal For The Penal Or Criminal Acts Of His Agent," *Michigan Law Review,* 11:93 (1912).

Case 28

Bridger v. International Business Machines Corp.

480 F.2d 566 (Fifth Cir. Ct. of App. 1973)

Introduction

Perhaps the most troublesome area of agency law is whether the agent's or employee's tort has been committed while he was acting within the scope of his employment. This is especially so where the principal furnishes his employee with a company car or reimburses him for his car expenses and requires his employee to be "on call" for emergencies *after* the conclusion of his normal working hours. Injured third parties usually sue the agent's employer because he is expected to have "deeper pockets" than his employee. And employers usually defend on the ground that the tort committed after normal working hours while technically "on call" does not impose liability under the doctrine of respondeat superior where the employee was not involved in any actual "call" at the time the tort was committed. The following case illustrates the judicial analysis exercised to determine whether such employees who are technically, but not actually, "on call" are deemed to be within the scope of their employment.

Thornberry, Circuit Judge

Appellant Bridger brought this suit in state court to recover damages for injuries to himself and the death of his wife, caused when the car occupied by appellant and his wife was struck from the rear by a car driven by Billy Farris Teasley, an employee of appellee International Business Machines Corporation (IBM). Alleging diversity of citizenship, IBM removed the case to the court below. Both sides moved for summary judgment; the trial court granted IBM's motion, holding that the facts established as a matter of law that Teasley was not acting within the scope of his employment with IBM at the time of the accident. Upon a careful review of the record, we have concluded that the issue of scope of employment should have been left to the jury. Accordingly, we reverse the judgment below and remand for trial.

Teasley was a "customer service engineer" or serviceman for IBM, performing repairs and service on IBM products (typewriters, dictation equipment, and the like) on the owners' premises. He was required to be at the day's first job by 8:30 a.m. and was permitted to cease work in time to return to IBM's Macon, Georgia, office by 5:15 p.m., although he was not required actually to return to Macon at the end of the day. For any work done outside these hours, Teasley was paid overtime. Although all customer service engineers were subject to call seven days a week, twenty-four hours a day, to perform emergency service work, Teasley had not received an emergency call for at least two years prior to the date of the accident, and the equipment he was trained to repair was not normally serviced after regular hours. Moreover, it is unclear from the record whether IBM could relay an emergency call to Teasley in the field; Teasley's supervisor testified only that "now we are actually using radios to contact them" (emphasis added).

Teasley drove his own car when making service calls, and was paid $2.70 per day for maintenance, whether he drove his car or not. In addition, IBM paid him mileage for the distance between his home in Warner Robins, Georgia, to the first job of each day, the distance he drove between job sites during the day, and the distance from the last job site back to Warner Robins, regardless of whether he actually returned to Warner Robins after finishing his last job.

On the day of the accident in question, after spending about two hours at IBM's Macon office, Teasley performed service work at Robins Air Force Base in Warner Robins for almost two hours. Thereafter he drove to the Agriculture Stabilization and Conservation Service office in Perry, Georgia, and did repair work there for approximately four hours. It is undisputed that this was his last service call for the day and that he received no emergency calls that night. He left Perry at roughly 5:00 p.m. and took the eastern-most of four alternate routes to Warner Robins, located roughly twelve miles northeast of Perry. At the town of Bonaire, Georgia, he drove east to the Flamingo Club, where he drank beer until ten o'clock that night. He then resumed his trip toward Warner Robins. Shortly after reaching the highway to Warner Robins, his car struck appellant's car from the rear, severely injuring Mr. Bridger and killing his wife. Teasley claimed and received mileage for the trip from Perry to Warner Robins.

In Georgia, an employer's liability for the torts of his employee is governed by statute:

> Every person shall be liable for torts committed by his wife, his child, or his servant, by his command or in the prosecution and within the scope of his business, whether the same shall be by negligence or voluntary. Ga. Code §105-108. Undeniably, Teasley was performing a purely personal mission while he was at the Flamingo Club for almost five hours drinking beer, and IBM cannot be liable for any tort he committed while engaged in that mission. . . . Under Georgia law, however, the employer's liability for his employee's torts is suspended only during the employee's "deviation" from his duties; upon the employee's resumption of his work, the employer's liability re-attaches. . . . Thus, the issue here is whether the trial court properly held that the evidence conclusively established that Teasley had not resumed the discharge of his duties at the time of the accident.

In Southern Gas Corp. v. Cowan, 1954, 89 GA. App. 810, 81 S.E.2d 488, the Georgia Court of Appeals held that facts substantially similar to those of the case at bar authorized a jury finding that an employee-driver was acting within the scope of his employment at the time of an automobile accident. Bowman, a salesman and serviceman for Southern Gas, collided with the plaintiff while driving home in a company-owned car roughly two hours after his last call of the day. The company paid operating expenses for the car, which Bowman could keep at home for his personal use subject to emergency business calls. Relying primarily on the fact that Bowman kept the car for his personal use subject to emergency calls, the court of appeals held that this evidence warranted a jury finding that Bowman was acting within the scope of his employment while driving home in the company car:

> To the extent that he was subject to call at all hours and had the automobile there to use in case he was so called, the keeping of the automobile at his home was in furtherance of his employment duties. . . . Bowman's driving of the company's automobile from the place of his last call to his home where he would keep it subject to using it on company business in the event he was called out by the company was within the scope of his employment.

81 S.E.2d at 490. The court expressly reserved the question whether Bowman would have been acting within the course of his employment while performing personal errands after reaching his home.

The holding in Cowan is somewhat ambiguous. Bowman was arguably benefiting his employer both by keeping the car subject to use on emergency business and by storing his employer's car at his home overnight. Whether either of these possible benefits was enough to impose vicarious liability on an employer, or whether both of them were necessary, was unclear until the Cowan court decided Price v. Star Service and Petroleum Corp., 1969, 119 Ga.App.171, 166 S.E.2d 593. There, an employee of Star Service had been involved in a collision while driving home from a Sunday church service in a company car. The opinion contains no mention of whether the employee was on call at the time of the accident. It was argued that the employee was benefiting his employer simply by driving the company car home for storage; but the court squarely rejected that argument, holding that company ownership of the car, standing alone, is an insufficient basis of employer liability. That holding makes it evident that the fact that Bowman was on call was the deciding factor in imposing liability on the employer in Cowan. It follows that, if Teasley was subject to call after resuming his trip home to Warner Robins, he was, no less than was Bowman, acting within the scope of his employment.

The trial court distinguished Cowan, however, on the ground that Teasley was not subject to emergency call. Noting that Teasley had not received an emergency call in at least two years, and pointing to IBM's doubtful ability to contact Teasley in the event of an emergency, the trial court held that the requirement of availability in emergencies was "never enforced and . . . not expected to be enforced" and was "at best a theoretical requirement." In our view, the question whether Teasley was on call was properly a question for the jury in the instant case. Merely because no emergency calls had been made is no evidence that IBM would not "enforce" the requirement that servicemen answer such calls if they were made. Nor is it as clear to us as it was to the trial court that IBM had no way of contacting Teasley in the event an emergency call was made. As noted above, Teasley's supervisor testified on deposition that "now we are actually using radios to contact them" (emphasis added). While it is reasonable to infer from this statement that at some point in the past IBM did not use radios to contact its servicemen, the statement says nothing about whether IBM had any means of contacting its servicemen before the installation of the radios. In brief, the question whether Teasley was in fact subject to emergency call—which, as we have seen above, is a critical factor in determining his employer's liability—was a disputed issue of fact that was inappropriate for the decision by the trial court on motions for summary judgment. Accordingly, the judgment below is reversed and remanded for further proceedings consistent with this opinion.

Discussion questions

1. The court held that whether the employee was in fact subject to emergency call is a critical factor in determining his employer's liability and that it was a disputed issue of fact which should not be decided by motions for summary judgment but rather by a jury. Would the court's decision be the same if the employee had never made any "calls" after normal working hours for a period of ten years? Why?
2. Assuming that being "on call" imposes liability upon the principal for all "after normal working hours" accidents, whether or not the employee was actually making a "call" at the time the tort was committed, would there be any instances when the employer would not be liable for the employee's torts? Why?
3. Would a private agreement between employer-employee that the employer would not have any liability for the employee's torts after normal working hours where the tort occurs at a time when the employee is not actually making a "call" bar recovery by an injured third party in his action against the employer? Why?
4. What steps could an employer take to reduce potential liability for employee's torts when such employees are "on call" after normal working hours? Why?
5. Assuming the employer is liable to the injured party, what recourse, if any, does he have against his employee? Why?

Case 29

Rappaport v. International Playtex Corp.

352 N.Y.S. 2d 241 (1974)

Introduction

It is a fundamental rule of agency law that a principal is liable for the torts of his agent, as is a master for the torts of his servant, if the tort of the employee was committed in the scope of his employment. The factual question often presented in such cases was whether the employee was acting in the scope of his employment where the employee had both a business motive and personal motive to be at the place where the tort was committed. The following case illustrates the rule of law applied in such cases.

Cooke, Justice

This is an appeal from an order of the Supreme Court at Special Term, entered June 29, 1973 in Broome County, which denied a motion pursuant to paragraphs (1) and (7) of CPLR 3211 to dismiss the complaints in both actions.

These actions for personal injuries and wrongful death arise out of an accident October 10, 1971 involving automobiles owned and operated respectively by Joel R. Davis and Henry Barnum, the latter having subsequently died. Actions by Barnum's representatives and by the other occupants of his car were instituted against Davis, during the course of which Davis was examined before trial on September 27, 1972. A month later, the instant actions were commenced against International Playtex Corporation, the gravamen of the complaints being that, at the time of collision, Davis was operating his vehicle in the course of and in the scope of his employment with said corporation. . . .

Proof was advanced that during October, 1971 Davis was employed as a salaried outside salesman by Playtex in a 16-county area surrounding Syracuse, New York, having been employed in such a capacity by said concern for 21 years; that his duties included selling the employer's products directly to retail stores and preparing reports and orders relating to such sales; that Davis did not have an office but worked out of his home at Cazenovia, New York; that he was required to own and operate a motor vehicle as a condition of his employment, for which he received a flat monthly reimbursement, most of his employment travel being by car; that he had no set hours of employment but worked whenever it was necessary including weekends; and that he was urged by his district manager to work evenings and weekends.

There was also a factual showing that on the day of the accident, a Sunday, Davis worked during a part of the morning at his home on the inventory of Dey Brothers of Syracuse, the customer he intended to visit the following day; that he left for his then separated wife's home at Cazenovia arriving about 1:30 P.M. and departing two hours thereafter with the unfinished paper work of the morning still in his vehicle; that his destination at the time of the accident was the Canastota home of Madeline Reynolds, whom he later married; that Davis stated the purpose of the trip to the Reynolds home was " . . . to do paper work and visit at my friend's house, and have dinner at my friend's house . . . "; that he also stated that besides visiting his friend he had another purpose in going to her home, that he intended to do more work on the Dey account, adding "I do my weekly call reports for two days over there on Sunday, and I have that with me and also I have some other records and orders that I have to make out, so on, key accounts and books to close"; and that it was normal for Davis to do paper work every Sunday wherever he happened to be.

Under the doctrine of respondeat superior, an employer will be liable for the negligence of an employee while the latter is acting in the scope of his employment . . . and "(a)n employee acts in the scope of his employment when he is doing something in furtherance of the duties he owes to his employer and where the employer is, or could be, exercising some control, directly or indirectly, over the employee's activities." . . . As a general rule, an employee driving to and from work is not acting in the scope of his employment, but an exception to this rule would exist, in the case of an employee who uses his car in furtherance of his work and while he is driving to a business appointment, since such a person is working and under his employer's control from the time he leaves the house in the morning until he returns at night. . . .

Davis testified at the examination before trial that he was enroute to Canastota to visit Madeline Reynolds and to do more paper work, the further work to be done after dinner. With relation to a trip, involving both business of the employer and a private purpose of the employee, it was said in Matter of Marks v. Gray, 251 N.Y.90 at pages 93, 94, 167 N.E.181 at page 183.

> To establish liability, the inference must be permissible that the trip would have been made though the private errand had been canceled. . . . The test in brief is this: If the work of the employee creates the necessity for travel, he is in the course of his employment, though he is serving at the same time some purpose of his own. Clawson v. Pierce-Arrow Motor Car Co., 231 N.Y. 273, 131 N.E. 914. If, however, the work has had no part in creating the necessity for travel, if the journey would have gone forward though the business errand had been dropped, and would have been canceled upon failure of the private purpose, though the business errand was undone, the travel is then personal, and personal the risk.

The Marks decision, involving a workmen's compensation claim, has been reaffirmed . . . and cited in tort cases on the issue of "course of employment". . . . It has been stated that its formula "*when rightly understood and applied,* has never yet been improved upon" (1 Larson, Workmen's Compensation Law (1972), . . .) and Professor Larson, referring to efforts to "write off" Marks, points out: "It is enough that the business motive is concurrent under the doctrine of Marks v. Gray and, so understood, the doctrine is still very much alive." . . .

While the deposition transcript and telephone interview indicate that Davis intended to perform employment related paper work at his girl friend's house following dinner and that he customarily did such work there on Sundays, he also stated that he normally did his paper work wherever he happened to be. The only reasonable inference that can be drawn is that the business purpose alone would not have launched the subject journey, and that, had Davis not known Madeline Reynolds socially or had the dinner engagement been canceled, the trip to her home at Canastota would not have been undertaken. Accordingly, it cannot be said that the employer's business was even a "concurrent cause" of the fateful trip, . . . and, therefore, Davis was not in the scope of defendant's business at the time and respondent superior does not apply. . . .

Order reversed, on the law, and the motion for dismissal of the complaints granted, without costs.

Discussion questions

1. What is meant by the test that "the business motive must be concurrent" with the personal motive in order for liability to be imposed upon the principal-master for the torts of the agent-employee? Why?
2. Would the court's decision be different if the employee had told his employer prior to the tort that he would do work at his girl friend's house on Sunday evenings and the employer did not object? Why?

Case 30

King v. Young

107 So.2d 751 (Fla. 1958)

Introduction

It is a fundamental rule of agency law that a principal is liable only for the torts of his agent committed during the scope of the agent's employment. If the agent is not an "employee" but only an "independent contractor", the principal is not liable for any torts committed during the course of the agency. The following case illustrates the judicial tests applied by courts to determine whether the agent is an "employee" or an "independent contractor".

Kanner, Chief Judge

This is a negligence action which arose from a collision occurring in the nighttime on a highway north of Haines City between two tractor-trailers, resulting in the death of both drivers and a passenger riding in one of the vehicles. A summary judgment was granted in favor of the appellee, J. W. Brown, a defendant, and against the appellant, W. D. King, plaintiff in the trial court. The appeal emerges from that judgment.

The appellant King, as the owner of one of the vehicles, instituted suit against Carl Young, the owner of the other vehicle driven by John G. Young, and also against J. W. Brown and Beverly, Inc., on the theory that at the time of the collision, John G. Young, the driver of Carl Young's tractor-trailer, was the agent of J. W. Brown and Beverly, Inc. Based on answers to interrogatories and depositions of Brown and Beverly, Inc., the trial court rendered summary judgment in favor of these parties. The appellant concedes the correctness of the judgment as to Beverly, Inc. The sole dispute, therefore, concerns the judgment rendered in favor of the appellee, Brown.

On the issue of agency there is the simple allegation in the complaint that John C. Young was driving the tractor-trailer as the agent of Brown and Beverly, Inc. In the answer, this allegation of agency was specifically denied.

The facts as they concern the existence or nonexistence of an agency relationship between the driver, John G. Young, and J. W. Brown, the appellee, are not in dispute. Brown was engaged in business as a transportation broker; Carl Young was engaged in the trucking business as a partner with his now deceased brother, John G. Young; and Beverly, Inc., was engaged in the business of growing vegetables. Beverly, Inc., had grown some green beans and had sold them to a concern in Georgia. Not having facilities of its own with which to transport the beans, it communicated with Brown to arrange to have them hauled to the Georgia destination. Brown telephoned John G. Young and arranged with him to transport the beans. Young, as directed, loaded the vegetables and started out for Georgia, and the collision occurred while he was en route. The arrangement between Brown and Young was that the buyer of the beans would sign the bill of lading and Young would have this returned to Brown; Brown would then pay Young $234.79 for the trip, less a commission of seven percent which would be retained by Brown. After paying Young this money, Brown would bill Beverly, Inc., for the full amount. The driver, Young, was to furnish his own gas and oil and bear all expenses of the trip; and Brown did not tell Young what route to take, but Young had the choice of routes to follow.

It is argued by the appellant that it was Brown who initiated and arranged for Young to drive his vehicle to Georgia, that it was Brown who directed Young where to pick up and deliver the beans, and that it was Brown who was to pay Young for the hauling of the produce and who thereby was to receive a financial benefit from the trip.

It is the position of Brown that he is simply a transportation broker and that his connection with the transaction was in that capacity, while that of Young was as an independent contractor.

The term "agency" may be defined as "a contract either express or implied upon a consideration, or a gratuitous undertaking, by which one of the parties confides to the other the management of some business to be transacted in his name or on his account, and by which that other assumes to do the business and render an account of it." . . . In an agency relationship, the party for whom another acts and from whom he derives authority to act is known and referred to as a principal, while the other party who acts for and represents the principal and who acquires his authority from him is known and referred to as an agent. Thus, the agent steps into the shoes of his principal and acts for him pursuant to the grant of authority vested in him by the principal. . . .

In the instant case, Brown was merely the intermediary in the transaction between the shipper and the transportation medium. What he did was to procure transportation for the shipper through the trucker Young, for which he, Brown, was to receive as his brokerage commission a percentage of the total transportation price. Although Brown arranged for Young to haul the beans, Young was to pay his own expenses; he had the control and choice of routes to follow; and he was completely independent of Brown after the load was arranged, except that Young had to bring back a receipt so as to show delivery of the beans before he could collect his freight charge.

The status of an independent contractor, as distinguished from that of an agent, consists of a contractual relationship by one with another to perform something for him, but the one so engaged is not controlled or subject to the control of the other in the performance of the engagement but only as to the result. Conversely, a principal in an agency relationship retains the right to control the conduct of an agent in regard to the engagement intrusted to him. It may be said that the recognized distinction between an agent and an independent contractor relationship is determined by whether the person is subject to or whether he is free from control with regard to the details of the engagement. . . .

The position assumed by appellant is inconsistent, because the agency relationship as applied to the instant case can only contemplate that one person, that is, the principal, is superior and that the other person, the agent, is subordinate. There is no indication whatever that Brown was a principal to either the shipper of the commodity or of the trucker. He was called upon by the shipper as a transportation broker to procure transportation and he then arranged with the trucker to haul the load, for which he was only to receive a commission for his services. If it could be said that an agency existed, the status of an agent would apply to the appellee Brown as a broker, rather than that of principal. . . .

It is conceded that Young was not an agent of Beverly, Inc. At most, the appellee Brown, so to speak, was the middleman, merely the nexus in the transaction. We must conclude therefore that the summary judgment should be affirmed.

Affirmed.

Discussion questions

1. Would the court's decision be different if the principal-broker selected the route to be taken by the truck owners and driver and supplied them with gasoline and oil? Why?
2. Was the court correct in impliedly holding that an independent contractor could not be an agent? Why?

Case 31

Chevron Oil Company v. Sutton

515 P.2d 1283 (New Mexico 1973)

Introduction

In the United States hundreds of thousands of businesses are conducted by licensees, franchisees and lessees who sell billions of dollars of goods and services annually which are supplied by their licensors, franchisors and lessors. The legal question then arises whether such licensors, franchisors and lessors assert "sufficient control" over their licensees, franchisees and lessees to create a master-servant relationship and whether the servant has been cloaked with apparent authority to act as agent for the master. Third parties who are injured by the torts committed by such licensees, franchisees and lessees usually claim the licensor, franchisor or lessor exercised "sufficient control" and therefore is liable for the resulting tort under the doctrine of respondeat superior. Licensors, franchisors and lessors seek to avoid this legal result and to immunize themselves from liability by including appropriate self-serving language in their contracts that the other parties are "independent" business parties and that the licensor, franchisor or lessor has no right to control their operations or to exercise any control over their employees. The following case illustrates the judicial analysis applied by courts to determine whether or not "sufficient control" is maintained to impose liability upon the licensor, franchisor or lessor under the doctrine of respondeat superior.

McManus, Chief Justice

This suit began in the District Court of Bernalillo County. Sutton, respondent, sought damages for death by wrongful act . . . against petitioner, Chevron Oil Company (Chevron), Lee Sharp (lessee for Chevron) and Herbert R. Buss (Sharp's employee). Sutton's wife had died from injuries sustained in a car accident when a wheel of a car repaired by Buss came off the vehicle. The district court granted Chevron's motion for a summary judgment. On appeal to the Court of Appeals, the summary judgment was reversed. . . . The matter is now before this court on certiorari to the Court of Appeals.

One of the grounds upon which the Court of Appeals based its decision was that of strict liability. We discussed this doctrine at length in Stang v. Hertz Corporation, 83 N.M. 730,497 P.2d 732 (1972). Nothing we said in our decision in that case can properly be enlarged or extended to embrace the factual situation here.

The main issue before this court is whether Chevron asserted enough control over its lessee to constitute a master-servant relationship. If such relationship is present, then Chevron could be found liable under the doctrine of respondeat superior. The district court granted Chevron a summary judgment on this issue and the Court of Appeals reversed on grounds that there were sufficient indicia of control to warrant the submission of the issue to a jury.

In the present case, there are two important contract provisions which must be considered. The first provided that Sharp was " . . . engaged in an independent business, and nothing herein contained shall be construed as granting to (Chevron) any right to control (Sharp's) business or operations, or the manner in which the same shall be conducted." This agreement, on its face, tends to show that there was no master-servant relationship present, but that Sharp was merely an independent contractor. However, the majority rule is that the manner in which the parties designate a relationship is not controlling, and if an act done by one person on behalf of another is in its essential nature one of agency, the one is the agent of the other, notwithstanding he is not so called. . . .

Furthermore, it has long been the rule that a third person who deals with an agent is not bound by any secret or private instructions given to an agent by the principal. . . . When such agreements do not control, "whether a station operator is an employee of an oil company or an independent contractor depends on the facts of each case, the principal consideration being the control, or right to control, of the operation of the station." (Emphasis added.) In Shaver, supra, the court granted summary judgment for the defendant when the defendant did not send its personnel to check the premises or deal directly with the operator of the station, but did allow the station operator to display the defendant's trade mark and signs, and use its credit card facilities. However, the court noted that "slight changes in facts may result in different conclusions as to the presence of an issue for determination by the jury." In addition, the court stated that when oil company personnel check the station for cleanliness and worthless check frequency, and suggest gas prices and ways to increase the business of the station, then these additional facts are enough to submit the case to a jury. . . .

In the present case, there is a substantial dispute as to a material fact, and this should foreclose summary judgment. The fact in dispute is whether or not Chevron exercised such control over Sharp as to bring the doctrine of respondeat superior into play. Independent stations of the appellant were required to: (1) diligently promote the sale of Chevron's brand products; (2) remain open for certain hours and days and "meet the operating hours of competitors"; (3) keep the premises, restrooms and equipment in a "clean and orderly condition"; (4) present a "good appearance"; and (5) promote Chevron's image to the motoring public. In addition, Sharp also (6) sold Chevron products and dispensed gasoline and oil provided by the Chevron organization; (7) received the benefit of Chevron advertising; (8) wore uniforms containing the Chevron emblem; (9) used calling cards which billed the station as "Lee Sharp Chevron and Four Wheel Drive Equipment" (apparently with Chevron's consent); and (10) the customers of the Sharp station were permitted to charge purchases of both products and repairs on Chevron credit cars. No one of these factors is controlling, but all are useful in determining whether or not control was present. By using all of these factors, there is a sufficient factual question as to whether or not there was an actual master-servant relationship.

Even if there were not a material issue as to whether or not Chevron asserted enough control as to create an actual master-servant relationship, there still exists a material issue as to whether or not Chevron had clothed the lessee with apparent authority.

In 3 Am.Jur.2d, Agency, § 74, at 477 (1962), it is stated:

> The apparent authority of an agent is to be determined by the acts of the principal, and not by the acts of the agent; a principal is responsible for the acts of an agent within his apparent authority only where the principal by his acts or conduct has clothed the agent with the appearance of authority. . . . The apparent authority of an agent results from statements, conduct, lack of ordinary care, or other manifestation of the principal's consent, whereby third persons are justified in believing that the agent is acting within his authority. . . . The acquiescense of the principal in an extension of his authority by an agent in the transaction in question may be sufficient to create the appearance of authority in the agent to such act. . . . In such case, the appearance of authority is created because of the fact that the third person is entitled to assume that the principal is cognizant of authority and would forbid it if it were unauthorized. . . .

Here, Chevron knew of and allowed Sharp to conduct his Four Wheel Drive Fixit Shop and it would be reasonable to assume that if Chevron did not want Sharp to continue such a business, it should have forbidden such activities or at least have put the public on notice that Sharp did not have the authority to make repairs and that it would not be responsible for such repair activities. Instead of putting the public on notice that Sharp did not have the authority to make such repairs, Chevron advertised in the telephone directory that its stations performed auto repairs, and that its repairmen were skillful. Sutton relied on such statements, in addition to relying on signs, uniforms, and credit card privileges which indicated to the public that Sharp was under the control of and was an agent of Chevron. . . . Thus, because Sutton relied on such statements and indicia of authority, there is a material question of fact present as to whether or not Sharp had been clothed with apparent authority by Chevron to act as Chevron's agent.

The second contractual provision is to the effect that Chevron " . . . has no right to exercise any control over any of (Sharp's) employees, all of whom are entirely under the control and direction of (Sharp) who shall be responsible for their actions and omissions."

The general rule is that a principal is not liable for the wrongful act of an assistant who has been procured by his agent unless the latter can be said to have been clothed with authority to employ help. . . . Such authority may, however, be implied from the nature of the work to be performed. As stated in Monetti v. Standard Oil Co., 195 So. 89 (La. App.1940):

> We find that . . . where the work for the performance of which the contract is entered into is such as to indicate the necessity of the employment of a subagent, there is liability in the principal for the acts of the subagent. . . .

Here, the record shows that it would be quite impracticable for Sharp to have operated the Chevron gas station by himself. In fact, various clauses in the contract show clearly that the parties contemplated that such an assistant, or possible more, should be employed. Furthermore, Gulf Refining Co. v. Brown, 93 F.2d 870, 116 A.L.R. 449 (4th Cir.1938) states:

> It is clear that a principal may not escape liability to third persons for the torts of a subagent, appointed by his agent with his consent, merely by entering into a contract with his agent under which the latter assumes sole responsibility for the subagent's conduct.

Therefore, if a master-servant relationship in fact existed, the liability of the subagent may be imputed to Chevron regardless of the language in the written contract to the contrary.

The cause is reversed and remanded to the District Court of Bernalillo County for action consistent with this opinion.

It is so ordered.

Discussion questions

1. What additional language should Chevron Oil Company have included in its contract with its lessee to help support its contention that it did not exercise "sufficient control" over its lessee?
2. What steps could Chevron Oil Company have taken to rebut any presumption that it had clothed its lessee with apparent authority?
3. What lessons can be learned from this case by the multi-billion dollar franchising industry?

Case 32

Collins v. City of New York

11MISC2d 76 (Supreme Court, 1958)

Introduction

Police departments throughout the United States usually require police officers to carry their regulation service revolvers at all times, while on duty and off duty. The police officer is also usually required to be available for police duty at all times.

However, before a municipal employer can be held liable by a judge or jury for a tort committed by its employee, the injured person must prove by a preponderance of the evidence that the tort was committed while the police officer was acting within the scope of his or her employment.

The following case illustrates how the court interpacts the essential requirement "within the scope of his or her employment."

Henry Clay Greenberg, J.

On September 28, 1953 Harold Kearney, a New York City policeman, while walking on the platform of a subway station on his way to report for duty, accidentally dropped a paper bag in which he was carrying his off-duty revolver. It went off when it hit the ground, the bullet striking plaintiff, who was walking about 20 feet to the rear of Kearney.

There is no problem in resolving the question of Kearney's liability. "A very high degree of care is required from all persons using firearms in the immediate vicinity of other people, no matter how lawful, or even necessary, such use may be" (4 Shearman and Redfield on Negligence [rev. ed.], 761, p. 1742). No. 192 of the Regulations of the Police Department provides that members of the department "shall exercise the utmost care in handling firearms". The carrying of a loaded revolver in a paper bag at arm's length, especially in a crowded city, is a clear disregard of basic standards of safety and constitutes actionable negligence. It may be observed that Kearney was found guilty after a hearing by the department of neglect of duty in the violation of the regulation requiring him to use the utmost care in carrying his revolver.

The serious problem in this case concerns the claimed liability to plaintiff of the codefendant, the City of New York. Plaintiff argues that the city is liable under the doctrine of *respondeat superior* for injuries resulting from the negligent carriage of a revolver by a policeman, who is required to carry it at all times, even when off duty. The city urges that it cannot be held liable, because Kearney was not at the time actually engaged in performing police work or police action within the scope of his employment.

The law is, of course, now well settled in this State that a municipality may be cast in liability for the negligence of an officer or employee in performing a governmental function. The waiver of sovereign immunity by section 8 of the Court of Claims Act included the civil divisions of the State and made them answerable for the wrongful acts of their officers and employees "in accordance with the same rules of law as applied to actions in the supreme court against individuals or corporations". This was paraphrased in *Runkel v City of New York.* "In other words, in each case the test now is whether an individual or private corporation, assuming that he or it were obligated to discharge the governmental duty involved, would be liable *to the injured person for a breach of that duty.*" Thus, the doctrine of *respondeat superior*—that the master is liable in damages for injuries caused by his servant's negligent performance of his duties—is now applicable with respect to municipal officers and employees.

The doctrine has always been consistently applied by our courts and was deemed so well stated in the early case of *Rounds v Delaware L. & W.R.R. Co.* as to merit quotation and emphasis in the fairly recent cases of *Sauter v New York Tribune:* "'the rule was declared to be, that the master was responsible *civiliter* for the wrongful act of the servant causing injury to a third person, whether the act was one of negligence or positive misfeasance, *provided the servant was at the time acting for the master, and within the scope of the business intrusted to him. The master is liable only for the authorized acts of the servant, and the root of his liability for the servant's acts in his consent, express or implied, thereto* * * * and this, although the servant departed from the private instructions of the master, *provided he was engaged at the time in doing his master's business, and was acting within the general scope of his employment.*"

The *Sauter* opinion, however, went on to point out, at page 445 (quoting now from *Mott v Consumers Ice Co.,* 73 N.Y. 543, 547): "'But if a servant goes outside of his employment, and without regard to his service, acting maliciously, or in order to effect some purpose of his own, wantonly commits a trespass, or causes damage to another, the master is not responsible."

The issue in this case, then, narrows down to the question as to whether Kearney, at the time he carried this revolver and negligently permitted it to go off, was engaged in acting for his master—the City of New York—within the scope of the business intrusted to him and general scope of his employment.

A member of the police force is required to carry his regulation service revolver at all times, with the qualification that he may substitute therefor a Colt or Smith & Wesson revolver of not less than .32 caliber when off duty and not in uniform (N.Y. City Police Dept. Reg., No. 281). The apparent basis for this rule is that the off-duty policeman is required to be available to perform in his employer's behalf at all times even though technically off duty. The fulfillment of this obligation to be available for service and to be prepared for service constitutes positive performance of the requisites of the policeman's employment. Such performance even in a negligent or imperfect manner contrary to the warrant of section 192 does not refute, alter or terminate the intrinsic character and nature of the act. In these circumstances there exists no affirmative pursuit by the policeman of an interest which could be termed personal, inimicable or otherwise separate and distinct from the performance of his employer's command. The employer is absolved of liability where the employee is not participating in any act or function beneficial to the employer's interest or where the employee is clearly acting in furtherance of his personal interest. The defendant policeman's employment is of a divisible character, viz., on tour or patrol—active duty; off duty—available for emergency duty. The instant circumstances demonstrate that the defendant policeman though technically within the off-duty classification was engaged in the execution of a function specifically prescribed by the defendant employer the City of New York and the careless or negligent performance of such duty—carrying a gun—nonetheless constituted performance of a requirement of his employment and in furtherance of his employer's interest. The employer is therefore responsible for the consequences of such acts.

It is unfortunate in my view that the regulations do not specifically state how the policeman shall carry his revolver when not in uniform, merely enjoining "utmost care", although a holster is required to be used when in uniform. This lack of specification might well be regarded as an added argument for holding the city responsible for the negligent, indeed reckless, manner in which this off-duty gun was being carried. But in any event, the city must be held responsible under the doctrine of *respondeat superior* for damages occasioned by negligent performance of a required function within the line of duty of a policeman.

To impose such liability it is not necessary that the policeman be then actively engaged in police "work". It is sufficient that he is performing some act in furtherance of his police function.

It is important to distinguish this situation from the cases wherein intoxicated or unbalanced police officers, generally after a tour of the bars, proceeded to shoot some innocent bystander. Absent proof of prior notice of such propensities on the part of the authorities, the city may not be held liable under the doctrine because the officer has then gone "outside of his employment, and without regard to his service, acting maliciously, or in order to effect some purpose of his own" (*Mott v Consumers Ice Co.*, 73 N.Y. 543, *supra*).

The injuries sustained by the plaintiff are serious in character both from the standpoint of pain, suffering and permanency and also from the standpoint of economic loss. The city did not in any respect challenge the extent of the injuries or the loss sustained. The plaintiff was examined by an orthopedist on behalf of the city, but he was not called to testify. On the basis of all the testimony, therefore, the court directs judgment in favor of plaintiff and against the defendants in the sum of $50,000. This constitutes the decision of the court pursuant to section 440 of the Civil Practice Act.

Discussion questions

1. Would the result of this case be the same if the accident occurred while the police officer was walking on the platform of a subway station on his way **home** after completing his tour of duty?
2. Would the result of this case be the same if the accident occurred while the police officer was walking on the platform of a subway station on his day off while he was using the subway for a personal reason such as to visit a friend?

Case 33

Joseph v. City of Buffalo

608 N.Y.S.2d 396 (1994)

Introduction

The following case demonstrates the legal reasoning employed by the courts to determine whether a tort committed by a police officer while off duty is within or outside the scope of his employment.

Smith, Judge.

The primary issue in this case is whether defendant City of Buffalo is entitled to summary judgment on the issue of its vicarious liability for the acts of defendant Joseph, an off-duty police officer, that resulted in severe injuries to his infant son.

On December 10, 1976, at approximately 8:00 A.M., defendant Randie Joseph, a police officer with the Buffalo Police Department, completed his eight-hour work shift and returned home carrying his loaded police service revolver. Defendant then went to the upstairs bedroom of his infant children, where he lay down on the bed of his three-year-old son, placed the unlocked, loaded revolver underneath the mattress, and observed his children as they played. As defendant later reclined downstairs on his living room couch, he heard the sound of a firearm being discharged. He ran upstairs to find his son underneath the mattress of his bed with a gunshot wound to his head. Defendant's son had apparently rolled up the mattress and found defendant's service revolver, which had discharged, injuring the infant.

Plaintiff, the child's mother, commenced this personal injury action against the City of Buffalo alleging vicarious liability under the doctrine of *respondeat superior.* The City initiated a third-party action against Joseph for a judgment declaring that defendant was not acting within the scope of his employment when he placed the gun under his son's mattress and when the accident occurred.

The Court expressly adopted the analysis set forth in the dissent on the prior appeal and concluded that Joseph, at the time of the conduct in issue, was not engaged in any police business and that the City is not vicariously liable for his conduct. This Court granted plaintiff's motion for leave to appeal.

Contrary to plaintiff's assertion, section 50-j of the General Municipal Law does not preclude summary judgment in this case. That statute governs the ultimate responsibility for negligence in the performance of duties by police officers. Subdivision (1) provides, in part, that a city shall assume the liability for the negligent act or tort of a duly appointed police officer of such municipality "provided such police officer, at the time of negligent act or tort complained of, was acting in the performance of his duties and within the scope of his employment." A police officer is deemed to be acting in the discharge of duty "when engaged in the immediate and actual performance of a public duty imposed by law and such public duty performed was for the benefit of the citizens of the community * * * and the municipal corporation * * * derived no special benefit in its corporate capacity" (General Municipal Law 50-j[2]).

Here, Joseph was not acting in the performance of his duties and within the scope of his employment when he placed the gun under his son's mattress and when the accident occurred as he napped in his home. Rather, he had returned home from work, placed the unlocked, loaded revolver underneath his son's mattress and gone downstairs to rest when his revolver accidentally discharged several hours later. Thus, it cannot be said that Joseph was engaged in the immediate and actual performance of a public duty imposed by law. The fact that rules 4.8.6 and 4.1.9 of Rules for the Government and Discipline of the Police Department of the City of Buffalo require police officers to carry their service revolvers while off duty, and to undertake the same responsibility for the suppression of disturbances and in the arrest of offenders when off duty as when on duty, does not warrant a different result. Furthermore, rule 4.8.3 states that police officers "shall be responsible for the security of their firearms at all times."

We must examine *Kull v. City of New York* and the impact, if any, of section 50-j. In *Kull*, a police officer was preparing to go on his tour of duty. He had just finished shaving and was walking toward his kitchen carrying his revolver. He placed the revolver on a television set in order to put on his shirt. Shortly thereafter, the infant plaintiff picked up the revolver and was injured when it accidentally discharged. That feature materially differentiates *Kull* from the present case, where the officer left his loaded service revolver unattended under his infant son's mattress for several hours while he napped in his own home. That conduct is wholly unrelated to any duty involving his employment.

Section 50-j which was intended to extend the applicability of the previous General Municipal Law

50-j, which was limited to the City of New York, "to all counties, cities, towns, villages, authorities and agencies to require them to assume the liability of and save harmless any duly appointed police officer for any negligent act committed in the performance of his duties and within the scope of his employment" (Mem. of Dept. of State, Bill Jacket, L.1975, ch. 843). The purpose of the statute is to protect police officers from liability for their negligent acts while in the furtherance of their employers interests, or in the statutory words "in the immediate and actual performance of a public duty imposed by law" (General Municipal Law 50-j[2]). This purpose does not affect the force of *Kull v. City of New York,* our distinguishing it, or the applicable common-law principles of vicarious liability.

We have examined plaintiff's remaining contentions and conclude that they are without merit.

Accordingly, the order of the Appellate Division should be affirmed, with costs.

Discussion question

1. Would the result be the same in this case if the police officer injured his infant son by negligently discharging his gun while removing his gun from his holster at home after returning from work?
2. Do you agree with the holding of *Kull v. City of New York* discussed in the case?

Case 34
Mastroianni v. Village of Hempstead
166 A.D.2d 560 (1990)

Introduction

The following case illustrates how the court distinguishes torts committed within or outside the scope of employment. In doing so, the court recognizes that a municipal employer may be liable for torts committed by its employees while off duty and even when the tort occurs beyond the geographical area of his employment, so long as the tort is committed while he or she was acting within the scope of his or her employment.

Opinion

The defendant Richard Gregory, against whom this action was already dismissed pursuant to CPLR 3211 (a) (8), was hired as a police officer by the defendant Incorporated Village of Hempstead, located in Nassau County, in 1965. During his 17-year tenure, Gregory was promoted to sergeant, was never the subject of any complaint concerning the excessive use of force, and was never reprimanded for any reason.

On September 11, 1982, one of his regularly scheduled days off, Gregory observed his wife at a gas station located in West Sayville, Suffolk County, with the plaintiff's decedent, Mustafa Koksal, under compromising circumstances. An altercation ensued between Gregory and Koksal, as a result of which Gregory filed criminal assault charges with the Suffolk County Police Department. Gregory withdrew his complaint when his wife assured him she would not see Koksal again, but on September 13, 1982, when Gregory was on vacation, his wife did not return from an errand as expected and Gregory went to search for her. He again found her in the company of Koksal, this time at a diner in Islip, also in Suffolk County. During the ensuing struggle, Gregory's gun went off and Koksal was killed. Gregory maintained to Suffolk County police called to the scene that at the time of the shooting he was attempting to effectuate Koksal's arrest on account of the assault two days earlier.

The plaintiff seeks compensatory and punitive damages for Koksal's pain and suffering and for his wrongful death, not only from Gregory but also from the village. Alleging that Gregory acted under color of State law and within the scope of his employment as a village police officer, he interposes theories against the village premised on 42 USC 1983, on vicarious negligence under the doctrine of respondeat superior, and on negligence in the hiring, training, supervision and retention of Gregory. He originally sought redress in the United States District Court, Eastern District of New York, but the village successfully moved for dismissal. In its oral decision in favor of the village, citing, *inter alia, Monell v New York City Dept. of Social Servs.*, the Federal District Court noted that the incident was "a personal affair" which belonged in State court and specified that the dismissal was without prejudice to instituting the "purely State court actions * * * in the appropriate forum".

Alleging virtually the same causes of action against both the village and Gregory, the plaintiff now seeks redress in this forum. Sometime after joinder of issue and dismissal of the action as against Gregory, the village moved for summary judgment dismissing the complaint as against it and for dismissal of the cross claim, which motion the supreme Court denied without prejudice to renewal after completion of discovery. In addition to ruling that an award of summary judgment would be premature, the Supreme Court noted that there appeared to be a question of fact as to whether Gregory was effectuating an arrest.

As implicitly noted by the Supreme Court, the motion with respect to the cross claim is moot. Since, however, there is no indication that any facts exist which cannot now be stated but which would justify opposition to the motion and since it is otherwise clear that the village is not here liable for the acts on which this litigation is premised, we conclude that the request by the village for summary judgment dismissing the complaint should have been granted.

We note as did the Federal District Court, that the plaintiff, as a matter of law, may not recover punitive damages from the village.

The plaintiff's common-law negligence claims fare no better. We recognize that neither the fact that Gregory was off duty at the time of the shooting nor the fact that he was then beyond the geographical area of his employment is dispositive of the issue of whether he was acting within the scope of his employment so as to render the village vicariously liable for his acts. We simply rule that, on the facts of this case, about which there is no material dispute, no jury could reasonably conclude that Gregory was acting in an official capacity and on a public matter while at the diner. In light of the plaintiff's failure to come forward with or suggest the existence of any facts to overcome those which establish that Gregory's hiring, training and retention were in accordance with acceptable standards, there is no basis for imposing liability on the village on account of substantive negligence. Since there is no theory which conforms with the facts on which the plaintiff could recover damages from the village, the complaint must be dismissed.

Discussion questions

1. Would the holding of the case be the same if the police officer was **not** on vacation (i.e., off duty) when he shot the victim but did so while he was on duty and in uniform?
2. Would the result of the case be the same if the police officer shot the victim in the diner while he was off duty at a time when the victim was attempting to rob the diner in order to obtain money to flee to South America with the police officer's wife? See Case 24.

Case 35

Clancy v. County of Nassau

142 A.D.2d 626 (1988)

Introduction

The following case illustrates how the courts apply the doctrine of respondeat superior to hold a municipal employer liable for the torts committed by its employees even when the employee disregards prescribed procedures and acts recklessly.

Opinion

Following a nonjury trial, the trial court dismissed the plaintiff's complaint, holding that the defendant Wagner did not negligently cause the death of the deceased and that the actions of the deceased were the proximate cause of his own death. We find this determination to be contrary to the weight of the credible evidence and so reverse the decision and enter judgment for the plaintiff on the issue of liability.

Martin Clancy, Jr. died as a result of four gunshot wounds inflicted by the defendant Detective William Wagner of the Nassau County Police Department on February 6, 1983, at about 1:30 A.M., during an altercation which occurred in a shopping center parking lot located on Route 25A in East Setauket, New York. Clancy had been out drinking with friends that night, while the defendant Wagner, who was in plain clothes, and his wife had just left a restaurant after having a few drinks. The altercation had started when the defendant Wagner, who had peered into Clancy's automobile to investigate the loud noises and shouts being made by two of Clancy's friends who were in the car, was pushed from behind by Clancy. The defendant Wagner pushed back, and then pulled out his gun. Although the defendant Wagner claims he told Clancy at that time that he was "a cop", he never showed his badge, nor did anyone else hear the statement. In any event, at that point, Clancy and one of his friends, a John Pizzitola, ran to a nearby club to get help, telling the manager that there was a "crazy man down the street with a gun". Thereafter, Clancy, who had returned to the car ahead of the others, tackled the defendant Wagner from behind as the defendant Wagner, with his weapon drawn, was holding the third of Clancy's friends, a James Kelly, against the vehicle. Clancy and the defendant Wagner fell to the ground with Clancy on top, and a few seconds later the defendant Wagner fired his weapon four times. Clancy died shortly thereafter from the gunshot wounds.

Where a trial has been held without a jury, the scope of the appellate court's factual review is not limited solely to whether the verdict is against the weight of the credible evidence, but the court may also weigh the relative probative force of conflicting inferences that may be drawn from the testimony and grant the judgment which it finds is warranted, taking into account that the trier of fact was able to observe the witnesses.

On review of the evidence presented at the trial, we find that the defendant Wagner's actions, through his negligence in the handling of the situation which developed, his failure to use proper police procedure, and his hasty and unwarranted resort to deadly force, were the proximate cause of the death of the deceased. We do not find from the evidence that it could be said that Clancy knew at the time of the second attack that the defendant Wagner was a police officer. Several witnesses testified that Clancy described the defendant Wagner as a crazy man with a gun. This was essentially corroborated by a defense witness who testified that as he drove his car into the parking lot, an unidentified young man came up to him and told him to "keep going, the guy's got a gun". Moreover, the evidence shows that the defendant Wagner, who was in plain clothes, failed to clearly indicate his status as a police officer in the first instance. The inference made by the Trial Judge that Clancy knew the defendant Wagner was a police officer merely because Clancy had told the manager of the club that the man had a gun is not a reasonable one.

The defendant Wagner further compounded the situation when he attempted to arrest Kelly, who had been in the back seat of the car throughout the first argument, when in fact Kelly, judging from the defendant Wagner's own testimony, did not do anything to warrant such an intrusion. The defendant Wagner's actions at this point indicate that he had lost objectivity and had engaged in reckless and careless conduct. That Clancy's second altercation with the defendant Wagner was an attempt to rescue his friend Kelly who was being held at gunpoint by one who he thought was "a crazy man" with a gun, is clearly supported by the evidence and commonsense inferences flowing therefrom. Inasmuch as the defendant Wagner's negligence and reckless conduct led to Clancy's mistaken belief that he was not a police officer, the subsequent events cannot be regarded as remote.

Further, the finding by the trial court that the defendant Wagner was in imminent peril of his life because Clancy was choking him was incorrect because there was no such testimony to this effect at the trial. In fact, it is upon this aspect of the evidence that we find that the defendant Wagner was most unreliable. At trial, the defendant Wagner did not testify that Clancy was choking him; rather he claimed that Clancy was banging his head on the pavement. However, not only was he unsure whether Clancy had him by the shoulders, or by his sweater; there was also no evidence in the hospital records to suggest that the defendant Wagner had suffered any serious head injuries. In addition, the autopsy report's indication that the deceased had suffered a gunshot wound to his right hand further refutes the defendant Wagner's story that he was being choked at the time. Moreover, the extremely short period of time within which the shots were heard after Clancy and the defendant Wagner fell to the ground, taken together with the fact that the deceased was unarmed, does not support the finding that the defendant Wagner feared being "mortally wounded" or was in a position of "imminent peril". In these circumstances, we find that the force used was unreasonable and stemmed from a situation brought about by the defendant Wagner's recklessness and negligence.

There was expert testimony as to the regulation requirement that police officers, off duty and in plain clothes, carry their weapons. This, together with the other circumstances of the case, establishes that, in shooting Clancy, the defendant Wagner was acting in the course of his employment. Accordingly, the County of Nassau is vicariously liable under the doctrine of respondeat superior.

Having granted the defendants motion, the trial court did not find it necessary to complete the trial on the issue of damages. Since we reverse and grant judgment to the plaintiff on the issue of liability, the case is remitted for a trial on the issue of damages only.

Discussion questions

1. Would the result be the same if the tort occurred not in Nassau County but in Queens County? In Buffalo, New York while the police officer was on vacation?
2. Would the result be the same if the police officer shot the victim while the police officer was intoxicated or high on drugs?

Name: ______________________________

PROBLEMS

Date: ______________________________

Section Number: ______________________________

1. A was employed by P as a driver of one of its delivery trucks. Under the terms of his employment he made deliveries daily along a designated route and brought the truck back to the store's garage for overnight storage. One day instead of returning to the garage as required, he drove the truck twenty miles north of the area he covered expecting to attend a social function unrelated to his employment or to his employer's affairs. Through his negligence in operating the truck while enroute, A seriously injured T. A caused the accident and was solely at fault. T entered suit in tort against the store for damages for personal injuries, alleging that the store, as principal, was responsible for the tortious acts of its agent. Under these circumstances

______ a. P is not liable because A was an independent contractor.

______ b. P is not liable because A had abandoned his employment and was engaged in an independent activity of his own.

______ c. P is liable based upon the doctrine of respondeat superior.

______ d. T can recover damages from both A and P.

2. Normally a principal will not be liable to a third party

______ a. On a contract signed on his behalf by an agent who was expressly forbidden by the principal to make it and where the third party was unaware of the agent's limitation.

______ b. On a contract made by his agent and the principal is not disclosed, unless the principal ratifies it.

______ c. For torts committed by an independent contractor if they are within the scope of the contract.

______ d. On a negotiable instrument signed by the agent in his own name without revealing he signed in his agency capacity.

3. T purchased an electric typewriter from P under a written contract. The contract provided that P retained title until the purchase price was fully paid and granted him the right to repossess the typewriter if T failed to make any of the required ten payments. A, an employee of P, was instructed to repossess the machine on the basis that T had defaulted in making the third payment. A took possession of the typewriter and delivered it to P. It was then discovered that T was not in default. Which of the following conclusions is supported by the above facts?

______ a. A is not liable to T.

______ b. T can sue either or both A and P for damages, but can collect only once.

______ c. Neither party is liable since it was apparently an honest mistake.

______ d. If A is sued and must pay the judgment obtained against him, he has no rights against P.

4. A was employed as a carpenter by P. He negligently constructed a scaffold at one of P's construction sites. The scaffold collapsed and injured D (a fellow employee), F (a supplier), and A.

______ a. P is not liable to F if A disobeyed specific instructions regarding construction of the scaffold.

______ b. P is liable to F even though A was grossly negligent.

______ c. A is not personally liable to D or F.

______ d. A cannot obtain workmen's compensation.

5. The liability of a principal to a third party for the torts of his agent

______ a. Can be effectively limited by agreement with the agent.

______ b. Can not extend to the inclusion of a criminal act committed by the agent.

______ c. Is less onerous if the agent is acting for an undisclosed principal.

______ d. Is an example of the imposition of liability without fault upon the principal.

6. A works as a welder for P. He was specially trained by P in the procedures and safety precautions applicable to installing replacement mufflers on automobiles. One rule of which he was aware involved a prohibition against installing a muffler on any auto which had heavily congealed oil or grease or which had any leaks. A disregarded this rule, and as a result a customer's auto caught fire causing extensive property damage and injury to A. Which of the following is correct?

_____ a. P is not liable to A under the worker's compensation laws.

_____ b. P is not liable to the customer because P's rule prohibited A from installing the muffler in question.

_____ c. A does not have any personal liability to the customer for the loss because A was acting for and on behalf of his employer.

_____ d. P is liable to the customer irrespective of its efforts to prevent such an occurrence and the fact that it exercised reasonable care.

7. Charles was a salesman for the Singer Company, selling its sewing machines in a prescribed territory. His contract provided that he was to be paid a commission on each sale he made and that he would devote himself full time to the company's business. Charles was to use his own automobile and was given $100.00 a week allowance for its use. The company reserved the right to prescribe and regulate not only what business he was to do but also the manner in which he was to do it. Moreover, the company reserved the right to prescribe and regulate the route Charles was to take and which prospective customers he was to visit.

a. Is Charles an employee or an independent contractor? Why?

b. Would your answer to a. be different if their contract provided expressly that Charles was an "independent contractor"? Why?

c. Would your answer to a. be different if the company did not exercise any of its rights to regulate Charles' business conduct? Why?

d. Why is it legally significant to determine whether a person is an employee or independent contractor?

8. Rapid Delivery Service, Inc., hired Dolson as one of its truck drivers. Dolson was carefully selected and trained by Rapid. He was specifically instructed to obey all traffic and parking rules and regulations. One day while making a local delivery, Dolson double parked and went into a nearby customer's store. In doing so, he prevented a car legally parked at the curb from leaving. The owner of the parked car, Charles, proceeded to blow the horn of the truck repeatedly. Charles was doing this when Dolson returned from his delivery. As a result of a combination of several factors, particularly Charles' telling him to "move it" and that he was "acting very selfishly and in an unreasonable manner," Dolson punched Charles in the nose, severely fracturing it. When Charles sought to restrain him, Dolson punched Charles again, this time fracturing his jaw. Charles has commenced legal action against Rapid.

   a. Will Charles prevail?

   b. What liability, if any, would Dolson have?

9. Harold Watts was employed by Superior Sporting Goods as a route salesman. His territory, route, and customers were determined by Superior. He was expected to work from 9:00 AM to 5:00 PM, Monday through Friday. He received a weekly salary plus time and one-half for anything over 40 hours. He also received a small commission on sales which exceeded a stated volume. The customers consisted of sporting goods stores, department stores, athletic clubs, and large companies which had athletic programs or sponsored athletic teams. Watts used his personal car in making calls or, upon occasion, making a delivery where the customer was in a rush and the order was not large. Watts was reimbursed for the use of the car for company purposes. His instructions were to assume the customer is always right and to accommodate the customer where to do so would cost little and would build goodwill for the company and himself.

   One afternoon while making a sales call and dropping off a case of softballs at the Valid Clock Company, the personnel director told Watts he was planning to watch the company's team play a game at a softball field located on the other side of town, but that his car would not start. Watts said, "Don't worry, it will be my pleasure to give you a lift and I would like to take in a few innings myself." Time was short and while on the way to the ballpark, Watts ran a light and collided with another car. The other car required $800 of repairs and the owner suffered serious bodily injury.

a. What is Superior's potential liability, if any, to the owner of the other car?

b. What is Valid's potential liability, if any, to the owner of the other car?

10. Charles Jackson was one of Ace Equipment Company's best salesmen. The company had placed him on a special incentive payment plan whereby he could double his salary if he doubled his sales volume. Jackson was very aggressive and used hard sell techniques. He had an opportunity to sell 15 fork lifts to a cargo handling company, a sale that would put him over the top in his incentive plan. The cargo company insisted upon an express warranty that the particular fork lifts would handle 8,000 pounds safely. Jackson, without authority and knowing the lifts were only guaranteed to handle 7,000 pounds, represented that the equipment had an 8,000 pound capacity. He thought that the lifts probably were adequate. Ace Equipment neither authorized this express warranty nor was aware of Jackson's misrepresentation.

    Two weeks after delivery of the fork lifts one of them gave way and dropped a carton containing computer equipment weighing 7,800 pounds. The cargo company seeks to return the fork lifts to Ace and to recover for the damage caused to the computer equipment. Ace refused to refund the money for the fork lifts and denies liability for Jackson's misrepresentation.

    In an action by the cargo company against Ace Equipment Company to rescind the contract and to recover damages caused to the computer equipment, judgment for whom? Explain.

11. Barbara purchased an electric typewriter from Stanley for $1,000 under a written contract which provided that Barbara was to pay the purchase price in ten equal monthly installments of $100 and that Stanley had the right to repossess the typewriter if Barbara failed to pay any installment on time. Three months later, Stanley instructed Arthur, his sales manager, to repossess the typewriter from Barbara on the ground that Barbara defaulted in making the third installment. Arthur, acting in good faith, repossessed the typewriter over Barbara's objection because she claimed she made the payment that month. Two days later Stanley discovered that Barbara had in fact made the payment and was not in default.

    a. In an action by Barbara against Stanley for wrongful repossession, judgment for whom? Explain?

    b. In an action by Barbara against Arthur for wrongful repossession, judgment for whom? Explain.

    c. Assuming that Barbara recovers damages from Arthur, does Arthur have the right of indemnification from Stanley? Explain.

12. Frank Anthony is a delivery truck driver for White Bakery Company. One afternoon while making deliveries, Anthony decided to watch a few innings of the home team's baseball game on television. Fearing detection if he remained in the neighborhood where his route was located, he drove to another part of town where the company did not have any customers. He parked his delivery truck on a side street and proceeded to the Lucky Horse Bar and Grill. While watching the game there, he became embroiled in a heated argument with William Watson, another customer of the bar. In a rage, Anthony pushed Watson off his bar stool. Watson suffered a broken hip and is suing White Bakery for $250,000.

    In an action by Watson against White Bakery Company judgment for whom? Explain.

13. Edwards, a driver employed by the Sun Oil Company was directed to drive a company truck to a freight yard and pick up a load of barrels. Edwards arrived at the freight yard, loaded the truck with barrels and also picked up some waste wood lying in the yard. When he left the yard, instead of proceeding to his employer's place of business, he went four blocks in the opposite direction to deliver the waste wood to his sister. After making the delivery to his sister, he drove the truck in the direction of the freight yard on the way back to the employer's place of business, but before he reached the yard, he negligently struck Taney, a pedestrian.

    a. In an action by Taney against Sun Oil Company, judgment for whom? Why?

    b. Assuming Sun Oil Company is liable to Taney, what rights, if any, does it have against Edwards? Why?

14. Saxon was engaged in the trucking business. Sunshine Milk Company sold milk to retail stores in New York. Sunshine and Saxon executed an agreement which provided that Saxon was to deliver Sunshine's milk to Sunshine's customers. The agreement further provided that (1) Sunshine assumed no responsibility for breakdown or damage to Saxon's trucks, (2) in case of truck accidents, Saxon was to furnish other trucks so that the "trucking is to be handled in such manner as to cause no delay to Sunshine, and (3) Saxon's drivers were to do all loading and Saxon was to be responsible for shortages and breakages. One of Saxon's truck drivers negligently killed a pedestrian while delivering an order for Sunshine.

    a. In an action by the estate of the decedent against Saxon, judgment for whom? Why?

    b. In an action by the estate of the decedent against Sunshine, judgment for whom? Why?

15. Gambels conducted a department store and advertised that it carried on the practice of dentistry in one of its departments. Hayley went to the appropriate department to have her teeth professionally treated by Dr. Casey, an employee of Dr. Hutton. She now claims that the work was done so negligently and unskillfully that her jaw and gums were injured. Gambels contends that it has no liability on the ground that Dr. Hutton, a licensed dentist, and his employees conducted the business of that department in his individual capacity as lessee under a lease agreement with Gambels.

    a. In an action by Hayley against Gambels, judgment for whom? Why?

    ____

    ____

    ____

    ____

    ____

    b. In an action by Hayley against Dr. Hutton and Dr. Casey, judgment for whom? Why?

    ____

    ____

    ____

    ____

    ____

16. On October 1 Great Puppet Shows, Inc. hired Mandrake as its new purchasing agent. The Company knew that Puppetland Corp. was interested in selling certain stage scenery and props but it believed that it could purchase the property for less money if it did not disclose its identity. Therefore, it instructed Mandrake to drive over to Puppetland's office the next day and negotiate for the purchase of the property in his own name without disclosing the Company's identity. Mandrake was authorized to spend up to $5,000.

    On October 2, Mandrake negotiated and signed a contract with Puppetland for the purchase of the property for $4,500 and for delivery and payment on October 15.

    After signing the contract Mandrake began to drive back to the Company office. On the way he stopped at a bar for a few drinks which he knew was in violation of a Company policy which prohibited drinking of alcoholic beverages during working hours. After becoming intoxicated he left the bar and began driving to the office. Enroute he negligently struck and killed a pedestrian. Upon learning these facts the Company immediately discharged Mandrake who then advised Puppetland that when he signed the contract in his own name he was really doing so for his former employer's benefit and that he wanted nothing more to do with the contract.

    a. Does Puppetland have the right to enforce the contract against the Company? State "yes" or "no" and discuss.

    ____

    ____

    ____

    ____

    ____

    ____

    ____

b. Does Puppetland have the right to enforce the contract against Mandrake? State "yes" or "no" and discuss.

____

____

____

____

____

c. Does the Company have the right to enforce the contract against Puppetland? State "yes" or "no" and discuss.

____

____

____

____

____

d. Does the pedestrian's estate have a right to recover against Mandrake and Great Puppet? State "yes" or "no" and discuss.

____

____

____

____

____

e. Does the Company have a right to recover against Mandrake if it incurs any liability to the pedestrian's estate? State "yes" or "no" and discuss.

____

____

____

____

____

17. If an agent has, within the scope of the agency relationship, committed both negligent and intentional acts resulting in injury to third parties, the principal

______ a. May be liable even if the agent's acts were unauthorized.

______ b. May effectively limit its liability to those third parties if the agent has signed a disclaimer absolving the principal from liability.

______ c. Will be liable under the doctrine of respondeat superior only for the intentional acts.

______ d. Will **never** be criminally liable unless it actively participated in the acts.

18. Long Corp. is a real estate developer and regularly engages real estate brokers to act on its behalf in acquiring parcels of land. The brokers are authorized to enter into such contacts, but are instructed to do so in their own names without disclosing Long's identity or Long's relationship to the transaction. If a broker enters into a contract with a seller on Long's behalf,

_____ a. Long will **not** be liable for any negligent acts committed by the broker while acting on Long's behalf.

_____ b. The broker will have the same actual authority as if Long's identity had been disclosed.

_____ c. The broker will **not** be personally bound by the contract because the broker has express authority to act.

_____ d. Long will be bound by the contract because of the broker's apparent authority.

19. A principal will **not** be liable to a third party for a tort committed by an agent

_____ a. Unless the principal instructed the agent to commit the tort.

_____ b. Unless the tort was committed within the scope of the agency relationship.

_____ c. If the agency agreement limits the principal's liability for the agent's tort.

_____ d. If the tort is also regarded as a criminal act.

20. Generally, a disclosed principal will be liable to third parties for its agent's unauthorized misrepresentations if the agent is an

	Employee	*Independent Contractor*
_____ a.	Yes	Yes
_____ b.	Yes	No
_____ c.	No	Yes
_____ d.	No	No

21. Pine, an employee of Global Messenger Co., was hired to deliver highly secret corporate documents for Global's clients throughout the world. Unknown to Global, Pine carried a concealed pistol. While Pine was making a delivery, he suspected an attempt was being made to steal the package, drew his gun and shot Kent, an innocent passerby. Kent will **not** recover damages from Global if

_____ a. Global discovered that Pine carried a weapon and did nothing about it.

_____ b. Global instructed its messengers **not** to carry weapons.

_____ c. Pine was correct and an attempt was being made to steal the package.

_____ d. Pine's weapon was unlicensed and illegal.

CHAPTER 9

TERMINATION OF THE PRINCIPAL-AGENT RELATIONSHIP

80. Introduction.

The principal-agent relationship may be terminated by (1) mutual agreement, or (2) the performance of their contract, or (3) one party giving the other notice that he terminates their agency relationship. Furthermore, certain events may occur during their agency relationship which will legally terminate it by operation of law, regardless of their different wishes or intentions. When the agency relationship is terminated, the important question remains: what are the rights, duties, and liabilities of the parties to each other and to third parties upon termination and after termination of the principal-agent relationship? Each will be discussed in the sections that follow.

81. Termination of the principal-agent relationship by mutual agreement.

The parties may agree at the time they enter into their agency relationship that it will terminate at a specified date or upon the happening of a specified event or condition.[1] However, regardless of the specified date, event or condition, the parties may terminate their agency relationship effective on any other date by mutual agreement, oral or written.[2] The legal effect of termination of the agency relationship is that the agent no longer has any actual authority to act for his principal as of the effective date of termination. However, as we will learn later in this chapter, the principal must give appropriate actual and constructive notice to third parties of the termination of the agency relationship to avoid liability on any contracts wrongfully made by his former agent after their agency relationship has been terminated.

82. Termination of the principal-agent relationship by performance of the contract.

Where the principal-agent agreement provides that the agency relationship is to continue until a specific purpose is achieved or until a certain date, it will terminate when the agent has achieved his purpose[3] or upon the date specified[4] without any notice of termination required to be given by either party to the other. And where the principal-agent agreement does not state a termination date, it will terminate at the end of a reasonable time based upon all the circumstances of each case[5] without any notice of termination required to be given by either party to the other. At the time the agency agreement has been performed or upon the expiration of the agency agreement, the agent has no actual authority to act any further on behalf of his principal.

However, in the event either party wrongfully terminates their agency relationship, before the specific purpose is achieved or before expiration of the date specified or before the expiration of a reasonable time if none is specified, he will be in breach of contract and liable to the other party for damages resulting from his breach of contract.[6]

83. Termination of the principal-agent relationship by act of either party.

It is a fundamental rule of agency law, subject to two exceptions, that the principal and agent each has the legal power to terminate the agency relationship at any time even though their agreement specifies that it is for a fixed term or until a certain event or condition occurs or is silent as to when it is to terminate.[7] The two exceptions are an agency for a security and an agency coupled with an interest, which cannot be revoked by act of the principal while he is indebted to his agent.

The rationale for this fundamental rule is that the agency relationship is a consensual relationship and may continue only so long as both consent. Any other rule which compels a principal to continue to employ his agent is contrary to public policy because it would materially prejudice the legal and economic interests of the principal against his will when he no longer wishes to entrust his fortune, reputation, and legal rights and responsibilities to his agent. Moreover, any other rule which compels an agent to continue to work for his principal after he no longer wishes to do so is contrary to public policy because it would constitute involuntary servitude which is prohibited by the United States Constitution.[8]

Although each party has the legal power to terminate the agency relationship at any time, subject to the two exceptions mentioned, the question remains whether the party terminating the agency relationship is liable to the other party for so doing. The answer depends on whether the termination is legally justified and therefore not a breach of contract or not legally justified and therefore a breach. If the party who exercises the power to terminate their agency relationship has no legal right to do so, then he is liable to the other party for all damages proximately caused by his breach of contract including loss of salary, commissions or profits.[9] However, where a principal is legally justified in terminating his agency relationship, he may do so at any time without any liability regardless of the specified duration as where the agent commits a breach of his fiduciary duty[10] or negligently or intentionally fails to comply with the requirements of their agreement or the principal's lawful instructions.[11] Similarly, where an agent is legally justified in terminating his agency relationship he may do so at any time without any liability regardless of its specified duration as where the principal requires that the agent commit unlawful acts or obey unlawful instructions or where the principal fails to cooperate with the agent which makes it difficult or impossible for the agent to perform his duties.

The question then arises under what circumstances is a principal legally justified in terminating an agency relationship where the agency agreement contains an express condition that the principal must be personally satisfied with the agent's performance? Such a provision is different from the usual provision in agency agreements which defines satisfactory performance by an objective standard, such as the agent must sell at least $1,000,000 a year of the principal's goods as a condition of continued employment. When the personal satisfaction test is used, also known as the subjective test, the courts require only that the principal act in good faith in concluding that he is not personally satisfied with the agent's performance.[12] Consequently, if the principal acts in good faith, he is legally justified in terminating their agency agreement, regardless of its specified duration, without liability to his discharged agent. In the application of this rule, the principal is the sole judge of whether he is personally satisfied. Thus, the test is not whether a reasonable principal would be personally satisfied. Moreover, when the court decides whether the principal acted in good faith, it will not consider whether the principal was motivated by some ulterior desire, as where he wishes to appoint a different agent or that the agent had developed a profitable business.[13] The discharged agent has the burden of proof that his former principal acted in bad faith in an action to recover damages from the principal for breach of contract where the agent claims that the principal was not legally justified in terminating their agency relationship.

The question arises as to how much advance notice of termination of the agency relationship must be given by one party to the other where their agreement is silent? The answer depends on whether the agency agreement is for a specified duration and whether he is legally justified in terminating the agency relationship. If he is, as where the other party has breached the agency agreement, no advance notice of termination is required regardless of the specified duration of their agency relationship. In such a case the agency relationship may be terminated at any time effective upon receipt of the notice of termination. If he is not legally justified in terminating the agency relationship, then he is liable for doing so prior to the expiration of the specified term of their agency agreement no matter how little or much advance notice of termination is given.

A related question arises as to what rules apply when one party wants to terminate the agency relationship which has no specified duration where neither has breached the agency agreement. An agency agreement which has no specified duration is called an agency at will, which many principals and agents deliberately enter into to avoid long-term commitments. Where there is an agency at will, the rule is universally recognized that although neither party has breached the agency relationship, either party may terminate it at any time without any liability by giving reasonable notice of termination to the other party if their agreement does not specify how much advance notice of termination shall be given. What constitutes reasonable notice is largely determined by the practices, customs and trade usages of the industry that the principal and agent are engaged in. In many industries, two weeks' notice is considered reasonable.

The notice of termination of the agency relationship may be given by either party in any manner, oral or written, directly or indirectly, unless their agreement expressly provides otherwise.[14] Such notice is effective not upon dispatch but only upon receipt by the other even though not read by the party receiving it and even though not given in the particular form required by their agreement unless their agreement expressly provides otherwise. As a matter of practice, termination clauses in written employment contracts are carefully drafted and their terms control.

84. Termination of the principal-agent relationship by operation of law.

In the evolution of agency rules of law certain events were judicially recognized to have the legal effect of terminating the principal-agent relationship automatically by operation of law without any notice being required to be given. These events are (1) death of the principal or agent, (2) incapacity of the principal or agent, (3) destruction or loss of the subject matter of the agency, (4) bankruptcy of the principal or agent, (5) outbreak of war, (6) frustration of the agency purpose, and (7) supervening illegality. Each of these events causes the agency relationship to terminate automatically by operation of law regardless of the intent of the parties or the terms of their agreement. Each will be discussed separately.

(1) Death of the principal or agent

The death of the principal or agent automatically terminates their agency relationship by operation of law, except where the agency is coupled with an interest or a statute provides otherwise.[15] The rationale of this rule is that in every principal-agent contract there is an implied condition that each natural person will continue to exist during the agency. When the condition fails by reason of the death of either party, their agency relationship is automatically terminated by operation of law. Where the principal dies, the agent's actual and apparent authority terminated automatically by operation of law even though the agent is unaware of his principal's death.[16] Moreover, where the principal is a partnership or a group of joint principals, the death of any partner or joint principal will also terminate the principal-agent relationship even though the surviving partners or joint principals want the agency relationship to continue.[17]

Applying these rules, an agent has no actual or apparent authority to make gifts or charitable contributions on behalf of his principal after the principal dies.[18] In such a case, the estate of the deceased principal can recover the property given to the third party. Furthermore, even where the agent and third party were unaware of the principal's death at the time the agent contracted in his principal's name, the estate of the deceased principal and third party have no liability to each other on the contract and neither can enforce the contract against the other. In such a case, the third party may recover damages against the agent based upon the agent's breach of warranty because every agent impliedly warrants when he contracts in the name of his principal with a third party that he has actual authority to contract. Since the agent's actual authority was automatically revoked by operation of law upon the principal's death, the agent breached his implied warranty of authority and is liable to the injured third party for damages suffered as a result of his breach of warranty. This result applies even where the agent has acted in good faith and in a reasonable manner. Moreover, he is not entitled to reimbursement or indemnification for his loss, no matter how great, because he did not act properly when he contracted in his principal's name since he had no authority to do so after his principal dies. Thus, an agent who contracts in the name of his deceased principal does so at his peril. This common law rule has been severely criticized by almost all legal commentators and the Restatement of Agency on two different grounds. One is the injustice to the third party who reasonably relies on the existence of the agent's authority to bind his principal and the other is the injustice to the agent, who becomes personally liable to the third party for breach of his implied warranty of authority. Accordingly, a few states have modified this common law rule by statute, but in the overwhelming number of states, including New York, the common law rule continues to be the law.

There are two exceptions to the general rule, the effect of which is that the principal's death will not terminate the agency relationship. The first exception is where the agent has an agency coupled with an interest which continues despite the principal's death until the debt owed by the deceased principal to the agent is paid in full or until the destruction of the subject matter of the agency occurs.

The second exception is the result of statutory law, found in the Uniform Commercial Code, applicable to bank depositors. The Code provides that the death of a principal who is a bank depositor will not terminate the agency relationship between the deceased principal and his agent, the bank, until his bank receives notice of his death.[19] And such notice does not become effective as to the bank until it has had a reasonable opportunity to act upon such notice. Moreover, even where the deceased principal's bank has received notice of the principal's death, the bank may pay or certify his checks for a period of ten days after the principal's death, unless the bank is ordered to stop payment by a person claiming an interest in that account.[20]

For the same reasons applicable to a principal who dies, the death of an agent will automatically terminate the agency relationship and any agent-subagent relationship by operation of law.[21] Moreover, while the death of one joint agent will not automatically terminate the agency relationship by operation of law, the principal has the right to terminate it even though the surviving joint agent wishes to continue the agency relationship unless the principal expressly or impliedly agreed at the time the agency relationship was formed that the surviving joint agent could continue the agency relationship.[22]

(2) Incapacity of the principal or agent

The second case where the principal-agent relationship will be automatically terminated by operation of law is when the principal or agent lacks legal capacity to act. If either is judicially determined to be insane, their relationship is terminated by operation of law, without any notice being required to being given to the other party.[23] A judicial decree of insanity is deemed to be effective notice to all parties that the agency relationship is terminated whether or not the other party to the agency relationship has actual knowledge of the insanity or the judicial decree. When a judicial decree of insanity is made, the agent from that date forward has no actual or apparent authority to contract on behalf of such a principal and any such contracts he makes in the principal's name are not binding on the principal. However, if an insane principal has not been judicially declared insane, he will be bound to third parties by contracts made by his agent on his behalf in good faith and in ignorance of his principal's insanity. If a principal has brief periods of insanity that are insufficient to have him judicially declared insane, their agency relationship is not terminated by operation of law even though during such periods of insanity he has no legal capacity to contract or to appoint an agent.[24]

By contrast, the agent's temporary or permanent insanity does not necessarily terminate the agency relationship because an agent is not required to be completely sane in order to have authority to act for his principal.[25] However, if the agent does not have legal capacity to do the authorized act, their agency relationship is terminated by operation of law.

(3) Destruction or loss of subject matter of agency

The third case where the agency relationship will be automatically terminated by operation of law is when the subject matter of the agency is destroyed or lost. Partial destruction will also terminate the agency relationship if continuation of the agency relationship with respect to the remaining subject matter is inconsistent with the best interests of the principal. Termination of the agency relationship under the foregoing circumstances becomes effective only upon the agent's receipt of notice of termination unless their agreement expressly provides that termination shall occur immediately upon destruction or loss without any notice being required to be given.

(4) Bankruptcy of principal or agent

The fourth case where the principal-agent relationship is automatically terminated by operation of law is where the principal is adjudicated a bankrupt. In such a case his interest and control over the subject matter of the agency is legally vested in the trustee in bankruptcy and the principal-agent relationship is terminated by operation of law even though the agent has not received notice of his principal's adjudication of bankruptcy.[26] By contrast, if a principal has severe financial problems or is insolvent without any adjudication of bankruptcy, the principal-agent relationship is not terminated by operation of law unless the purpose of the agency is frustrated.

In comparison with a bankrupt principal, it is the general rule that an agent's adjudication of bankruptcy will not terminate the agency relationship unless the agent's adjudicated bankruptcy will have a detrimental effect on the business or credit of his principal if the agency were to continue.[27] Generally, the agent's adjudicated bankruptcy will terminate the agency relationship where his personal credit is important or where the principal's obligations will increase. Applying this rule, the bankruptcy of a *del credere* agent, who guarantees that he will pay the debts of customers to whom he sells his principal's goods on credit, will terminate the agency relationship because the agent's personal credit is relied on by his principal.

(5) Outbreak of war

The fifth case where the agency relationship will be automatically terminated by operation of law is when the principal resides in a foreign country which subsequently goes to war with the United States where the agent resides. The rationale of this rule is that the foreign principal has become a non-resident alien enemy upon the outbreak of war whose instructions may not be lawfully obeyed by his United States agent.[28] However, more recent cases have held that the outbreak of war does not terminate such an agency relationship *per se.* Such cases have held that whether termination occurs by operation of law depends upon whether it would still be legal for the agent to act[29] and whether the agent could reasonably believe that the principal would no longer desire him to act.[30] Thus, if a non-resident alien-principal engaged a United States resident-agent to sell his property in contemplation of war, the subsequent outbreak of war would not terminate the principal-agent relationship.[31]

(6) Frustration of the agency purpose

The sixth case where the agency relationship will be automatically terminated by operation of law is when there is a fundamental change in circumstances which frustrates the purpose for which the agency relationship was created, unless the principal agrees otherwise.[32] Among the circumstances which may frustrate the business purpose of the agency are substantial changes in the value of the subject matter or significant changes in the general business environment.

(7) Supervening illegality

The seventh and last case where the agency relationship will be automatically terminated by operation of law is when the principal's rights in the subject matter of the agency are divested by law or the agent cannot lawfully continue to perform the acts required by the agency. This will occur because of what is traditionally called supervening illegality. Applying these rules, the agency relationship will be terminated by operation of law where an agent's license is revoked subsequent to the formation of the agency relationship because it is now illegal for the agent to perform the act[33] or where there is a change in the law making the agent's proposed action illegal.

85. When notice of termination is required to be given by principal to third parties.

We have seen that the agency relationship may be terminated either by mutual agreement, performance of their contract, one party giving notice of termination to the other, or by operation of law. Upon the effective date of termination, the agent's actual authority, express or implied, is revoked. However, in many cases the former agent continues to have apparent authority to bind his former principal to third parties after his actual authority has been revoked. The question arises as to what the principal must do to revoke his former agent's apparent authority when it continues after termination of the agency relationship and how and when he may effectively terminate his former agent's apparent authority in order to avoid liability on contracts wrongfully made in his name by his former agent.

It is a fundamental rule of agency law that a principal must notify all third parties with whom his former agent previously contracted that his agent's authority has been revoked in order to avoid liability to such third parties on contracts made in his name by his former agent after his authority has been revoked.[34] Such notice may be oral or written and is effective when received by the third party.[35] In addition, the principal must also give notice to the public at large, called constructive notice,[36] that his agent's authority has been revoked in order to avoid liability on contracts wrongfully made in his name by his former agent with all other third parties after his authority has been revoked. When the principal gives both actual and constructive notice he has no liability on contracts wrongfully made in his name by his former agent after his authority has been revoked.

Constructive notice may be given and is effective when the principal publishes a public notice in a newspaper of general circulation in the area where the agency was regularly carried on or in a trade journal that is published for customers in the principal's trade informing the public that the named person is no longer an agent for the principal. The public notice is required to be published only once and is binding on all third parties who never previously contracted with the former agent even though such third parties never read the notice or otherwise had any knowledge that the agent's authority had been revoked. Third parties who never previously dealt with the former agent will usually obtain information about the public notice if they purchase a credit report concerning the principal in whose name the former agent contracts before giving the former agent goods or money. Credit reporting agencies read, collect and disseminate the published information as part of their credit report concerning the principal to those who purchase their credit reports.

The rationale of the rule that requires the principal to give both actual and constructive notice is that third parties usually rely on a person's apparent authority to contract on behalf of his principal. The apparent authority is originally created by the principal providing the agent with one or more of the following: business cards and stationery, business forms (order forms, sales invoices) company literature and brochures, company products, company uniforms, and company credit cards. After termination, the principal may not recover all of these items from his agent, thus adding even more substance to the former agent's continuing apparent authority. Although either the principal or agent may have terminated the agency relationship, third parties may not be aware of the termination and therefore continue to rely in good faith on the continuing apparent authority of the former agent to contract on behalf of the principal. Consequently, if the principal fails to give both actual notice and constructive notice, he will be bound to all third parties on contracts made in his name by his former agent. The following examples illustrate the application of these rules.

Example

P discharges A. P publishes a notice the next day in a newspaper of general circulation where the agency was formerly carried on that A is no longer an agent for P. One week later, A contracts in P's name to buy and receive goods on credit from T who never dealt previously with A. A absconds with the goods. T was not aware of the public notice. T sues P to recover the purchase price of the goods under the contract.

Held

T loses. T is bound by P's constructive notice even though he was not aware of it. A's actual authority was revoked on the date of discharge while his apparent authority was revoked on the date the newspaper notice was published.

Example

P discharges A. P publishes a notice in a newspaper of general circulation where the agency was formerly carried on that A is no longer an agent for P. P gives no other notice to anyone else. One week later, A contracts in P's name to sells P's goods to T who has previously dealt with A on a regular basis. A collects a deposit for such goods from T as well as $1,000 due on a prior purchase. A had prior actual authority to collect money owed to P. A absconded. T was not aware of the public notice. T sues P to when P fails to deliver the goods to him and when P fails to credit T for the $1,000 payment that T made to A.

Held

T wins. P was required to give T actual notice of termination of A's authority. P's constructive notice was not legally sufficient because T was not aware of such notice. Although A had no actual authority to bind P, he had apparent authority to do so.

86. When notice of termination is not required to be given by principal to third parties.

The rules requiring the principal to give both actual notice and constructive notice of the termination of the agency relationship do not apply where the principal dies, becomes bankrupt, or is judicially declared insane. In each such case, the agent's actual and apparent authority is revoked by operation of law, and the third parties who contract with the former agent in the principal's name have no rights against the principal or his estate. Moreover, neither the principal nor his estate can enforce the contract against the third party. In such a case, the third party's sole recourse is to recover from the former agent who contracted in the name of the principal because he has breached his implied warranty that he had authority to contract on behalf of the named principal. In that event, the former agent is not entitled to any reimbursement or indemnity from his former principal no matter how great his loss is and regardless of his good faith because he did not act properly when he contracted in his former principal's name as he was no longer his agent.

Notes

1. Shelton v. Lemmon, 268 S.W. 177 (Tex. Civ. App. 1924).
2. Shapiro v. Stahl, 195 F. Supp. 822 (M.D. Pa. 1961).
3. One Twenty Realty Co. v. Baer, 260 Md. 400, 272 A.2d 377 (1971); Freed Fin. Co. v. Preece, 14 Utah2d 409, 385 P.2d 156 (1963); In Re Szabo's Estate, 10 N.Y. 2d 94, 217 N.Y.S.2d 593 (1961).
4. Wilson Sullivan Co. v. International Paper Makers Realty Corp., 307 N.Y. 20, 119 N.E.2d 573 (1954).
5. Rutter v. Rutter, 74 N.M. 737, 398 P.2d 259 (1964); Beaucar v. Bristol Fed. Sav. & Loan Ass'n, 6 Conn. Cir. 148, 268 A.2d 679 (1969). A reasonable time is measured by whether the agent could reasonably believe that the principal still wanted him to act. Restatement, Second, Agency, Sect. 105, comment b (1958).
6. Kerr S.S. Co. v. Kerr Nav. Corporation, 113 Misc. 56, 184 N.Y.S. 646 (1920); McDonald v. Davis, 389 S.W.2d 494, (Tex. Civ. App. 1965); Helsby v. St. Paul Hospital & Casualty Co., 195 F. Supp. 385 (D. Minn. 1961), where the court emphasized that the principal in such a case has the power to revoke but not the right.
7. Smith v. Conway, 198 Misc. 886, 101 N.Y.S.2d 529 (1950); Sarokhan v. Fair Lawn Memorial Hospital, Inc., 83 N.J. Super. 127, 199 A.2d 52 (1964); Guerin Mills v. Barrett, 254 N.Y. 380, 173 N.E. 553 (1930), whereby the courts held that a power of attorney which was made irrevocable by statute could still be revoked by the principal; Century Refining Co. v. Hall, 316 F.2d 15 (10th Cir. 1963), where the court held that where no time is set for termination, the agent's authority may be terminated at any time at the election of either party.
8. 13th Amendment.
9. Wilson Sullivan Co. v. International Paper Makers Realty Corp., 307 N.Y. 20 (1954); Century Refining Co. v. Hall, 316 F.2d 15 (10th Cir. 1963).
10. Finnerty v. Frenchman, 118 N.Y.S.2d 790 (1952).
11. Getty v. Roger Williams Silver Co., 162 App. Div. 513, 147 N.Y.S. 1083 (1914).
12. The "personal satisfaction" test is sometimes found in the agency agreement as an unrestricted reservation by the principal of a right to cancel. Such a right, in the absence of bad faith, will be enforceable. See, Schweinburg v. Altman, 145 A.D. 377, 130 N.Y.S 37 (1911).
13. Brown v. Restsoff Min. Co., 127 App. Div. 368, 111 N.Y.S. 594 (1908).
14. NLRB v. Marcus Trucking Co. Inc., 286 F. 2d 583 (2d Cir. 1961); Tinney v. Duckett, 141 A. 2d 192 (D.C. Mun. App. 1958).
15. In Re Steinrich's Estate, 133 N.Y.S. 2d 137 (1954); In Re Szabo's Estate, 217 N.Y.S. 2d 593 (1961). An analysis of the rule that death terminates an offer by operation of law is found in "Death As Affecting Offers And Agencies," *Washington Law Review,* 3:133-144, July 1928. Wisconsin enacted, in Wisconsin Laws, 1943, C. 49, that "the death of the principal shall not operate as a revocation as to the attorney or agent until he shall have notice of the death, or as to one who, without notice of such death, in good faith deals with the attorney or agent; and this shall apply whether the agency was created in writing or not." In a number of states legislation has been enacted, but limited to those in the armed services or overseas on national business. See Restatement, Second, Agency, Vol 3, Appendix (1958).
16. In Re Grand's Estate, 43 N.Y.S. 2d 803 (1943); Thornton v. Lewis, 106 Ga. App. 328, 126 S.E. 2d 869 (1962); Mubi v. Broomfield, 108 Ariz. 39, 492 P. 2d 700 (1972); King v. Beale, 198 Va. 802, 96 S.E. 2d 765 (1957).
17. Shumate v. Sohon, 56 App. D.C. 290, 12 F. 2d 825, 59 A.L.R. 291 (1926); Ferguson v. Pilling, 231 Iowa 520, 1 N.W. 2d 662 (1942).
18. City Bank Farmers Trust Co. v. Housman, 59 N.Y.S. 2d 880 (1945); In Re Levine's Estate, 26 Misc. 2d 307, 203 N.Y.S. 2d 643 (1960); see, also, Glennan v. Rochester Trust and Safe Deposit Co., 209 N.Y. 12, 102 N.E. 537 (1913). However, New York General Obligations Law 2-501 provides that the death of a member of the armed forces does not terminate a written power of attorney so long as neither the agent nor the third person has actual knowledge or notice of death, and they act in good faith.
19. Section 4-405 of the Uniform Commercial Code relieves the bank of liability if it deposits, pays or collects a depositor's check without knowledge of his death.
20. Ibid.
21. In Re Chinese Merchant's Bank Ltd., 151 Misc. 425, 272 N.Y.S. 764 (1934).
22. Matthews v. Phoenix Mut. Life Ins. Co., 316 F. Supp. 1076 (W.D. Pa. 1970); Salisbury v. Brisbane, 61 N.Y. 617 (1874).
23. In Re Berry's Estate, 69 Misc. 2d 397, 329 N.Y.S. 2d 915 (1972); Jackson v. Hall, 139 Kan. 832, 32 P. 2d 1055 (1934).
24. First National City Bank v. Gonzalez & Co. Sucursal Corp., 308 F. Supp. 596 (D.P.R. 1970), where the court required a judicial decree of insanity of the principal in order to terminate the agent's authority.
25. For a contrary holding, see Millman v. First Fed. Sav. & Loan Association, 198 So. 2d 338 (Fla. App. 1967) and Harrington v. Bailey, 351 S.W. 2d 946 (Tex. Civ. App. 1961).

26. Dubois v. U.S. Fidelity & Guar. Co., 341 Pa. 85, 18 A. 2d 802 (1941).
27. Florance v. Kresge, 35 Am. Bankr. R (N.S.) 209, 93 F. 2d 784 (4th Cir. 1938).
28. Howell v. Gordon, 40 Ga. 302 (1869). See, Tiffany, *Agency* (2d ed. 1924), sect.87; Mechem, *Outlines of Agency* (3d. ed. 1923), sect. 216; note, *Yale Law Journal* 37:379-380, January 1928.
29. Johnson v. Eisentrager, 70 S. Ct. 936, 339 U.S. 763 (1950).
30. Insurance Co. v. Davis, 95 U.S. 425 (1877); Keppelmann v. Keppelmann, 89 N.J. Eq. 390, 105 A. 140 (1918), reversed 91 N.J. Eq. 67, 108 A. 432 (1919) on other grounds; Williams v. Paine, 18 S. Ct. 279, 165 U.S. 55 (1898).
31. Springer v. Garvan, 276 F. 595 (S.D. Ohio 1920).
32. Warfel v. United States, 120 Ct. Cl. 279, 98 F. Supp. 340 (Ct. Cl. 1951), cert. denied 343 U.S. 914 (1952).
33. Restatement, Second, Agency, Sect. 111 (1958).
34. Doctor v. Gilmartin, 14 Daly 206, 6 N.Y.S. 296 (1897).
35. McNeilly v. Continental Life Ins. Co., 66 N.Y. 23 (1876); Austin v. Holland, 69 N.Y. 571 (1877).
36. Menschke v. Riley, 159 Mo. App. 331, 140 S.W 639 (1911); Restatement, Second, Agency, Sect. 136 (3) (a) (b) (1958), provides that constructive notice is sufficient "by advertising the fact (of termination of the agent's authority) in a newspaper of general circulation in the place where the agency is regularly carried on or giving publicity by some other method reasonably adopted to give the information to such third person".

Case 36

F.L.&T. v. Wilson

139 N.Y. 284 (1893)

Introduction

The death of a principal automatically terminates the agency relationship by operation of law except in the case of an agency coupled with an interest. The question then arises whether payments made by a third party to an agent after the principal's death in good faith and without notice of the principal's death will be binding upon the principal's estate. The following case decided nearly 100 years ago represents the rule of law today in the United States.

O'Brien, J.

The plaintiff, as general guardian of infants, heirs and devisees of one William Maden, has recovered judgment against the defendant for rent claimed to be due under a lease of certain real estate, executed in the lifetime of the testator. Maden died in Cuba on the 6th of August, 1884, having by will devised the real estate in Brooklyn, the rent of which was claimed in this action, to his infant children, who are represented by the plaintiff. He had been for many years before his death a resident of Cuba, and the owner of the real estate in question. The will was duly proved and established under the laws of that country on the 27th of August, 1884, and such proceedings were afterwards had here that it was admitted to record in the office of the surrogate of New York on the 10th of June, 1885, and the plaintiff was appointed guardian December 19, 1888. The real estate had been for many years managed and rented by an agent of the owner, who acted under a verbal authority. The judgment was for rent accruing under the lease subsequent to the death of the owner from the month of May, 1885. It is undisputed that the defendant paid all the rent claimed to the agent subsequent to the death of his principal, but as it does not appear that the agent ever accounted for the same, the sole question presented by this appeal is whether the defendant is protected by such payment in this action. On the 8th of April, 1884, the testator, by his agent, and the defendant, executed the lease which appears to be under seal, acknowledged and recorded. By this instrument, Maden, who is described as "of Cortenas, Island of Cuba," demised to the defendant for the term of five years from May 1 thereafter the buildings in respect to which the rent is claimed to have accrued, at the yearly rate of $3,500, payable monthly in advance. The lease contains a provision for renewal for five years, at $4,000 per year, payable in like manner. The defendant, on his part, covenanted to pay the rent as stipulated and to surrender the premises at the expiration of the term. The defendant had, during the four years prior to the execution of this lease, occupied the premises as tenant under agreement with the agent, and had paid the rent to him, and it appears that the defendant never had any personal dealing with the owner, though he knew he was in fact the landlord and where he resided. At the time that the defendant paid the rent in question to the agent neither of them had any knowledge or information in regard to the death of the owner.

The rule is well settled by authority that the power of an agent to collect and receive payment of rents falling due to his principal, when such power is not coupled with an interest, terminates and ceases upon the death of the principal, and that payment made thereafter to the agent does not bind the estate of the principal, though the payment be made in ignorance of the principal's death. . . . The rule seems to have originated in the presumption that those who deal with an agent knowingly assume the risk that his authority may be terminated by death without notice to them. The case of an agency coupled with an interest is made an exception to the rule. . . . It is urged that the exception applies to this case for the reason that the agent was entitled to commissions upon the rents collected, and to be allowed his disbursements for repairs, insurance and taxes. The trial court refused to find that he had such an interest as would prevent the revocation of the power upon the death of the principal. There was no proof to show that the agent, at the time of the death, had any claim on account of repairs, insurance or taxes, and, therefore, it is needless to inquire how far, if at all, these elements, if shown to exist, would change the case. It may be assumed that the agent was entitled to compensation for his services, in the form of commissions, upon the money collected, while the agency was in force. But this would not give him such an interest as would continue his power after his principal's death. Agents are quite frequently paid by commissions upon sales of property, or upon moneys collected, and to hold that this constitutes such an interest as would save the power from revocation by the death of the principal, would be, in effect to abrogate the rule in most cases. The interest which can protect a power after the death of the person by whom it was created, must be an interest in the thing itself. The power must be engrafted upon some estate or interest in the things to which it relates. . . . Here the agent had no estate or interest in the property nor in the rents as such. The most that can be said is that he was entitled to commissions upon what was to be produced by the exercise of the power, and hence it cannot be said that the power and the interest are united in the same person at the time of their creation. It cannot, we think, be claimed for a moment that the principal in the creation of the power, conferred upon the agent any interest in the subject to which it was intended to relate. At no time could the agent act except in the name of his principal, and a power thus limited must necessarily cease with the death of the person in whose name it is to be exercised. The learned counsel for the defendant in an interesting and ingenious argument, has attempted to take this case out of the operation of the general rule, but, while much impressed with the equity of his position, we have not been able to make any satisfactory distinction between the facts as they appear in the records and that that appeared in the cases to which reference has been made. The result which we feel constrained to reach will illustrate how a rule or principle of law will operate harshly and produce what might seem to be injustice in a particular case. This conclusion must, however, be modified when we consider that either the defendant or the infant children of the deceased must bear the loss which has occurred by the default of the agent. The defendant could have foreseen what has happened and protected himself against loss by insisting upon payment to the owners alone, or by proper stipulations in the lease. There can be no doubt that a party may, by his contract, estop his personal representatives or his estate from recovering money paid to his agent in good faith, after his death, under such circumstances as appear in this case, but we see no reasonable way that the children of the owner, who are the real plaintiffs in this case, could have avoided the result. The presumption that every man knows the law implies that they will act with reasonable caution and vigilance in their business affairs, and that in entering upon contracts or carrying them out they will become informed by competent advice of the risks and dangers that beset them. When a man knowingly deals with the agent of a principal who resides in a foreign country, it must be assumed that he will guard against the perils that the transaction necessarily involves, and while courts are disposed to exercise all their power to relieve parties who have acted in good faith, from the result of their neglect to provide, in the first instance, against accidents which might have been foreseen, there seems to be no way open for such a result in this case, without disregarding or refining away an important rule of law. This would practically be judicial legislation. We feel bound to follow the current of authority, and to leave the work of reforming the law on this question, if reform be necessary or desirable, to the legislature.

There would seem to be an incongruity in the law of agency with respect to the effect of a revocation of the agent's powers by the act of the principal himself and a revocation produced by his death. In the former case, the revocation does not affect third parties, dealing with the agent in good faith, without notice. . . . While in the latter, as we have seen, the revocation operated upon all parties, without notice, unless the power is coupled with an interest, in which case the agent may execute it in his own name, notwithstanding the death of the principal. The civil law protected third parties who dealt in good faith with the agent without notice in all cases, whether the power was revoked by the act of the principal or his death, but as Chancellor Kent has observed this equitable principle does not prevail in the English law . . . from which the rule that obtains in this state was derived, though in other jurisdictions, and perhaps in England, the harshness of the common law has been modified by statute. . . . The common-law rule has become too firmly established in this state to be disturbed by judicial action, though a change by the law-making power would be in harmony with more enlightened views and would promote the interests of justice.

The judgment must, therefore, be affirmed, with costs.

All concur.

Judgment affirmed.

Discussion questions

1. What provision could the third party and principal have agreed to which would have changed the result of this case?
2. If the principal will not agree to any provision which would change the rule of law, how can the third party protect himself against the operative effect of this rule if the principal should die?

Case 37

Schnee v. Jonas Equities

109 Misc.2d 221 (Supreme Court, Appellate Team, 2nd Dept., 1981)

Introduction

As a general rule, the death of the principal revokes the agent's authority by operation of law. This case illustrates an important exception to the general rule where the deceased principal is a party to a lease agreement involving real property.

Opinion of the Court

Memorandum.

Judgment of the court below unanimously modified by reducing the amount to $127.09, plus costs and disbursements in the court below, and, as so modified, affirmed, without costs.

This is a small claims proceeding wherein the administratrix of a deceased tenant seeks to recover two months security in the amount of $424.53 from defendant, landlord. Tenant resided in the premises under a lease running from May 1, 1976 until April 30, 1979 at a monthly rental of $209.31. Tenant died on March 17, 1978. The keys to the apartment were given to the defendant on March 28, 1978. Defendant, in turn, relet the apartment on May 1, 1978 at a rental of $225 per month. Insofar as is relevant to this appeal, the deceased tenant's lease provided that the landlord had the option to relet the premises as tenant's agent and that no surrender of the premises would be valid unless accepted in writing.

A lease for a term of years is not terminated by the death of the lessee prior to the expiration of the term. The lease passes as personal property to the estate, which remains liable for payment of the rent. Moreover, the personal representative has the same remedies as the lessee had for any breach of the agreement. Thus, the trial court's finding that the agency created in the lease was terminated by tenant's death is incorrect. As a general rule, the death of the principal acts as an absolute revocation of an agent's authority. However, this rule is not applicable where, as here, the estate replaced the deceased tenant as a party to the lease by operation of law. In effect, the death of the tenant effectuated a substitution of the estate as the principal and not a revocation of defendant's option to relet the premises as plaintiff's agent.

Discussion questions

1. Would a provision in the lease that expressly provided that the agency be terminated upon the principal's death change the result of this case?
2. Would a landlord usually agree to such a provision?

PROBLEMS

Name: ____________________

Date: ____________________

Section Number: ____________________

1. P is totally dissatisfied with the agency relationship he has with A and wishes to terminate it. In which of the following situations does P not have the power to terminate the relationship?

_____ a. P and A have agreed that their agency is irrevocable.

_____ b. A has been appointed as P's agent pursuant to a power of attorney.

_____ c. A is an agent coupled with an interest.

_____ d. The agency agreement is in writing and provides for a specific duration which has not elapsed.

2. P dismissed A, its purchasing agent, for incompetence. It published a notice in the appropriate trade journals which stated: "this is to notify all parties concerned that A is no longer employed by P and the corporation assumes no further responsibility for his acts." A called on several of P's suppliers with whom he had previously dealt, and when he found one who was unaware of his dismissal, he would place a substantial order for merchandise to be delivered to a warehouse in which he had rented space. P had rented warehouse space in the past when its storage facilities were crowded. A also called on several suppliers with whom P had never dealt; he would present one of his old business cards to the secretary and then make purchases on open account in the name of P. A then sold all the merchandise delivered to the warehouse and absconded with the money. In this situation

_____ a. A had continuing express authority to make contracts on P's behalf with suppliers with whom he had previously dealt as P's agent, if they were unaware of his dismissal.

_____ b. The suppliers who previously had no dealings with P cannot enforce the contracts against P even if the suppliers were unaware of A's lack of authority.

_____ c. P is liable on the A contracts to all suppliers who had dealt with A in the past as P's agent.

_____ d. Constructive notice via publication in the appropriate trade journals is an effective notice to all third parties regardless of whether they had dealt with A or read the notice.

3. P dismissed A, its purchasing agent. P published a notice in appropriate trade journals which stated: "This is to notify all parties concerned that A is no longer employed by P, and the corporation assumes no further responsibility for his acts." A called on several of P's suppliers with whom he had previously dealt, and when he found one who was unaware of his dismissal, he placed a substantial order for merchandise to be delivered to a warehouse in which A rented space. P had rented space in the warehouse in the past when its storage facilities were crowded. A also called on several suppliers with whom P had never dealt and made purchases from them on open account in the name of P. The merchandise purchased by A was delivered to the warehouse. A then sold all the merchandise and absconded with the money. Which of the following most accurately describes the legal implications of this situation?

_____ a. A had apparent authority to make contracts on P's behalf with suppliers with whom A was currently dealing as P's agent if they had no actual knowledge of his dismissal.

_____ b. The suppliers who previously had no dealings with P can enforce the contracts against P if the suppliers had no actual knowledge of A's lack of authority.

_____ c. P is liable on the A contracts to all suppliers who had dealt with A in the past as P's agent and who have not received personal notice, even though they had read the published notice.

_____ d. Constructive notice by publication in the appropriate trade journals is an effective notice to all third parties regardless of whether they had previously dealt with A or read the notice.

4. An agent's power to bind his principal to a contract is generally terminated

_____ a. Automatically upon the commission of a tort by the agent.

_____ b. Instantly upon the death of the principal.

_____ c. Upon the bankruptcy of the agent.

_____ d. Without further action by the principal upon the resignation of the agent.

5. A was a general agent of P with authority to sell, make collections, and adjust disputes. A was caught padding his monthly expense account by substantial amounts and was dismissed. P hired another general agent, X, to replace A. X was slowly but steadily calling upon A's accounts to make sales and was informing them that A's services had been terminated. P also published a notice in the appropriate trade journals and the local newspaper announcing the replacement of A with X. A, after he was let go, called on all the customers who had outstanding accounts payable and quickly made whatever collections he could in cash and absconded. Which of the following statements is correct regarding P's legal right against the customers?

_____ a. P can regain possession of the goods since title did not pass because A's actions constituted a fraud.

_____ b. P can obtain payment from the customers despite A's wrongful acts since it had published a notice of A's dismissal.

_____ c. P will have to absorb the loss since A had continuing implied authority to make collections.

_____ d. P will have to absorb the loss unless P can prove the customers had actual notice of A's dismissal.

6. P hired A as a traveling salesman to sell goods manufactured by P. A also sold a line of products manufactured by a friend. He did not disclose this to P. The relationship was unsatisfactory and P finally fired A after learning of A's sales of the other manufacturer's goods. A, enraged at P for firing him, continued to make contracts on P's behalf with both new and old customers that were almost uniformly disadvantageous to P. P, upon learning of this, gave written notice of A's discharge to all parties with whom A had dealt. Which of the following statements is incorrect?

_____ a. P can bring an action against A to have him account for any secret profits.

_____ b. Prior to notification, A retained some continued authority to bind P despite termination of the agency relationship.

_____ c. New customers who contracted with A for the first time could enforce the contracts against P if they knew that A had been P's salesman but were unaware that A was fired.

_____ d. If P had promptly published a notification of termination of A's employment in the local newspapers and in the trade publications, he would not be liable for any of A's contracts.

7. A has been P's agent in the liquor business for ten years and has made numerous contacts on P's behalf. Under which of the following situations could A continue to have power to bind P?

_____ a. The passage of a federal constitutional amendment making the sale or purchase of alcoholic beverages illegal.

_____ b. The death of P without A's knowledge.

_____ c. The bankruptcy of P with A's knowledge.

_____ d. The firing of A by P.

8. Arlene, as agent for Hector, made a particularly desirable written contract with Terry in Hector's name for the sale of Hector's real estate for $125,000. Terry, realizing he has made a bad bargain, seeks to avoid the contract. Terry learns that one day prior to the date the contract was executed by Arlene and Terry, Hector had a fatal heart attack. This was unknown to either party at the time the contract was made and both parties acted in good faith. The executor of Hector's estate seeks to enforce the contract against Terry.

   In an action by the executor of Hector's estate against Terry, judgment for whom? Explain.

9. Allen was the New York agent for Potter, who conducted a retail camera store as a sole proprietorship in San Francisco. Potter wrote Allen a letter on July 9 instructing Allen to purchase up to $100,000 of cameras from New York camera distributors. On July 14 Potter died suddenly. Mrs. Potter did not notify Allen of her husband's death. On July 18 Allen ordered in the name of Potter $100,000 of cameras from Zeiss Wholesale Cameras, unaware of Potter's death.

   a. In an action by Zeiss Wholesale Cameras against the estate of Potter, judgment for whom? Why?

   b. If the estate of Potter wishes to enforce the contract against Zeiss Wholesale Cameras may it do so? Why?

   c. What rights, if any, does Zeiss Wholesale Cameras have against Allen? Why?

10. Prince Realty Corporation orally employed Baker, 17 years old, as an assistant manager to manage an apartment house it owned. Prince Realty instructed Baker not to contract for any repair work without its prior approval. Prince Realty also instructed Baker to collect in person the monthly rent from the 100 tenants. Contrary to these instructions, Baker contracted with Trinity Plumbing Company to repair some plumbing for $200 and a bill for the services rendered has been submitted to Prince Realty for payment. In addition, Corbin, a tenant, asserted a claim against Prince Realty alleging that he was assaulted by Baker who was attempting to collect past due rent. Although Baker was discharged after managing the apartment for three months, he collected the rent for the fourth month on all apartments and absconded. After learning this, Prince Realty has billed the tenants for the fourth month's rent.

    a. In an action by Trinity Plumbing Company against Prince Realty Company, judgment for whom? Explain.

    b. In an action by Corbin against Prince Realty Company, judgment for whom? Explain.

    c. In an action by Prince Realty Company against the tenants to recover the fourth month's rent, judgment for whom? Explain.

11. Andrew was a travelling salesman employed by the Paper Box Corporation. His express authority included the solicitation of orders and the collection of accounts. After Andrew had worked for the corporation for five years, he was discharged. The corporation published a notice of Andrew's discharge in a newspaper of general circulation in the geographical area where Andrew formerly worked. Three days later, Andrew called upon Richard, an old customer, and collected $1,000 from him. The publication by the corporation had not come to Richard's attention. He also called upon Charles, a new prospect who knew of Andrew's express authority but who had never dealt with the corporation. Andrew secured a substantial order from Charles, collected the price of the goods, sent the order to the corporation, and disappeared. The corporation delivered the goods to Charles in accordance with the order.

    a. Will the corporation recover if it sues Richard to recover $1,000? Explain.

    b. Will the corporation recover if it sues Charles for the agreed price of the goods? Explain.

12. Pulitzer was a manufacturer of consumer products. Atlas was a travelling salesman for Pulitzer who regularly called on retail stores in a six state area. While on a selling trip, Atlas received a telegram from Pulitzer terminating his services as a salesman immediately. Atlas was furious and continued to call on old and new customers. Pulitzer did not notify anyone that he had terminated Atlas' employment or otherwise publish any notice of such termination. Two days later Atlas sold $1,500 worth of goods to Tompkins, an old customer he had regularly dealt with for the last three years and took a 20% cash deposit of $300 as had been the practice for many years. Atlas also sold $1,000 worth of goods to a new customer, Gomez, and took a cash deposit of $250. Atlas forwarded the orders to Pulitzer and absconded with the $550 he collected. Pulitzer refused to perform or return the deposit claiming he had no liability to either party because Atlas had been fired two days earlier.

    a. Is Pulitzer liable to Tompkins? Why?

b. Is Pulitzer liable to Gomez? Why?

____

____

____

____

____

13. Polk is in the business of leasing farm equipment to farmers. Tyler is and has been his agent for the last seven years with authority to collect rent each month from farmers under the leases. Polk revoked Tyler's authority to collect rent four months ago but Tyler nevertheless continued to collect rent from Hancock who had been renting Polk's equipment for many years. Tyler absconded with the collected rent for the next three months. Polk now makes demand upon Hancock to pay the overdue rent.

a. In an action by Polk against Hancock to recover three months' rent, judgment for whom?

____

____

____

____

____

b. Suppose Tyler's authority to collect rent terminated by the death of Polk and the facts are otherwise the same. Must Hancock pay the estate of Polk? Why?

____

____

____

____

____

14. Generally, an agency relationship is terminated by operation of law in all of the following situations **except** the

_____ a. Principal's death.
_____ b. Principal's incapacity.
_____ c. Agent's renunciation of the agency.
_____ d. Agent's failure to acquire a necessary business license.

15. Bolt Corp. dismissed Ace as its general sales agent and notified all of Ace's known customers by letter. Young Corp., a retail outlet located outside of Ace's previously assigned sales territory, had never dealt with Ace. Young knew of Ace as a result of various business contacts. After his dismissal, Ace sold Young goods, to be delivered by Bolt, and received from Young a cash deposit for 20% of the purchase price. It was not unusual for an agent in Ace's previous position to receive cash deposits. In an action by Young against Bolt on the sales contract, Young will

_____ a. Lose, because Ace lacked any implied authority to make the contract.
_____ b. Lose, because Ace lacked any express authority to make the contract.
_____ c. Win, because Bolt's notice was inadequate to terminate Ace's apparent authority.
_____ d. Win, because a principal is an insurer of an agent's acts.

16. A general agent's apparent authority to bind her principal to contracts with third parties will cease without notice to those third parties when the

_____ a. Agent has fulfilled the purpose for which the agency relationship was created.

_____ b. Time set forth in the agreement creating the agency relationship has expired.

_____ c. Principal and agent have mutually agreed to end their relationship.

_____ d. Principal has received a discharge in bankruptcy under the liquidation provisions of the Bankruptcy Code.

17. Trent was retained, in writing, to act as Post's agent for the sale of Post's memorabilia collection. Which of the following statements is correct?

I. To be an agent, Trent must be at least 21 years of age.

II. Post would be liable to Trent if the collection was destroyed before Trent found a purchaser.

_____ a. I only.

_____ b. II only.

_____ c. Both I and II.

_____ d. Neither I nor II.

18. Baker Corp. dismissed Abel as its general sales agent. Baker notified all of Abel's known customers by letter. Fam Corp., a retail outlet located outside of Abel's previously assigned sales territory, had never dealt with Abel. However, Fam knew of Abel as a result of various business contacts. After his dismissal, Abel sold Fam goods, to be delivered by Baker, and received from Fam a cash deposit for 25% of the purchase price. It was not unusual for an agent in Abel's previous position to receive cash deposits. In an action by Fam against Baker on the sales contract, Fam will

_____ a. Win, because a principal is an insurer of an agent's acts.

_____ b. Win, because Baker's notice was inadequate to terminate Abel's apparent authority.

_____ c. Lose, because Abel's conduct constituted a fraud for which Baker is **not** liable.

_____ d. Lose, because Abel lacked any express or implied authority to make the contract.

19. Harris is a purchasing agent for Elkin, a sole proprietor. Harris has the express authority to place purchase orders with Elkin's suppliers. Harris typically conducts business through the mail and has very little contact with Elkin. Elkin was incapacitated by a stroke and was declared incompetent in a judicial proceeding. Subsequently, Harris placed an order with Ajax, Inc. on behalf of Elkin. Neither Ajax nor Harris were aware of Elkin's incapacity. With regard to the contract with Ajax, Elkin (or Elkin's legal representative) will

_____ a. Not be liable because Harris was without authority to enter into the contract.

_____ b. Not be liable provided that Harris had placed orders with Ajax in the past.

_____ c. Be liable because Harris was acting within the scope of Harris authority.

_____ d. Be liable because Ajax was unaware of Elkin's incapacity.

20. The apparent authority of a general agent for a disclosed principal will terminate without notice to third parties when the

_____ a. Principal dismisses the agent.

_____ b. Principal or agent dies.

_____ c. Purpose of the agency relationship has been fulfilled.

_____ d. Time period set forth in the agency agreement has expired.

21. Young was purchasing agent for Wilson, a sole proprietor. Young had the express authority to place purchase orders with Wilson's suppliers. Young conducted business through the mail and had little contact with Wilson. Young placed an order with Vanguard, Inc. on Wilson's behalf after Wilson was declared incompetent in a judicial proceeding. Young was aware of Wilson's incapacity. With regard to the contract with Vanguard, Wilson (or Wilson's legal representative) will

______ a. Not be liable because Vanguard dealt only with Young.

______ b. Not be liable because Young did **not** have authority to enter into the contract.

______ c. Be liable because Vanguard was unaware of Wilson's incapacity.

______ d. Be liable because Young acted with express authority.